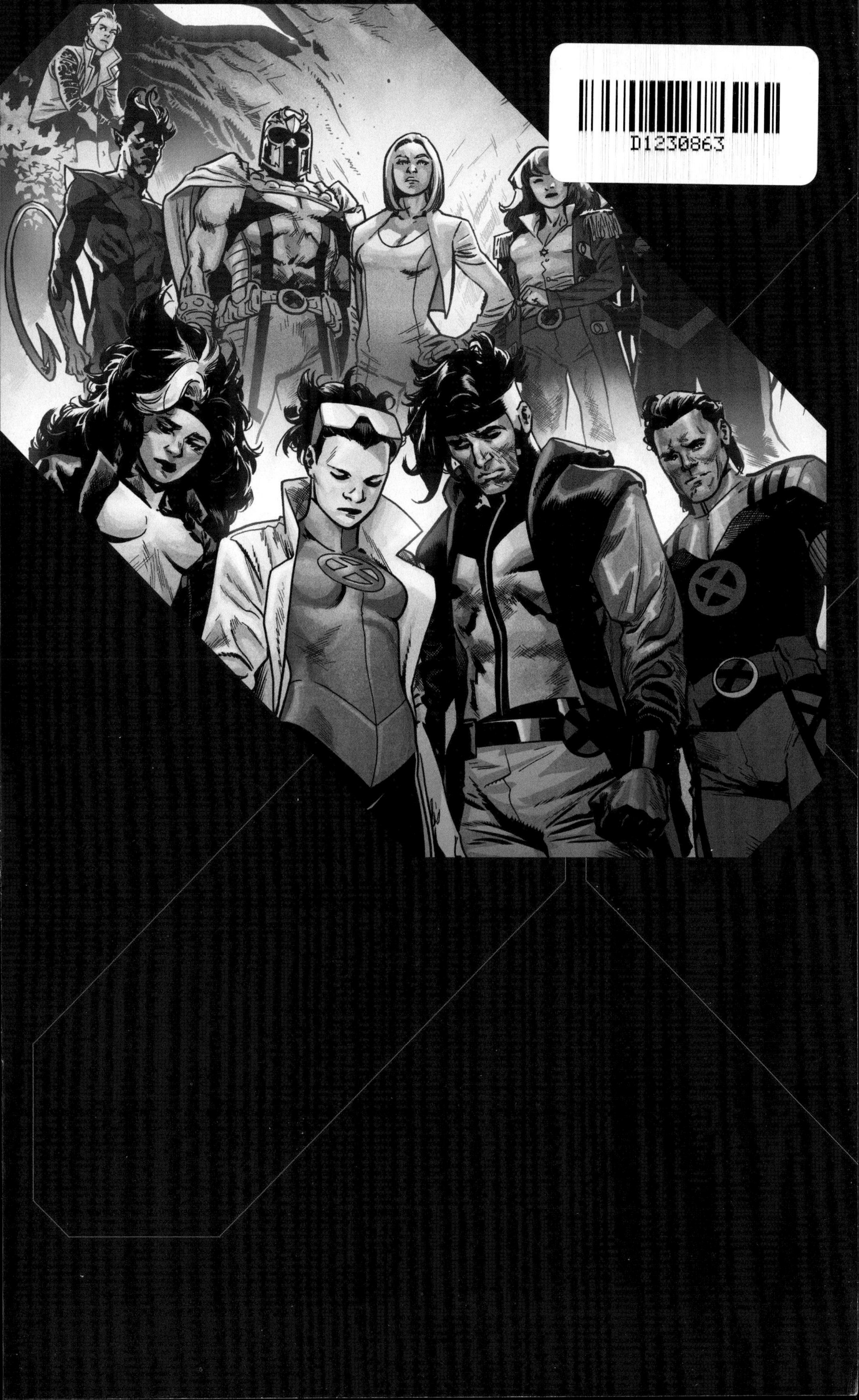

REIGN OF X VOL. 5. Contains material originally published in magazine form as EXCALIBUR (2019) #18-19, S.W.O.R.D. (2020) #2,3 and KING IN BLACK: MARAUDERS (2021) #1. First printing 2021. ISBN 978-1-302-93172-8. Published by MARVEL WORLDWIDE, INC., a subsidiary of MARVEL ENTERTAINMENT, LLC. OFFICE OF PUBLICATION: 1290 Avenue of the Americas, New York, NY 10104. © 2021 MARVEL No similarity between any of the names, characters, persons, and/or institutions in this magazine with those of any living or dead person or institution is intended and any such similarity which may exist is purely coincidental. **Printed in the Canada.** KEVIN FEIGE, Chief Creative Officer; DAN BUCKLEY, President, Marvel Entertainment; JOE QUESADA, EVP & Creative Director; DAVID BOGART, Associate Publisher & SVP of Talent Affairs; TOM BREVOORT, VP, Executive Editor; NICK LOWE, Executive Editor, VP of Content; Digital Publishing; DAVID GABRIEL, VP of Print & Digital Publishing; JEFF YOUNGQUIST, VP of Production & Special Projects; ALEX MORALES, Director of Publishing Operations; DAN EDINGTON, Managing Editor; RICKEY PURDIN, Director of Talent Relations; JENNIFER GRÜNWALD, Senior Editor, Special Projects; SUSAN CRESPI, Production Manager; STAN LEE, Chairman Emeritus. For information regarding advertising in Marvel Comics or on Marvel.com, please contact Vit DeBellis, Custom Solutions & Integrated Advertising Manager, at vdebellis@marvel.com. For Marvel subscription inquiries, please call 888-511-5480. **Manufactured between 8/27/2021 and 9/28/2021 by SOLISCO PRINTERS, SCOTT, QC, CANADA.**

10 9 8 7 6 5 4 3 2 1

REIGN OF X

Volume
5

X-Men created by Stan Lee & Jack Kirby

Writers:	Tini Howard, Al Ewing & Gerry Duggan
Artists:	Marcus To, Valerio Schiti, Ray-Anthony Height, Bernard Chang, Nico Leon & Luke Ross
Color Artists:	Erick Arciniega, Marte Gracia & Carlos Lopez
Letterers:	VC's Ariana Maher & Cory Petit
Cover Art:	Mahmud Asrar & Matthew Wilson; Valerio Schiti & Marte Gracia; and Russell Dauterman & Matthew Wilson
Head of X:	Jonathan Hickman
Design:	Tom Muller
Associate Editor:	Annalise Bissa
Editors:	Jordan D. White & Mark Basso
Collection Cover Art:	Mahmud Asrar & Matthew Wilson
Collection Editor:	Jennifer Grünwald
Assistant Editor:	Daniel Kirchhoffer
Assistant Managing Editor:	Maia Loy
Assistant Managing Editor:	Lisa Montalbano
VP Production & Special Projects:	Jeff Youngquist
SVP Print, Sales & Marketing:	David Gabriel
Editor in Chief:	C.B. Cebulski

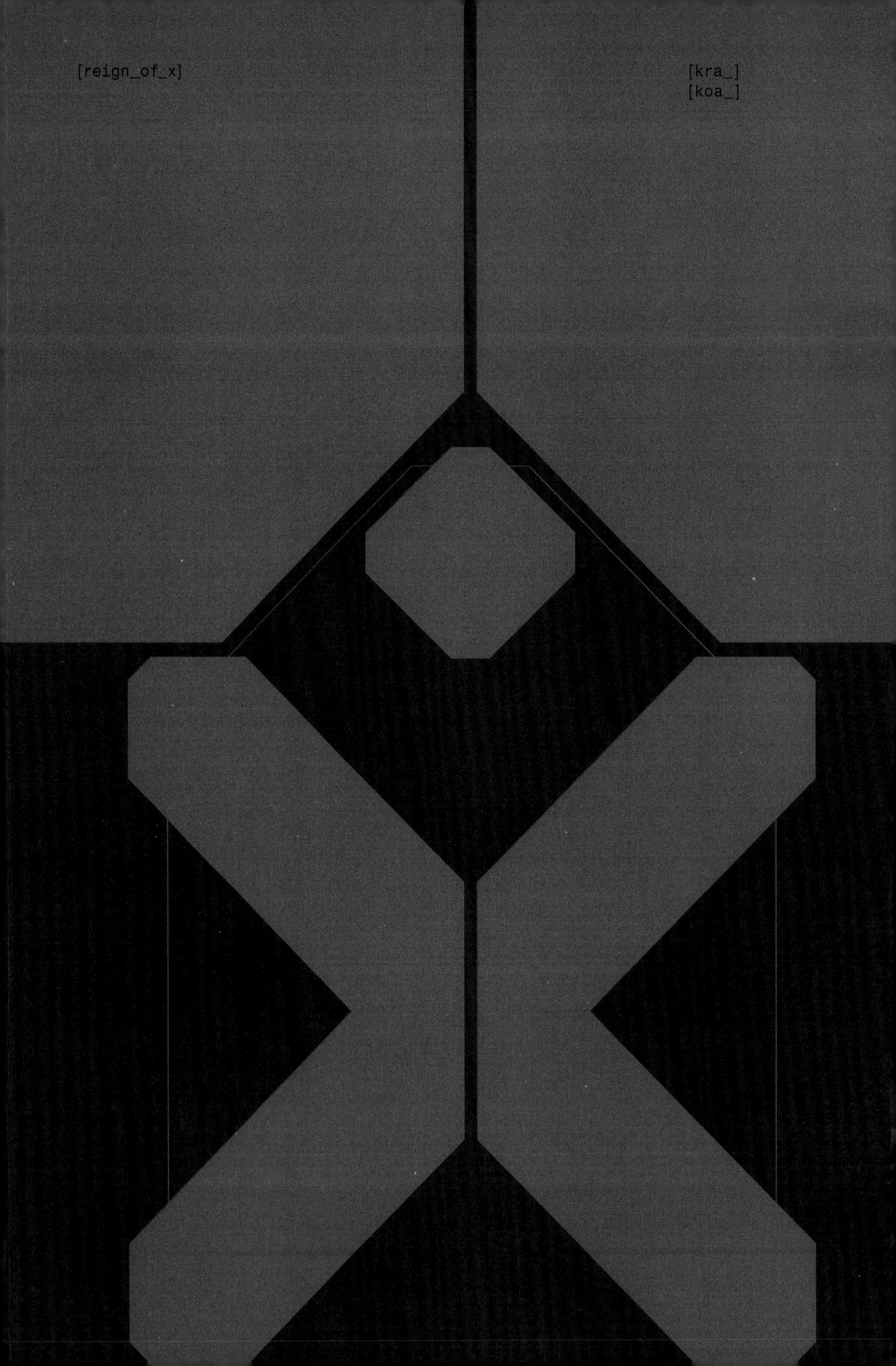
[reign_of_x]
[kra_]
[koa_]

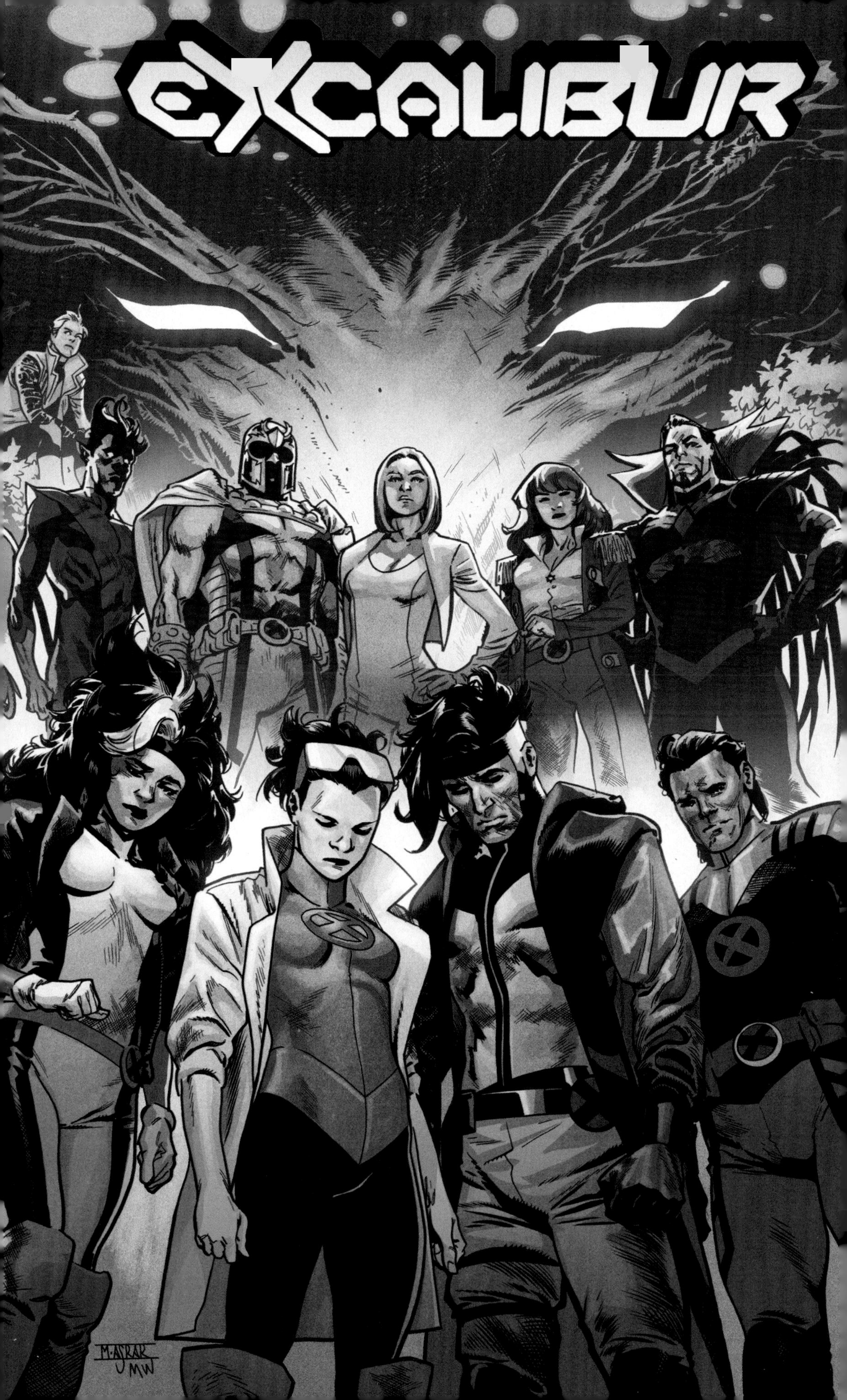
EXCALIBUR
M.ASRAR
MW

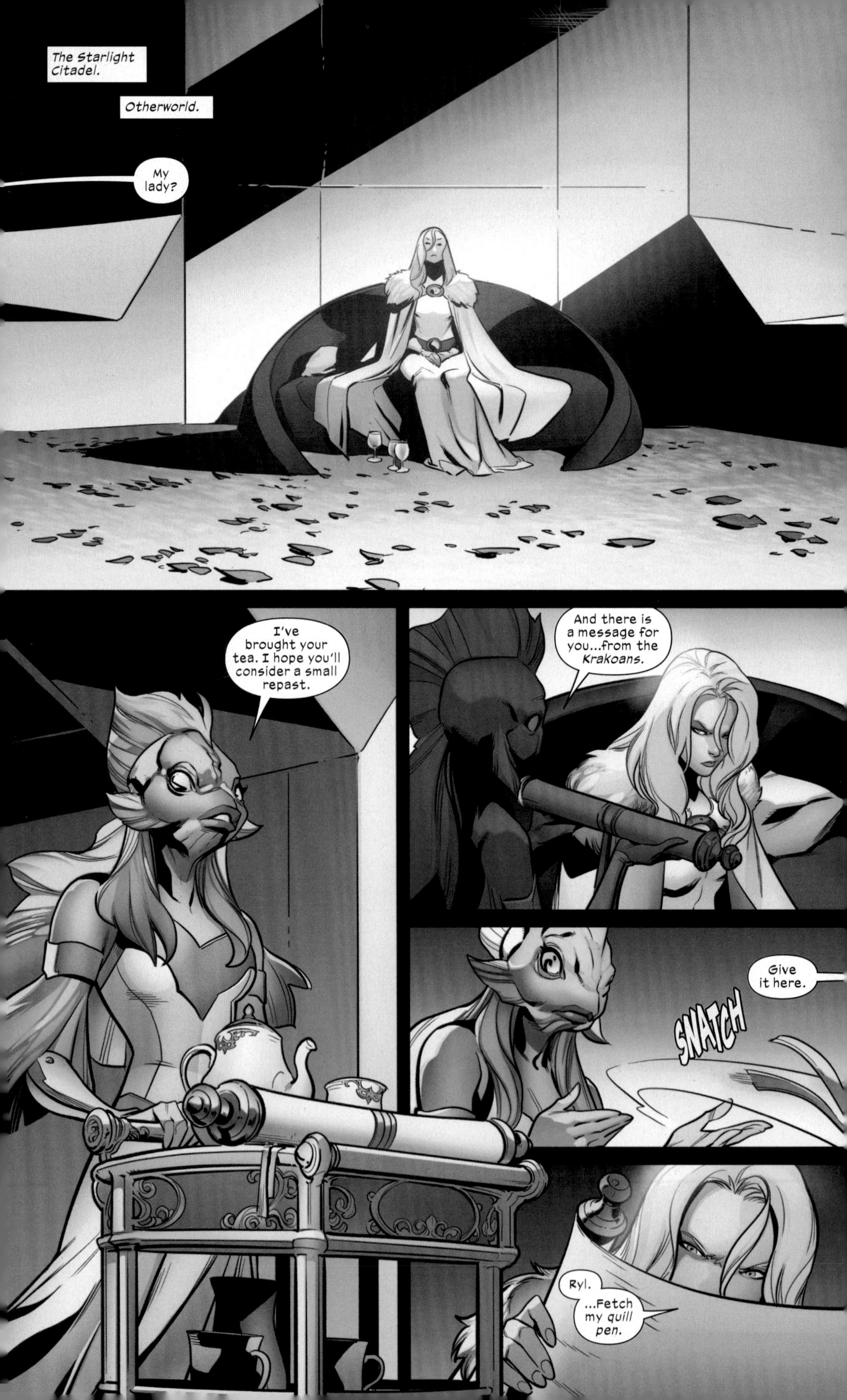
The Starlight Citadel.
Otherworld.
My lady?
I've brought your tea. I hope you'll consider a small repast.
And there is a message for you...from the *Krakoans.*
Give it here.
SNATCH
Ryl.
...Fetch my quill pen.

FROM THE DESK OF THE OMNIVERSAL MAJESTRIX

"Consider the message, consider the time,
consider many things before you bother Saturnyne!"

To Whom it May Concern,

Thank you for your letter!

The Omniversal Majestrix is hard at work ensuring the proper proceedings of Otherworld in her role as overseer of the Otherworldly Parliament and Courts both Foul and Fair.

Unfortunately, the Majestrix cannot meet with you at this time, as the representative of your home reality cannot be identified. Representatives of home realities are determined by the presence of a Captain Britain, your officer to Otherworld.

Ordinarily we'd ask you to submit your request to Captain Britain and have them submit your complaints at the next tribunal. Unfortunately, we have looked into the tomes and discovered that your reality currently lacks a Captain Britain!

With that in mind, the Majestrix will not be able to hear your request until the matter is rectified.

Best wishes and warmest regards,

Opal Luna Saturnyne

The Court of Omniversal Majestrix, Opal Luna Saturnyne

BETSY'S BACK (?)

When Captain Britain went missing, EXCALIBUR leapt into action to find her -- and now she's returned.

That was easy... Right?

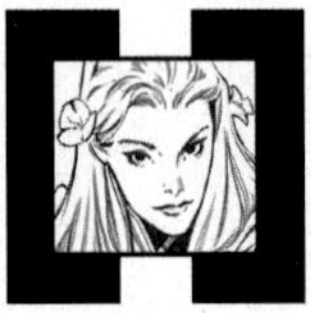
Captain Britain

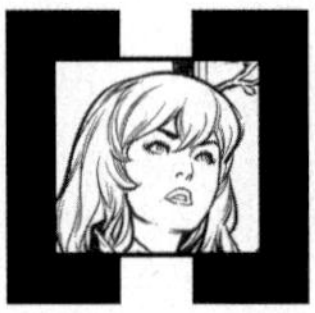
Rogue

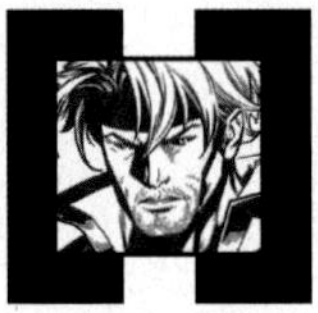
Gambit

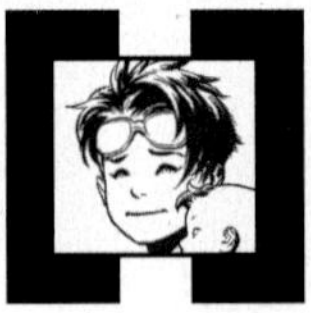
Jubilee

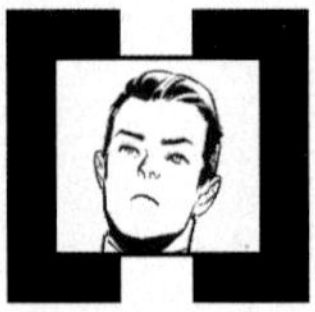
Rictor

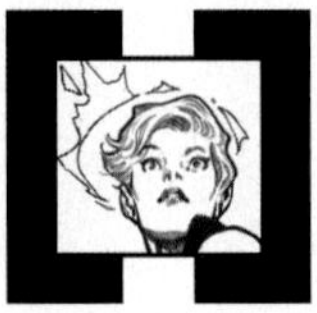
Rachel Summers

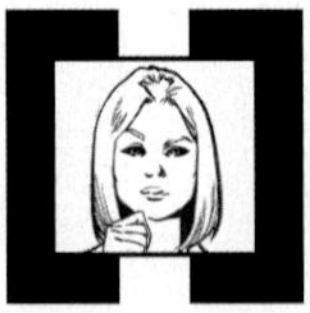
Emma Frost

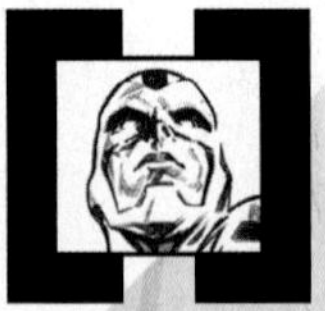
Captain Avalon

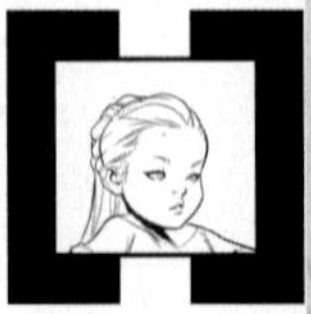
Maggie Braddock

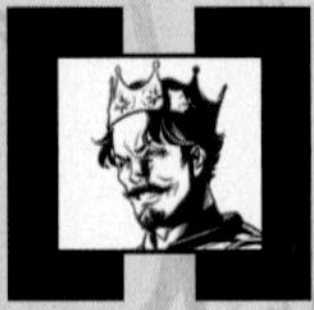
Monarch

[00_Reign]
[00___ofX]

EXCALIBUR
[X_18]

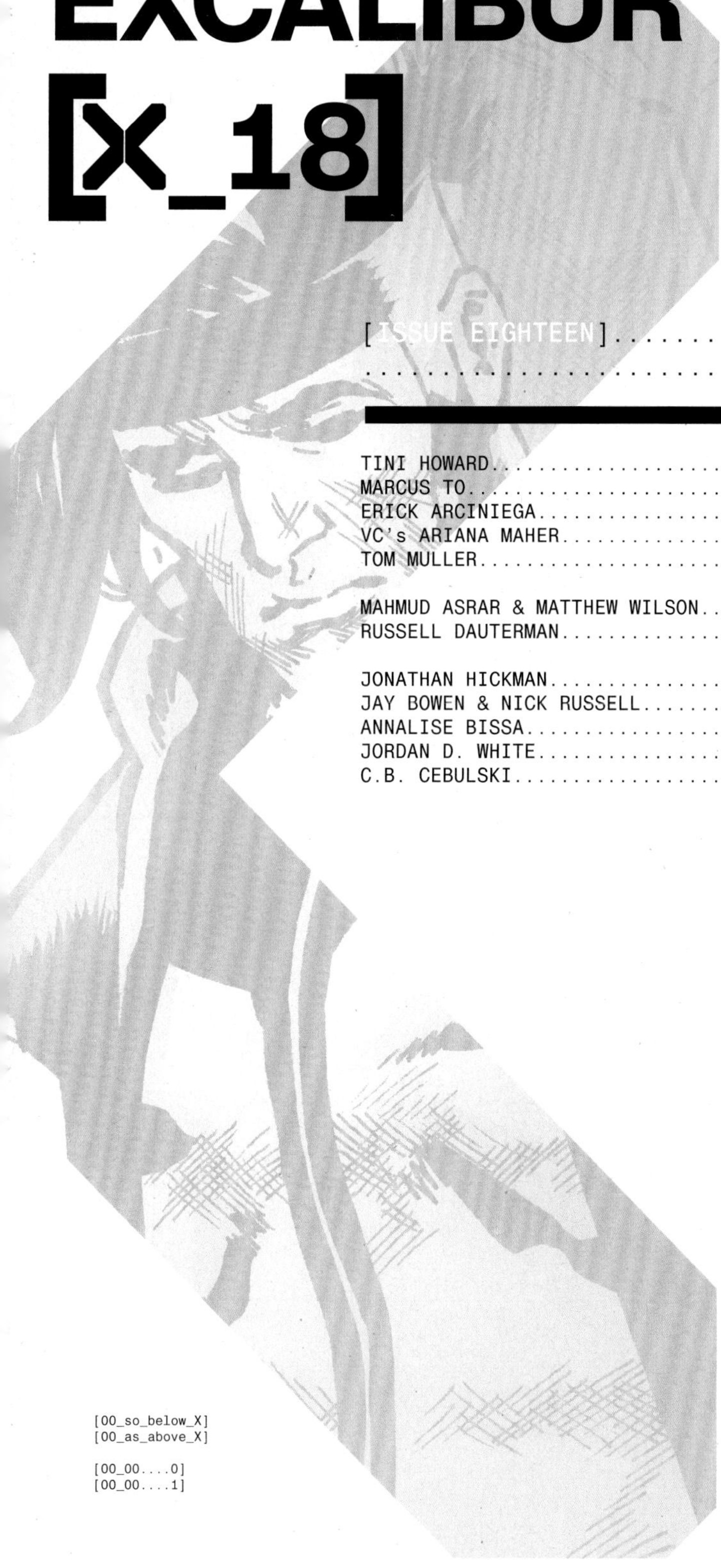

[ISSUE EIGHTEEN]................................
....MAD WOMEN

TINI HOWARD..[WRITER]
MARCUS TO..[ARTIST]
ERICK ARCINIEGA.............................[COLOR ARTIST]
VC's ARIANA MAHER.............................[LETTERER]
TOM MULLER..[DESIGN]

MAHMUD ASRAR & MATTHEW WILSON...............[COVER ARTISTS]
RUSSELL DAUTERMAN....................[VARIANT COVER ARTIST]

JONATHAN HICKMAN...............................[HEAD OF X]
JAY BOWEN & NICK RUSSELL......................[PRODUCTION]
ANNALISE BISSA...........................[ASSOCIATE EDITOR]
JORDAN D. WHITE......................................[EDITOR]
C.B. CEBULSKI..............................[EDITOR IN CHIEF]

[00_so_below_X]
[00_as_above_X]

[00_00....0]
[00_00....1]

[00_this____]
[00_world___]

[00_and_the_]

[00___other_]

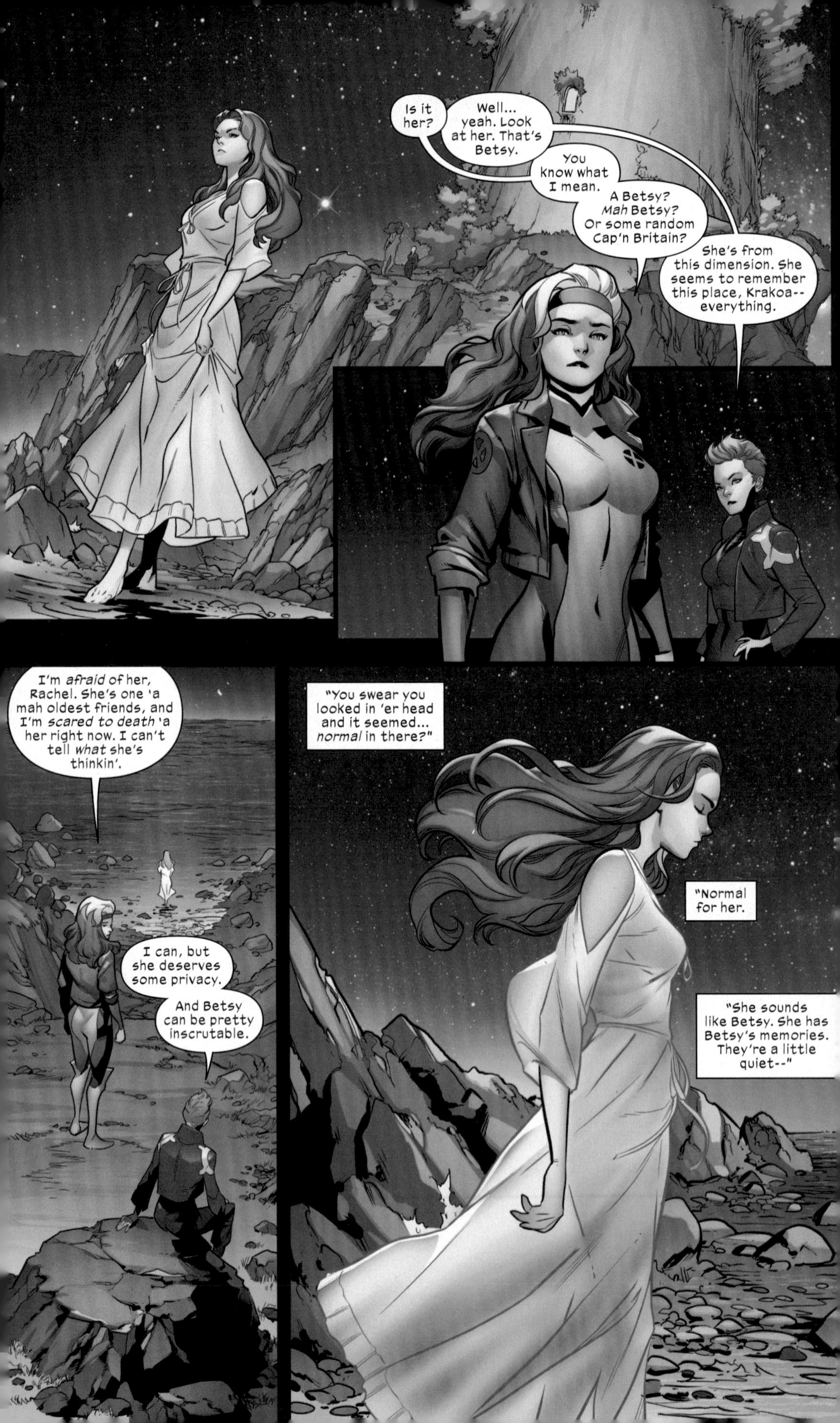
Is it her?
Well... yeah. Look at her. That's Betsy.
You know what I mean.
A Betsy? *Mah* Betsy? Or some random Cap'n Britain?
She's from this dimension. She seems to remember this place, Krakoa-- everything.
I'm *afraid* of her, Rachel. She's one 'a mah oldest friends, and I'm *scared to death* 'a her right now. I can't tell *what* she's thinkin'.
I can, but she deserves some privacy.
And Betsy can be pretty inscrutable.
"You swear you looked in 'er head and it seemed... *normal* in there?"
"Normal for her.
"She sounds like Betsy. She has Betsy's memories. They're a little quiet--"

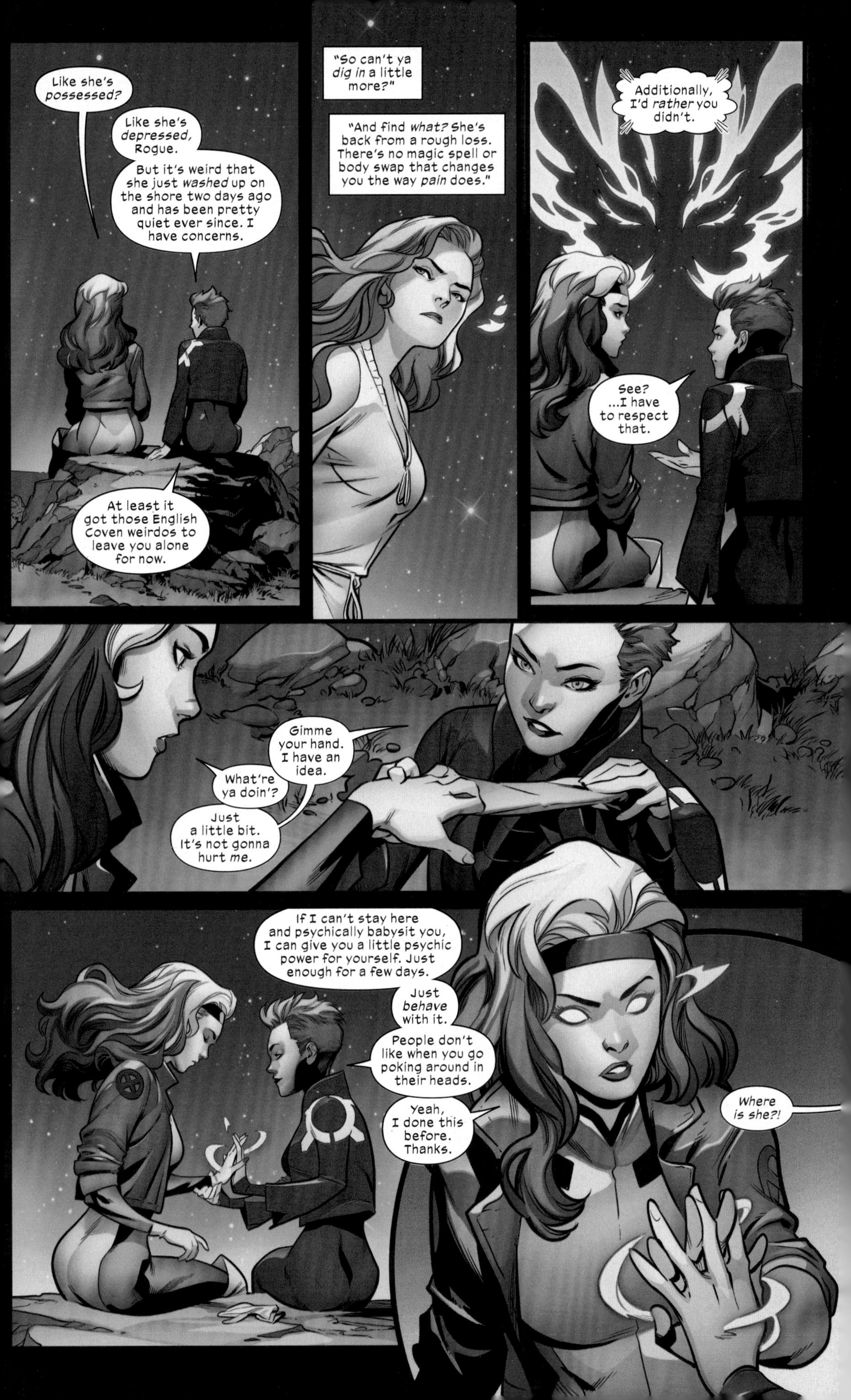

Like she's *possessed?*
Like she's *depressed,* Rogue.
But it's weird that she just *washed* up on the shore two days ago and has been pretty quiet ever since. I have concerns.
At least it got those English Coven weirdos to leave you alone for now.
"So can't ya *dig in* a little more?"
"And find *what?* She's back from a rough loss. There's no magic spell or body swap that changes you the way *pain* does."
Additionally, I'd *rather* you didn't.
See? ...I have to respect that.
Gimme your hand. I have an idea.
What're ya doin'?
Just a little bit. It's not gonna hurt *me.*
If I can't stay here and psychically babysit you, I can give you a little psychic power for yourself. Just enough for a few days.
Just *behave* with it.
People don't like when you go poking around in their heads.
Yeah, I done this before. Thanks.
Where is she?!

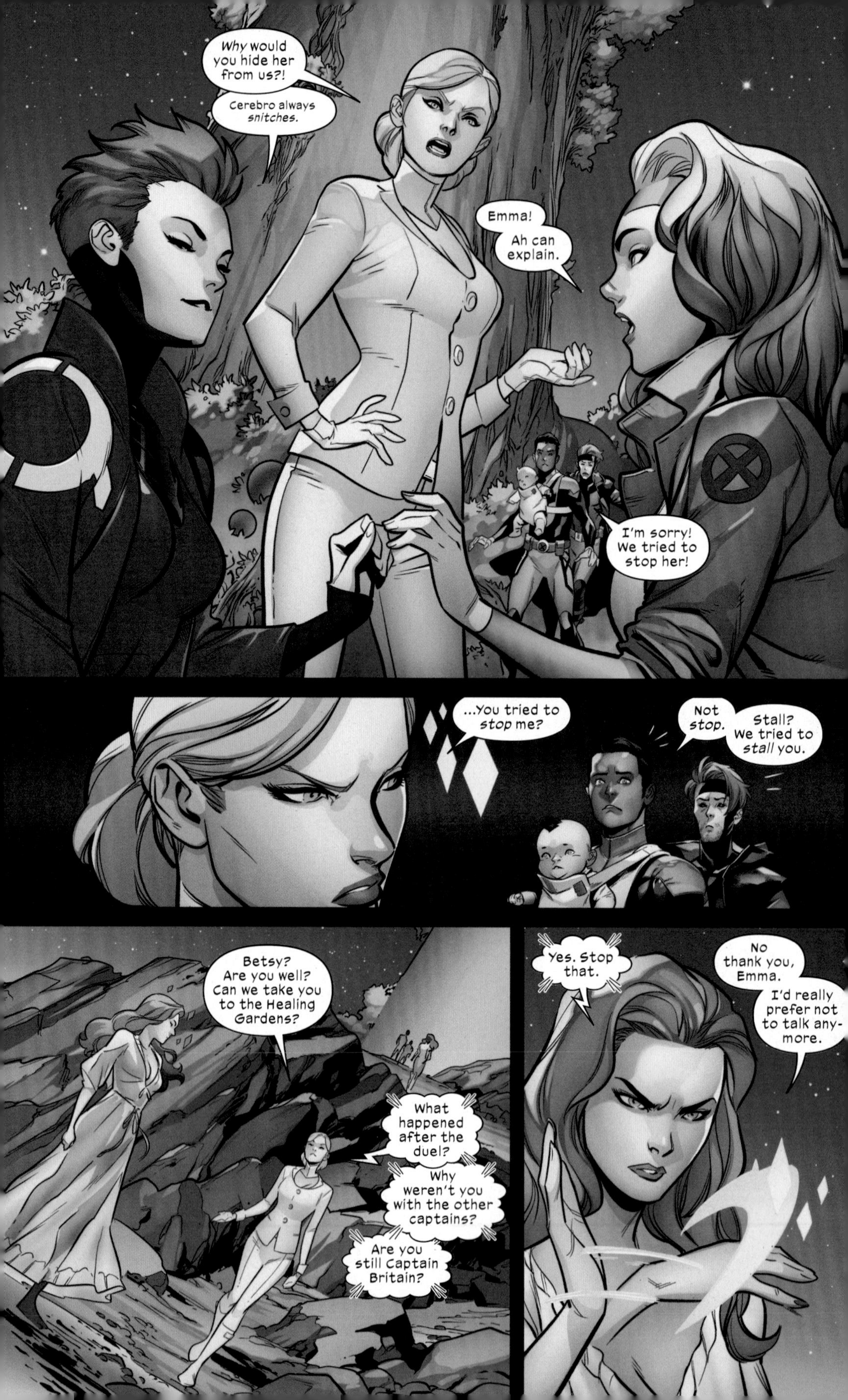
Why would you hide her from us?!
Cerebro always snitches.
Emma! Ah can explain.
I'm sorry! We tried to stop her!
...You tried to stop me?
Not stop.
Stall? We tried to stall you.
Betsy? Are you well? Can we take you to the Healing Gardens?
What happened after the duel?
Why weren't you with the other captains?
Are you still Captain Britain?
Yes. Stop that.
No thank you, Emma.
I'd really prefer not to talk any-more.

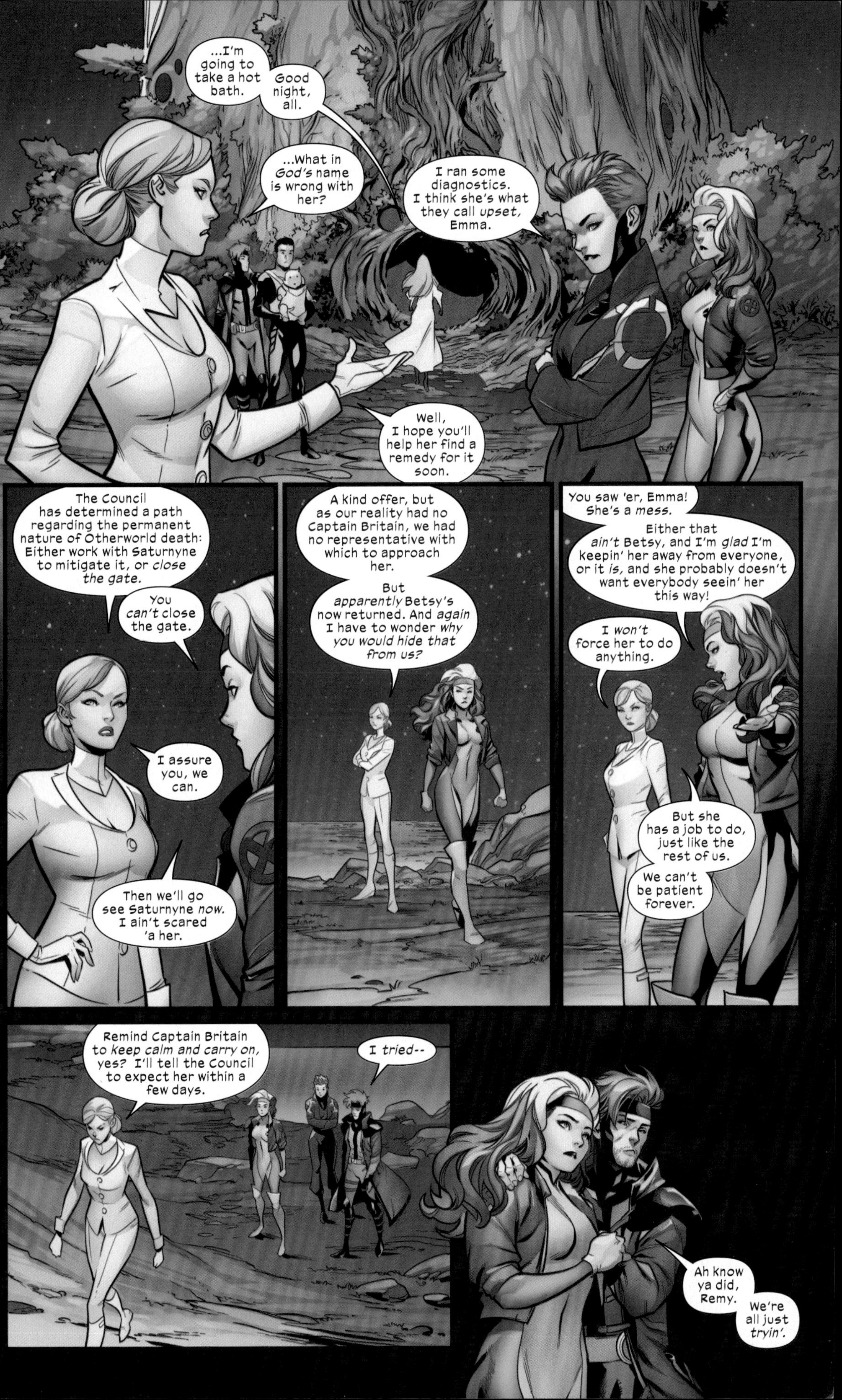
...I'm going to take a hot bath.
Good night, all.
...What in *God's* name is wrong with her?
I ran some diagnostics. I think she's what they call *upset*, Emma.
Well, I hope you'll help her find a remedy for it soon.
The Council has determined a path regarding the permanent nature of Otherworld death: Either work with Saturnyne to mitigate it, or *close the gate.*
You *can't* close the gate.
I assure you, we can.
Then we'll go see Saturnyne *now.* I ain't scared 'a her.
A kind offer, but as our reality had no Captain Britain, we had no representative with which to approach her.
But *apparently* Betsy's now returned. And *again* I have to wonder *why you would hide that from us?*
You saw 'er, Emma! She's a *mess.*
Either that *ain't* Betsy, and I'm *glad* I'm keepin' her away from everyone, or it *is*, and she probably doesn't want everybody seein' her this way!
I *won't* force her to do anything.
But she has a job to do, just like the rest of us.
We can't be patient forever.
Remind Captain Britain to *keep calm and carry on,* yes? I'll tell the Council to expect her within a few days.
I tried--
Ah know ya did, Remy.
We're all just *tryin'.*

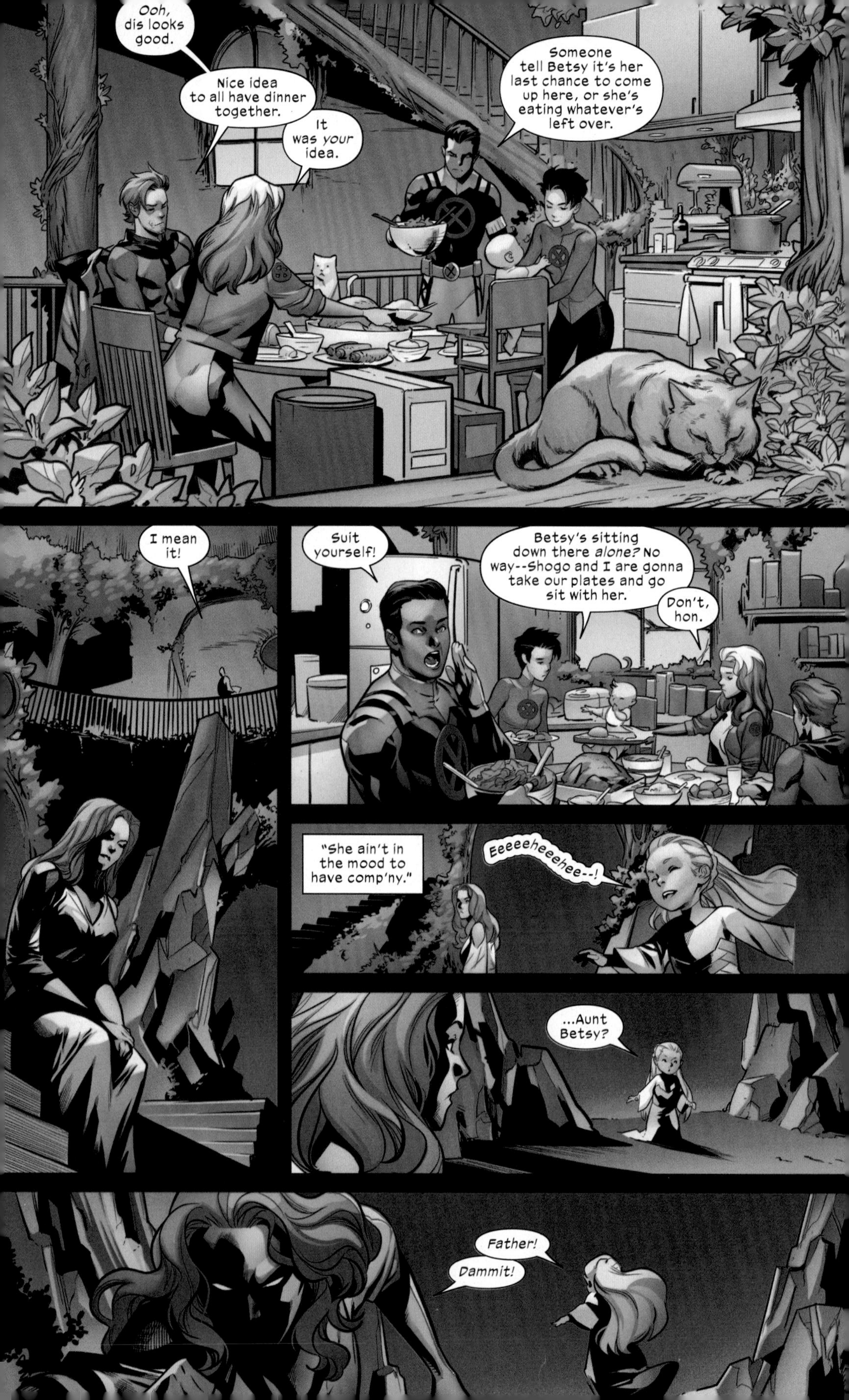
Ooh, dis looks good.
Nice idea to all have dinner together.
It was your idea.
Someone tell Betsy it's her last chance to come up here, or she's eating whatever's left over.
I mean it!
Suit yourself!
Betsy's sitting down there alone? No way--Shogo and I are gonna take our plates and go sit with her.
Don't, hon.
"She ain't in the mood to have comp'ny."
Eeeeeheeehee--!
...Aunt Betsy?
Father!
Dammit!

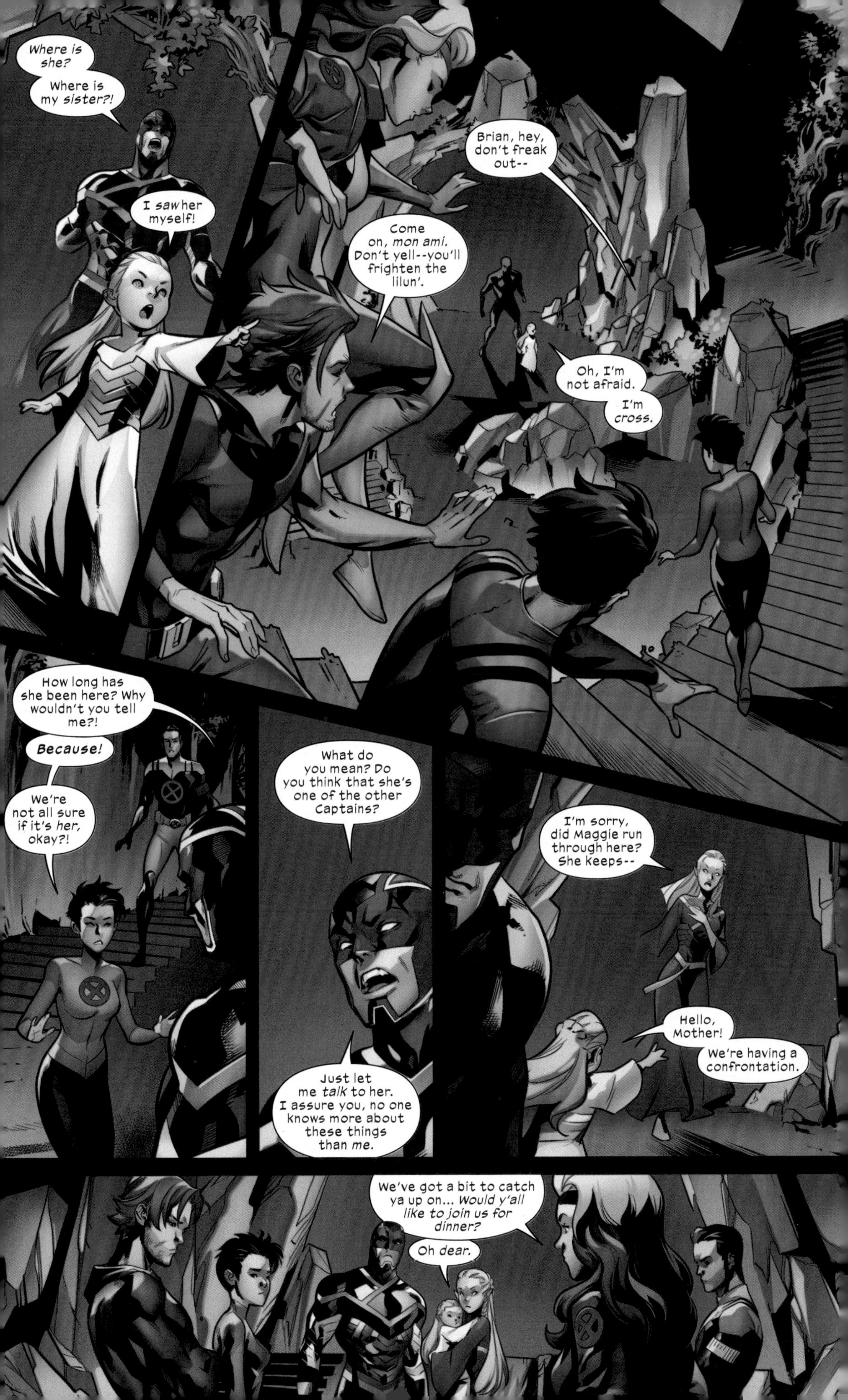
Where is she?
Where is my *sister?!*
I saw her myself!
Brian, hey, don't freak out--
Come on, *mon ami.* Don't yell--you'll frighten the lilun'.
Oh, I'm not afraid.
I'm *cross.*
How long has she been here? Why wouldn't you tell me?!
Because!
We're not all sure if it's *her,* okay?!
What do you mean? Do you think that she's one of the other Captains?
Just let me *talk* to her. I assure you, no one knows more about these things than *me.*
I'm sorry, did Maggie run through here? She keeps--
Hello, Mother!
We're having a confrontation.
We've got a bit to catch ya up on... *Would y'all like to join us for dinner?*
Oh dear.

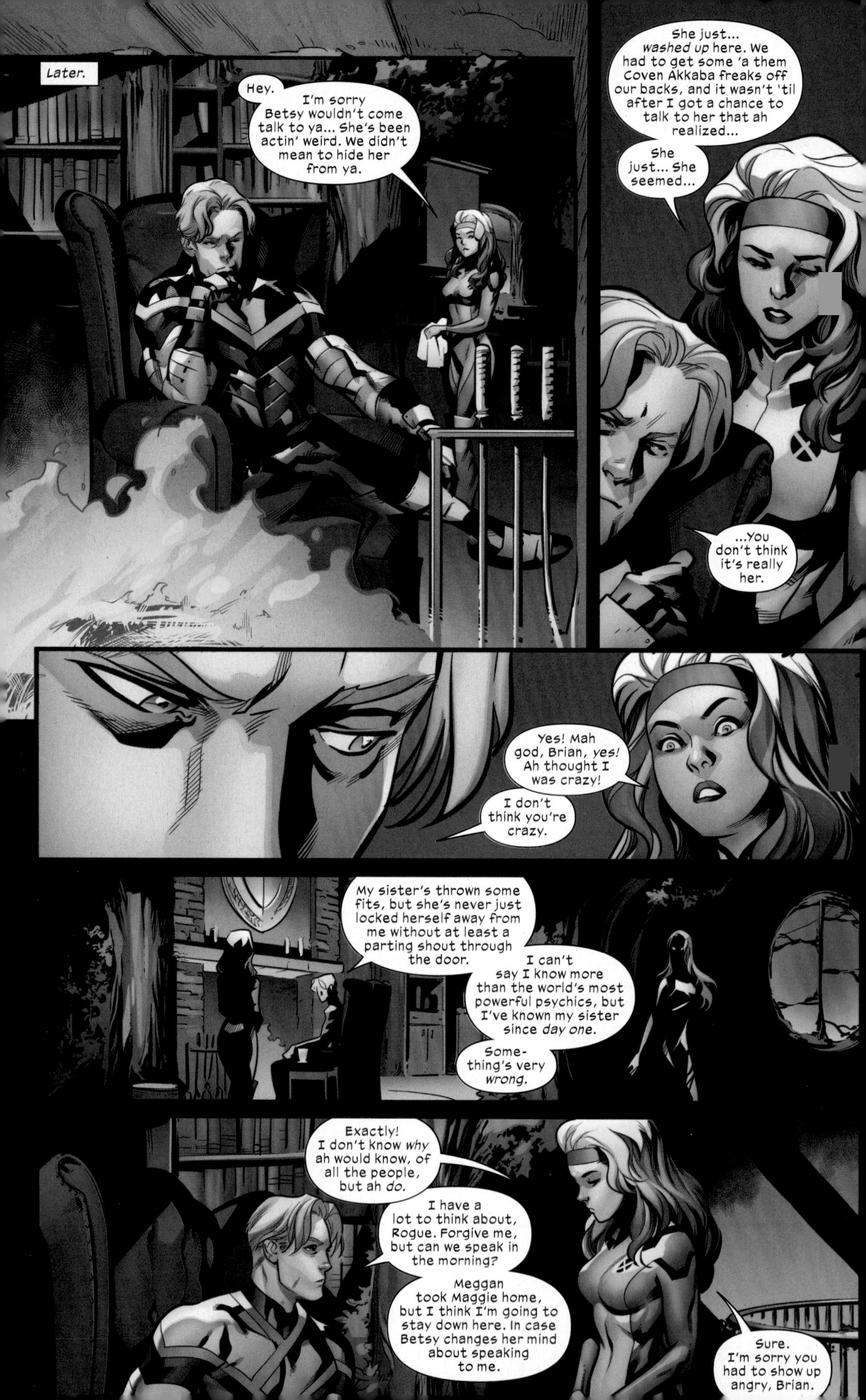

Later.
Hey.
I'm sorry Betsy wouldn't come talk to ya... She's been actin' weird. We didn't mean to hide her from ya.
She just... washed up here. We had to get some 'a them Coven Akkaba freaks off our backs, and it wasn't 'til after I got a chance to talk to her that ah realized...
She just... She seemed...
...You don't think it's really her.
Yes! Mah god, Brian, yes! Ah thought I was crazy!
I don't think you're crazy.
My sister's thrown some fits, but she's never just locked herself away from me without at least a parting shout through the door.
I can't say I know more than the world's most powerful psychics, but I've known my sister since day one.
Some-thing's very wrong.
Exactly! I don't know why ah would know, of all the people, but ah do.
I have a lot to think about, Rogue. Forgive me, but can we speak in the morning?
Meggan took Maggie home, but I think I'm going to stay down here. In case Betsy changes her mind about speaking to me.
Sure. I'm sorry you had to show up angry, Brian.

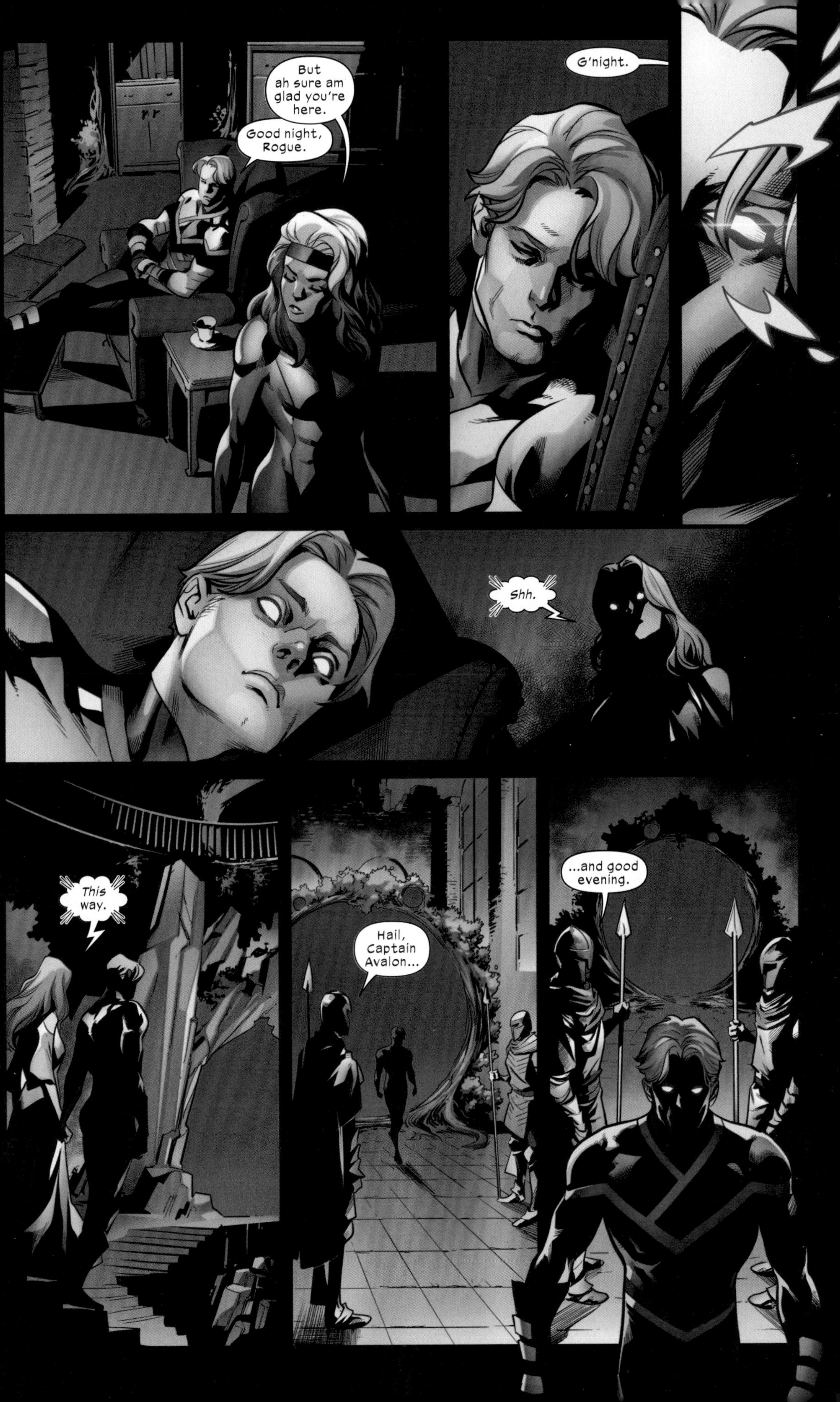

But ah sure am glad you're here.
Good night, Rogue.
G'night.
Shh.
This way.
Hail, Captain Avalon...
...and good evening.

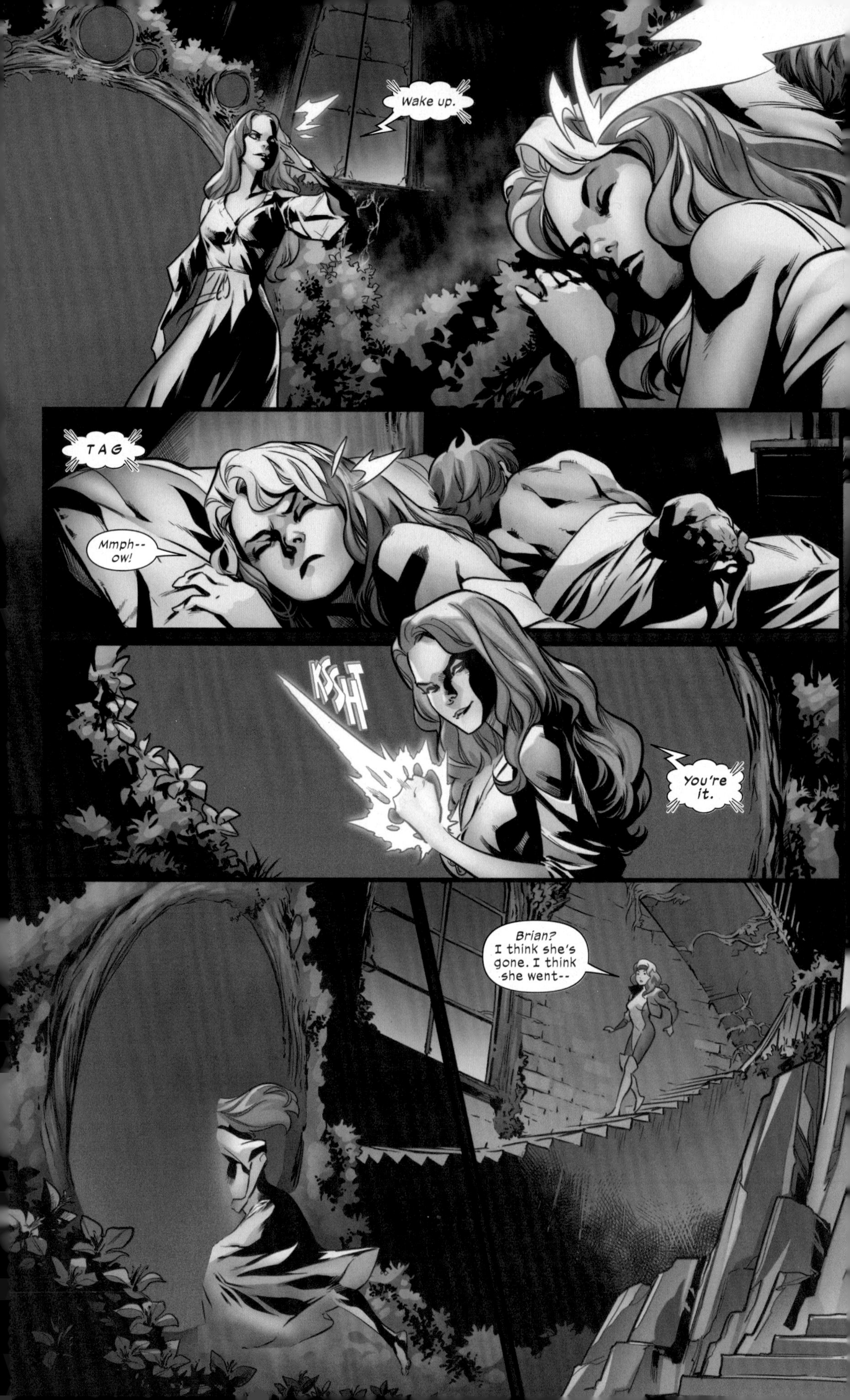

Wake up.
TAG
Mmph-- ow!
KSSHT
You're it.
Brian? I think she's gone. I think she went--

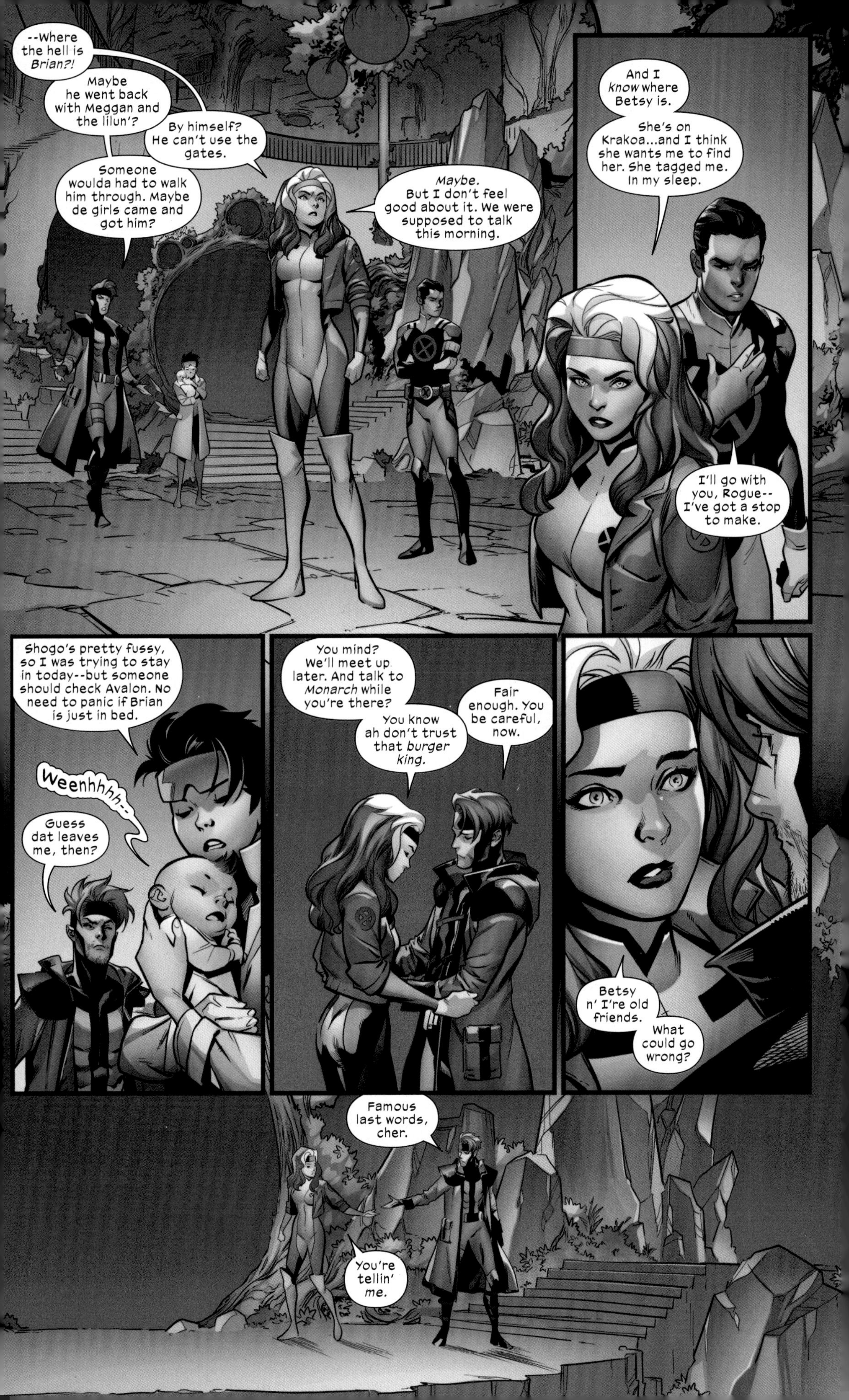
--Where the hell is *Brian?!*
Maybe he went back with Meggan and the lilun'?
By himself? He can't use the gates.
Someone woulda had to walk him through. Maybe de girls came and got him?
Maybe. But I don't feel good about it. We were supposed to talk this morning.
And I *know* where Betsy is.
She's on Krakoa...and I think she wants me to find her. She tagged me. In my sleep.
I'll go with you, Rogue--I've got a stop to make.
Shogo's pretty fussy, so I was trying to stay in today--but someone should check Avalon. No need to panic if Brian is just in bed.
Weenhhhh--
Guess dat leaves me, then?
You mind? We'll meet up later. And talk to *Monarch* while you're there?
You know ah don't trust that *burger king.*
Fair enough. You be careful, now.
Betsy n' I're old friends.
What could go wrong?
Famous last words, cher.
You're tellin' *me.*

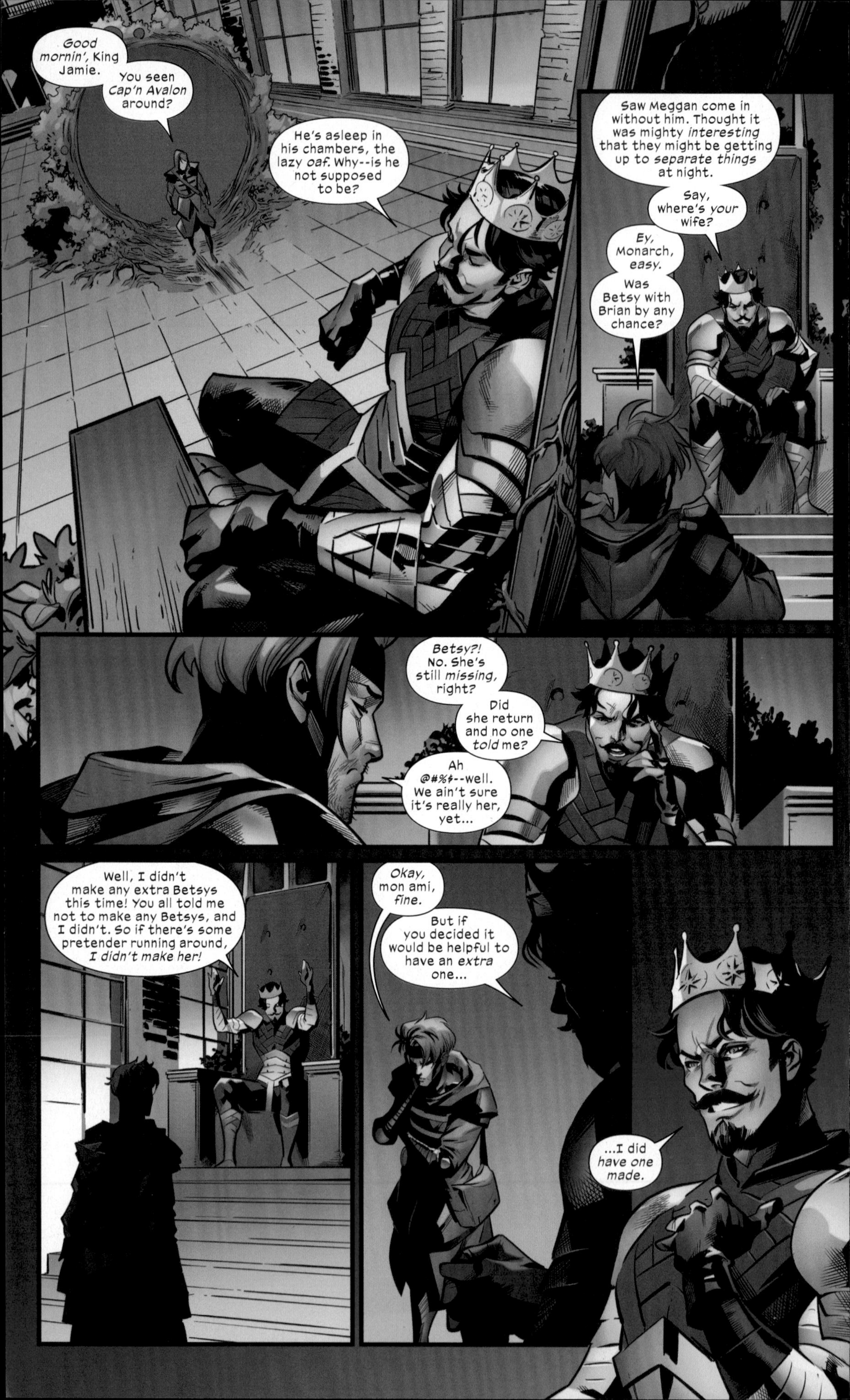
Good mornin', King Jamie.
You seen Cap'n Avalon around?
He's asleep in his chambers, the lazy oaf. Why--is he not supposed to be?
Saw Meggan come in without him. Thought it was mighty interesting that they might be getting up to separate things at night.
Say, where's your wife?
Ey, Monarch, easy.
Was Betsy with Brian by any chance?
Betsy?! No. She's still missing, right?
Did she return and no one told me?
Ah @#%$--well. We ain't sure it's really her, yet...
Well, I didn't make any extra Betsys this time! You all told me not to make any Betsys, and I didn't. So if there's some pretender running around, I didn't make her!
Okay, mon ami, fine.
But if you decided it would be helpful to have an extra one...
...I did have one made.

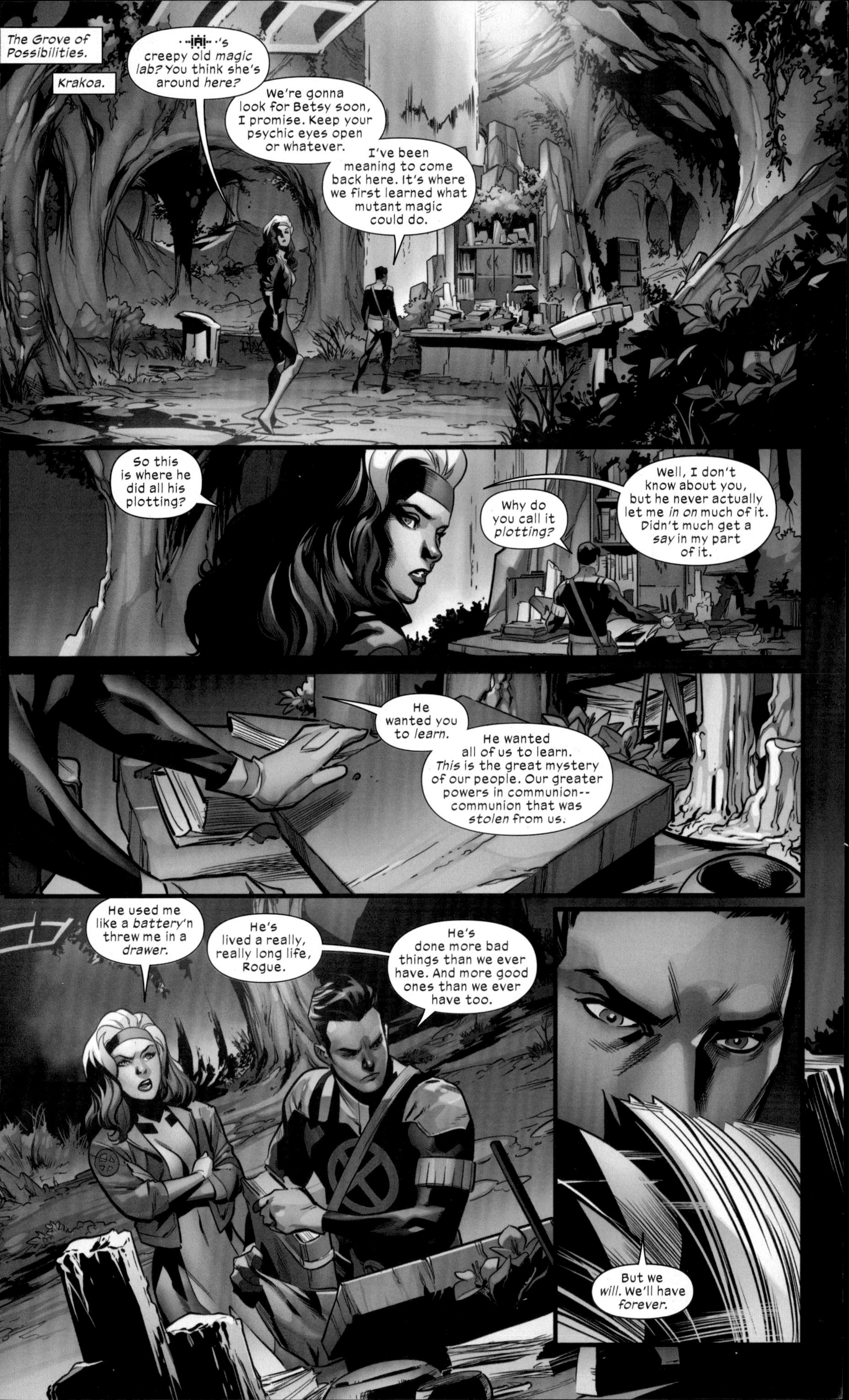
The Grove of Possibilities.
Krakoa.
's creepy old magic lab? You think she's around here?
We're gonna look for Betsy soon, I promise. Keep your psychic eyes open or whatever.
I've been meaning to come back here. It's where we first learned what mutant magic could do.
So this is where he did all his plotting?
Why do you call it plotting?
Well, I don't know about you, but he never actually let me in on much of it. Didn't much get a say in my part of it.
He wanted you to learn.
He wanted all of us to learn. This is the great mystery of our people. Our greater powers in communion-- communion that was stolen from us.
He used me like a battery'n threw me in a drawer.
He's lived a really, really long life, Rogue.
He's done more bad things than we ever have. And more good ones than we ever have too.
But we will. We'll have forever.

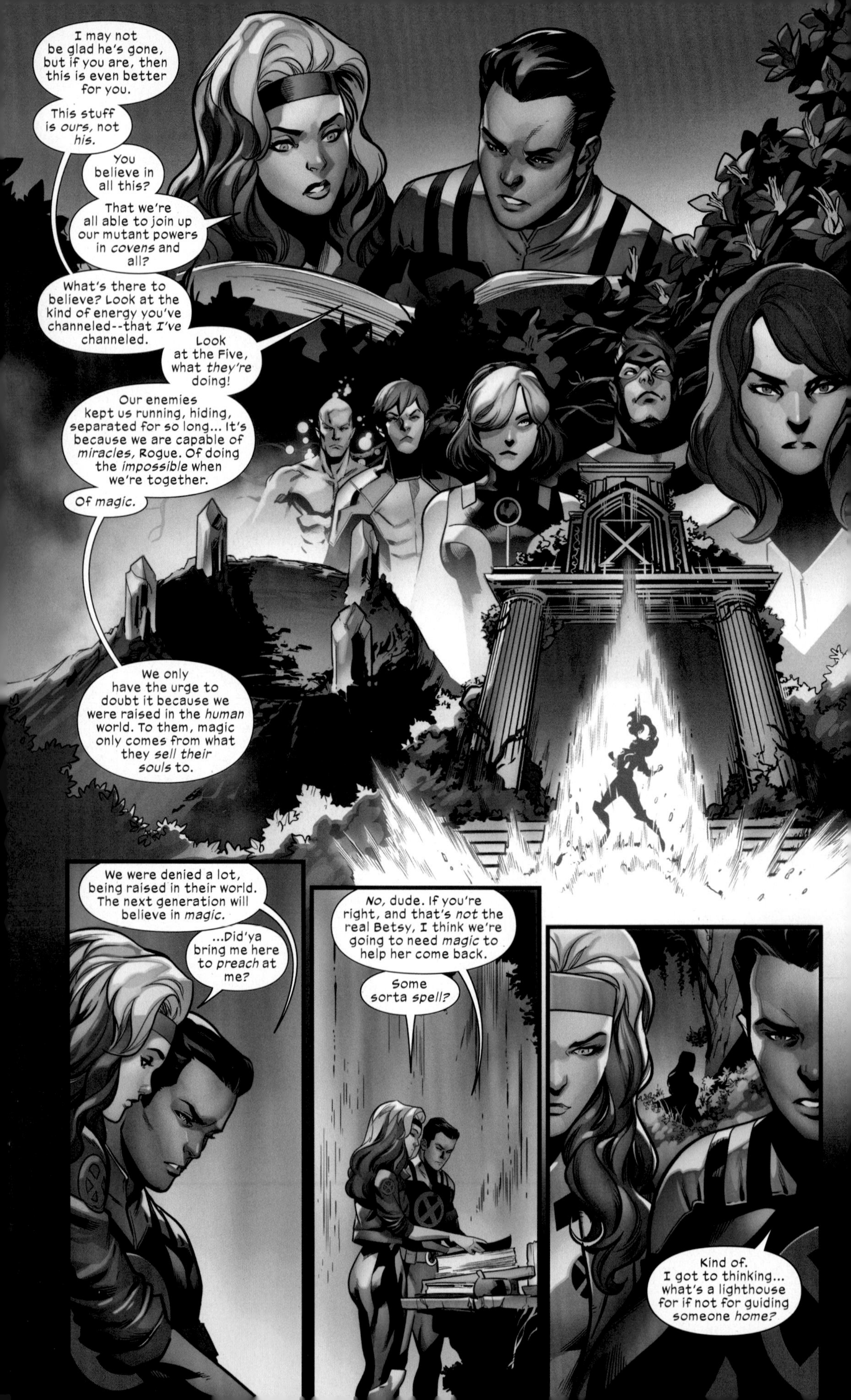

I may not be glad he's gone, but if you are, then this is even better for you.
This stuff is *ours*, not *his*.
You believe in all this?
That we're all able to join up our mutant powers in *covens* and all?
What's there to believe? Look at the kind of energy you've channeled--that *I've* channeled.
Look at the Five, what *they're* doing!
Our enemies kept us running, hiding, separated for so long... It's because we are capable of *miracles*, Rogue. Of doing the *impossible* when we're together.
Of *magic*.
We only have the urge to doubt it because we were raised in the *human* world. To them, magic only comes from what they *sell their souls* to.
We were denied a lot, being raised in their world. The next generation will believe in *magic*.
...Did'ya bring me here to *preach* at me?
No, dude. If you're right, and that's *not* the real Betsy, I think we're going to need *magic* to help her come back.
Some sorta *spell*?
Kind of. I got to thinking... what's a lighthouse for if not for guiding someone *home*?

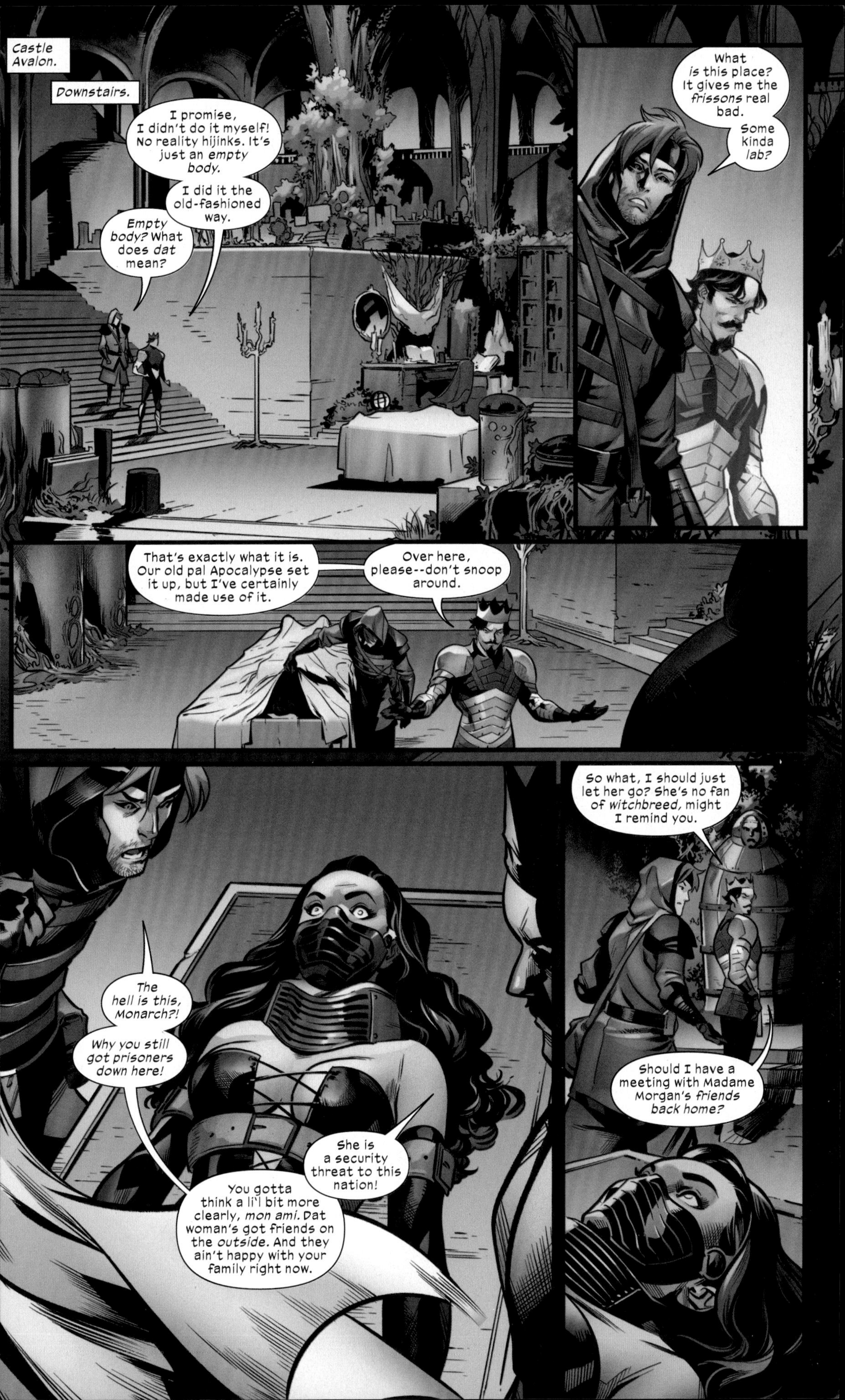
Castle Avalon.
Downstairs.
I promise, I didn't do it myself! No reality hijinks. It's just an *empty body.*
I did it the old-fashioned way.
Empty body? What does *dat* mean?
What *is* this place? It gives me the *frissons* real bad.
Some kinda *lab?*
That's exactly what it is. Our old pal Apocalypse set it up, but I've certainly made use of it.
Over here, please--don't snoop around.
The hell is this, Monarch?!
Why you still got prisoners down here!
She is a security threat to this nation!
You gotta think a li'l bit more clearly, *mon ami.* Dat woman's got friends on the *outside.* And they ain't happy with your family right now.
So what, I should just let her go? She's no fan of *witchbreed,* might I remind you.
Should I have a meeting with Madame Morgan's *friends back home?*

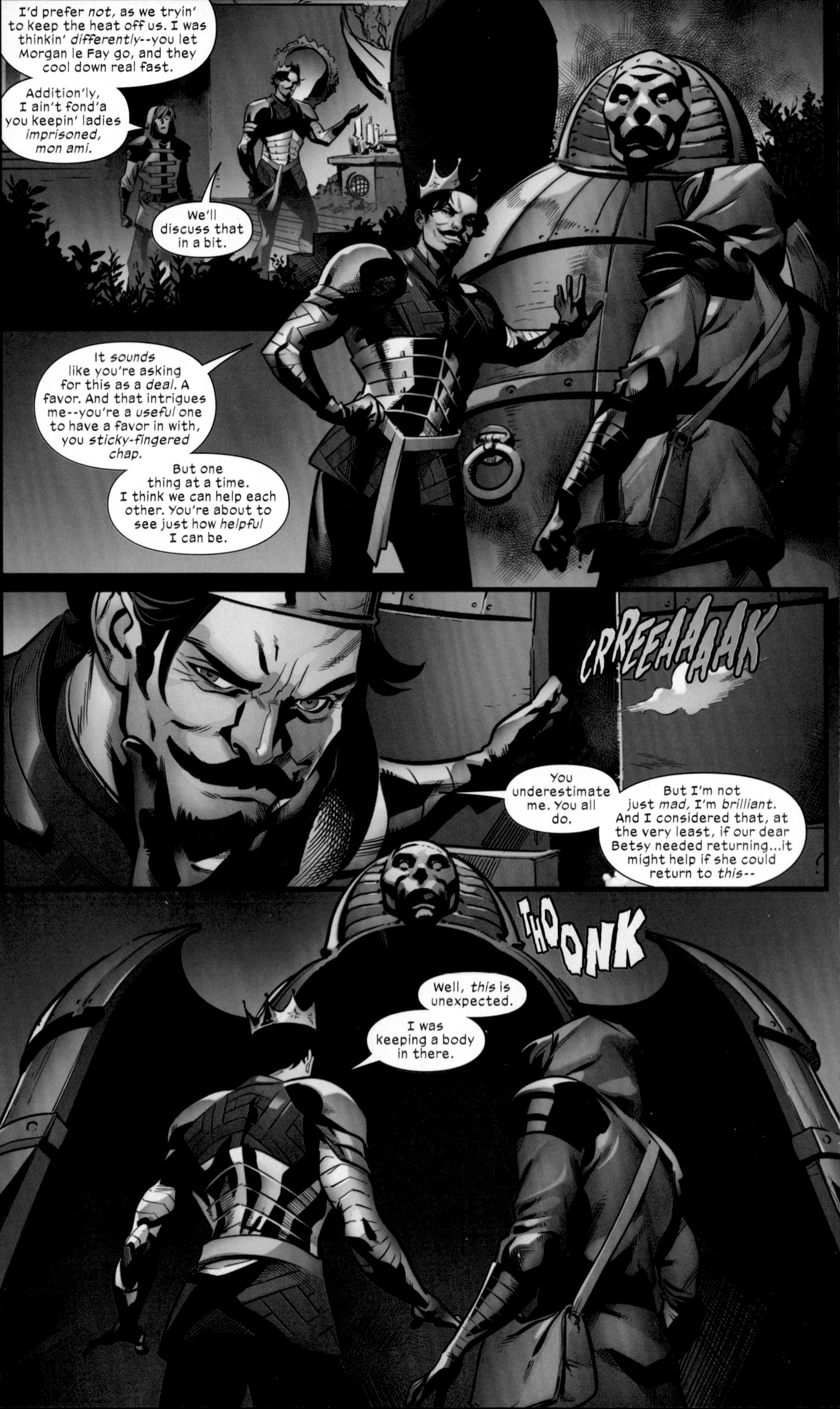
I'd prefer *not*, as we tryin' to keep the heat off us. I was thinkin' *differently*--you let Morgan le Fay go, and they cool down real fast.
Addition'ly, I ain't fond'a you keepin' ladies *imprisoned*, *mon ami*.
We'll discuss that in a bit.
It *sounds* like you're asking for this as a *deal*. A favor. And that intrigues me--you're a *useful* one to have a favor in with, you *sticky-fingered chap*.
But one thing at a time. I think we can help each other. You're about to see just how *helpful* I can be.
CRREEAAAAK
You underestimate me. You all do.
But I'm not just *mad*, I'm *brilliant*. And I considered that, at the very least, if our dear Betsy needed returning...it might help if she could return to *this*--
THOONK
Well, *this* is unexpected.
I was keeping a body in there.

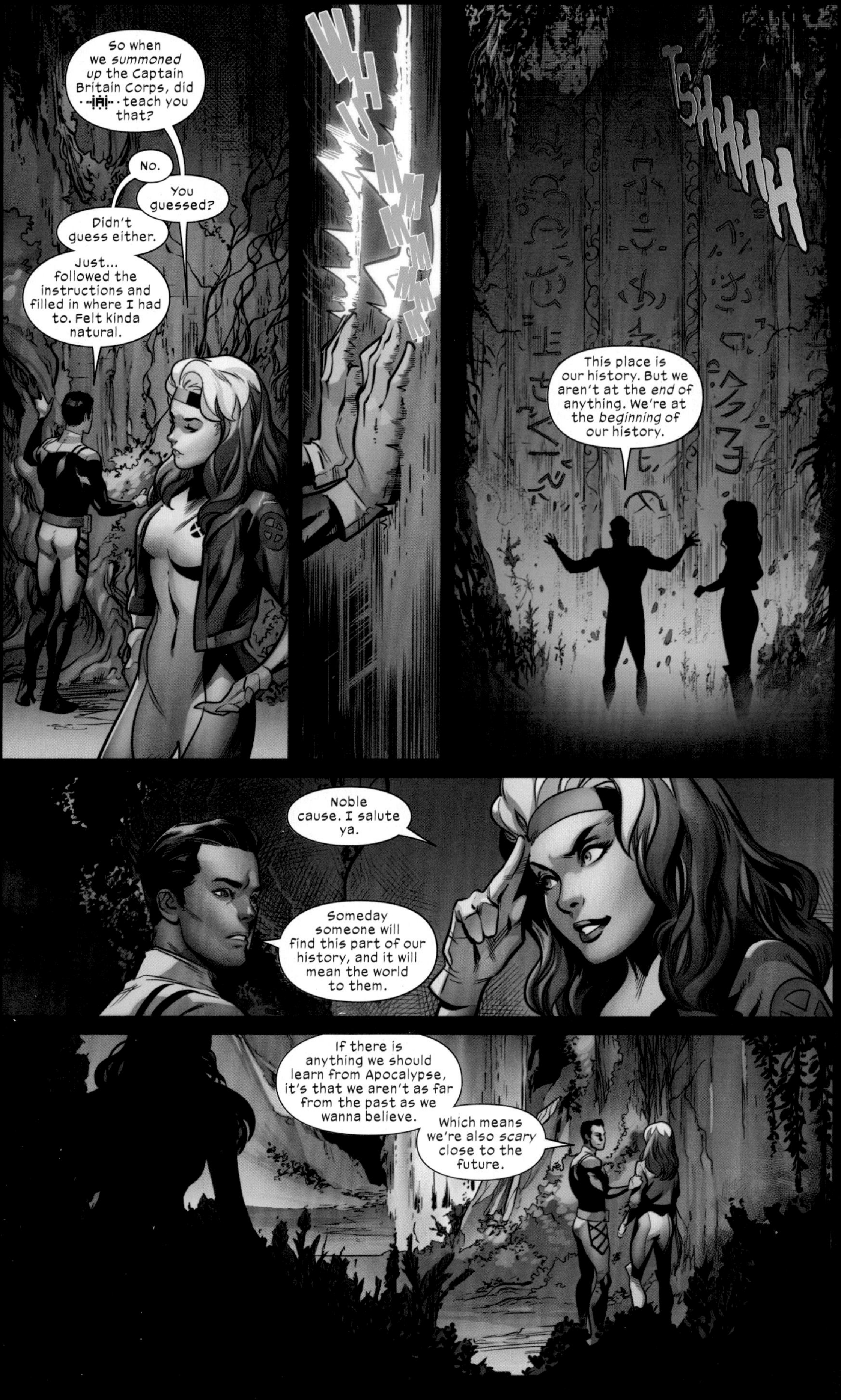

So when we *summoned up* the Captain Britain Corps, did teach you that?
No.
You guessed?
Didn't guess either.
Just... followed the instructions and filled in where I had to. Felt kinda natural.
This place is our history. But we aren't at the *end* of anything. We're at the *beginning* of our history.
Noble cause. I salute ya.
Someday someone will find this part of our history, and it will mean the world to them.
If there is anything we should learn from Apocalypse, it's that we aren't as far from the past as we wanna believe.
Which means we're also *scary* close to the future.

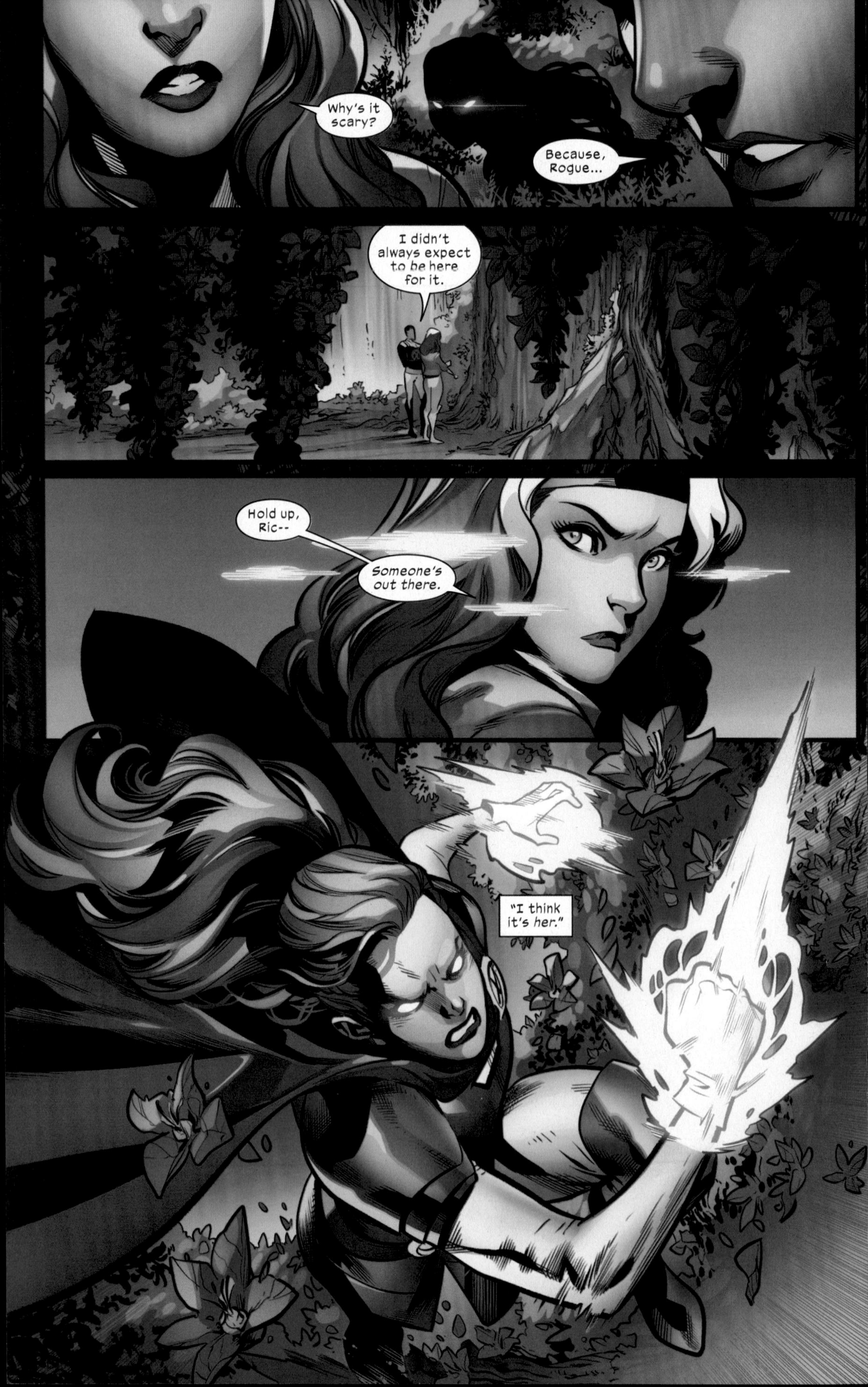

Why's it scary?
Because, Rogue...
I didn't always expect to be here for it.
Hold up, Ric--
Someone's out there.
"I think it's her."

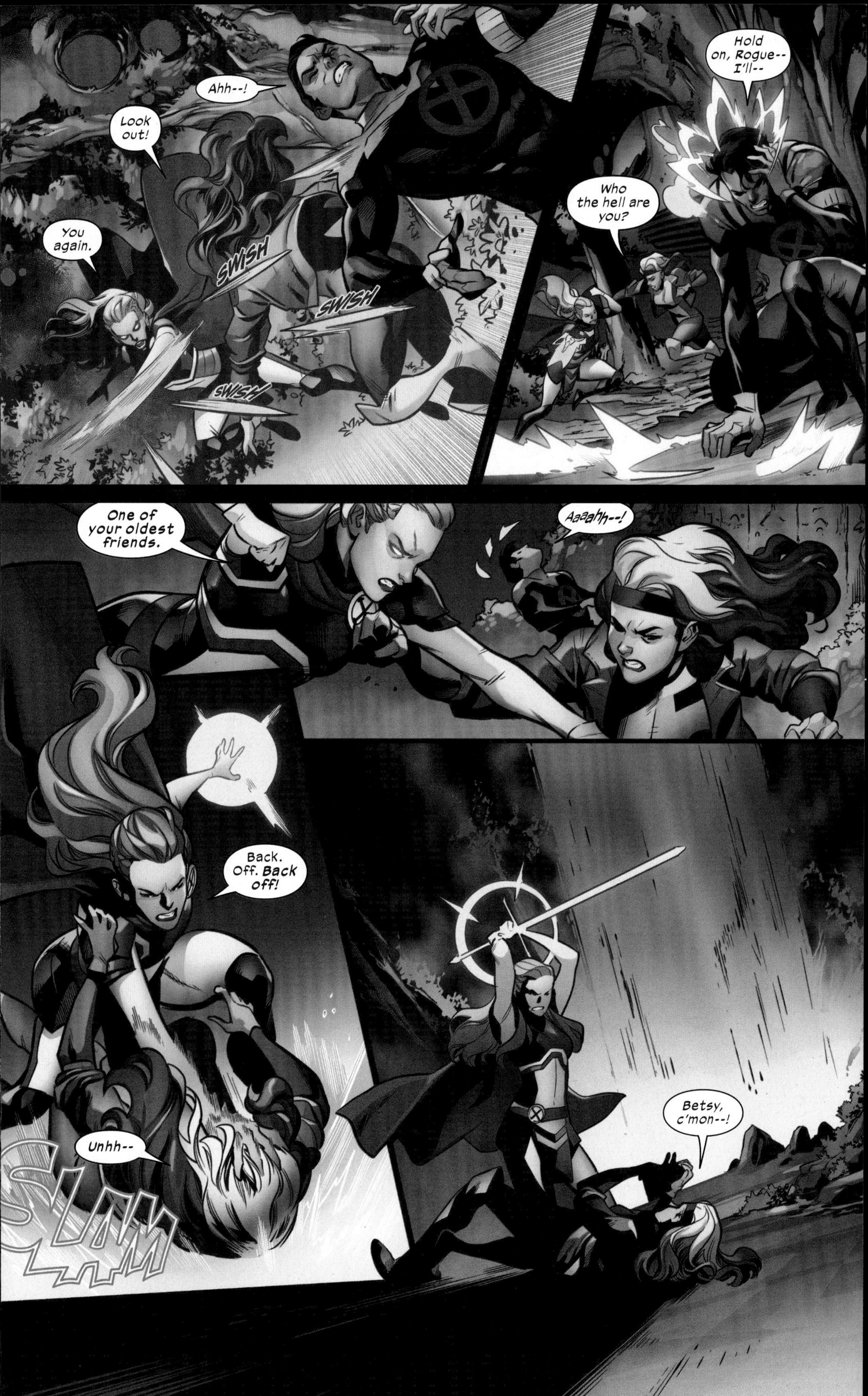
Ahh--!
Look out!
You again.
SWISH
SWISH
SWISH
Hold on, Rogue-- I'll--
Who the hell are you?
One of your oldest friends.
Aaaahh--!
Back. Off. Back off!
Unhh--
SLAM
Betsy, c'mon--!

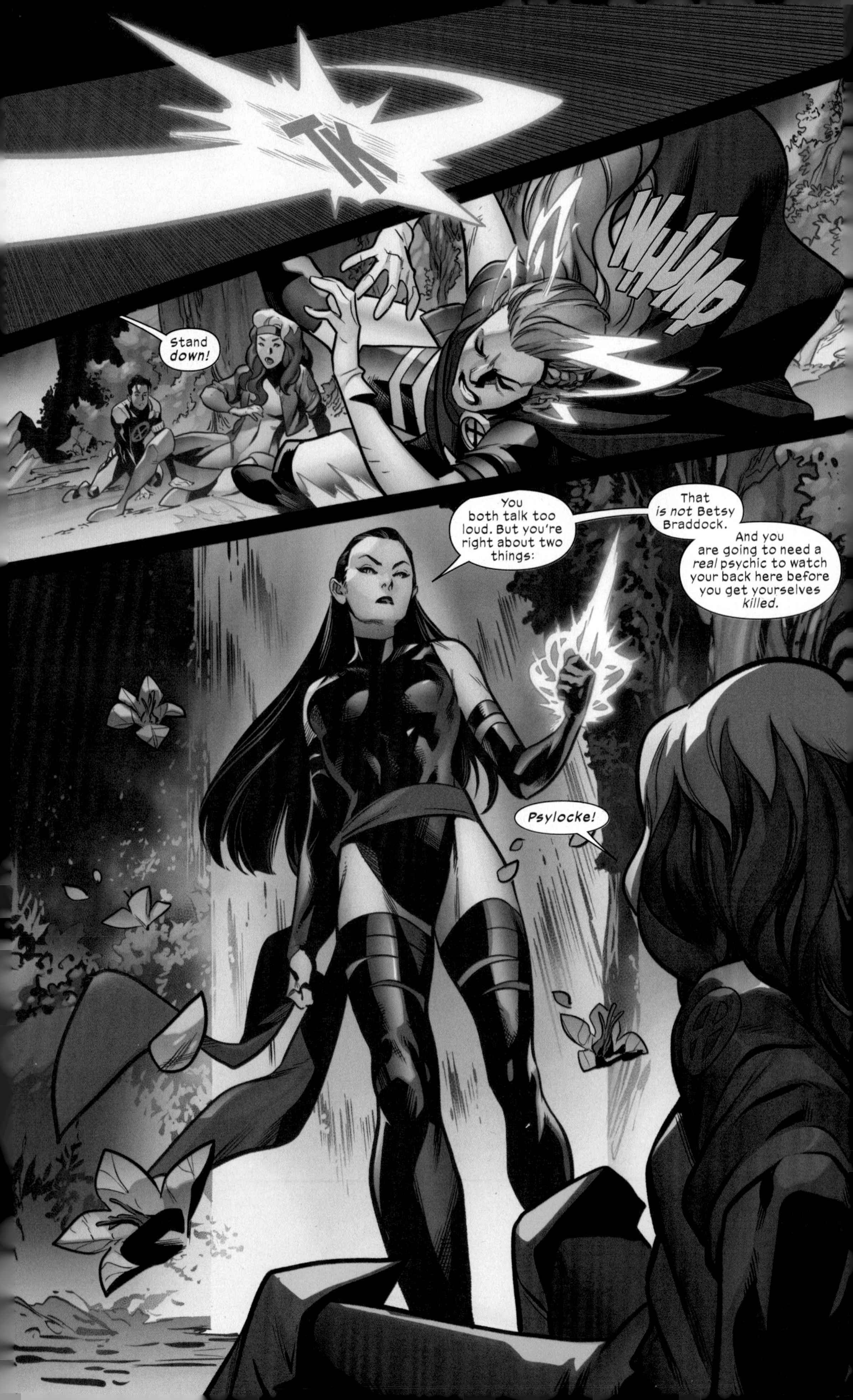
TK
WHUMP
Stand down!
You both talk too loud. But you're right about two things:
That *is not* Betsy Braddock.
And you are going to need a *real* psychic to watch your back here before you get yourselves *killed.*
Psylocke!

RICTOR -

I translated what you showed me on the wall - that's an old language. Not one that was ever commonly used anywhere. He must've known someone would bring it to me, so we can keep it pretty private. I filed a copy of this with the Council. Just in case. Congratulations?

-CYPHER

TRANSLATION BEGINS:

As we have defeated death, it did not occur to me that we might have a need for wills or other mortal codices. But I know that I am leaving soon, and have affairs to settle.

I, 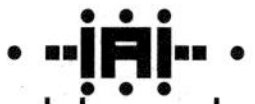 of Krakoa, declare this Will of my intent after I am gone, and hereby revoke any existing wills or codices.

To my apprentice, I leave everything.

(Rictor - In the place in your heart where you have always seen a failure, there is instead a fault - a deep aching split in you that exposes a molten heat. You have always endured it. It is what I have always known about you - the great secret of the powers of Earth is that you must have a spirit that can stand to the heat beneath.)

Like Cypher is the only one who can hear Krakoa's words, you are the only one that can hear her heartbeat. This era among us has given you the power of the land, made you powerful in a way previously undreamt. It is why this magic must be yours. All I have learned and gathered of our magic, I leave to you.

As you read this, you know by now why I have done what I have done. Everything before now is pre-history.

I leave it all in your hands.

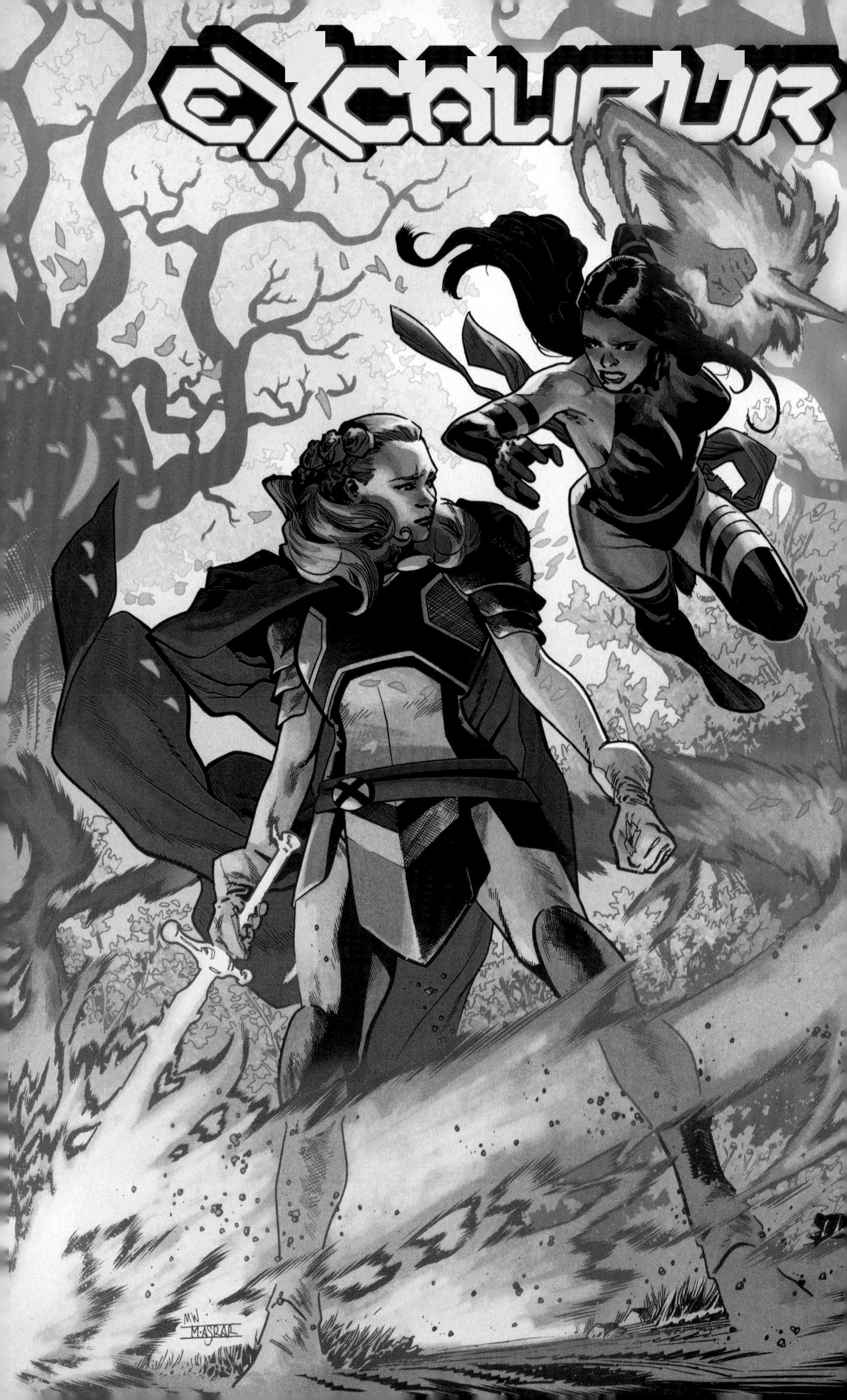
EXCALIBUR

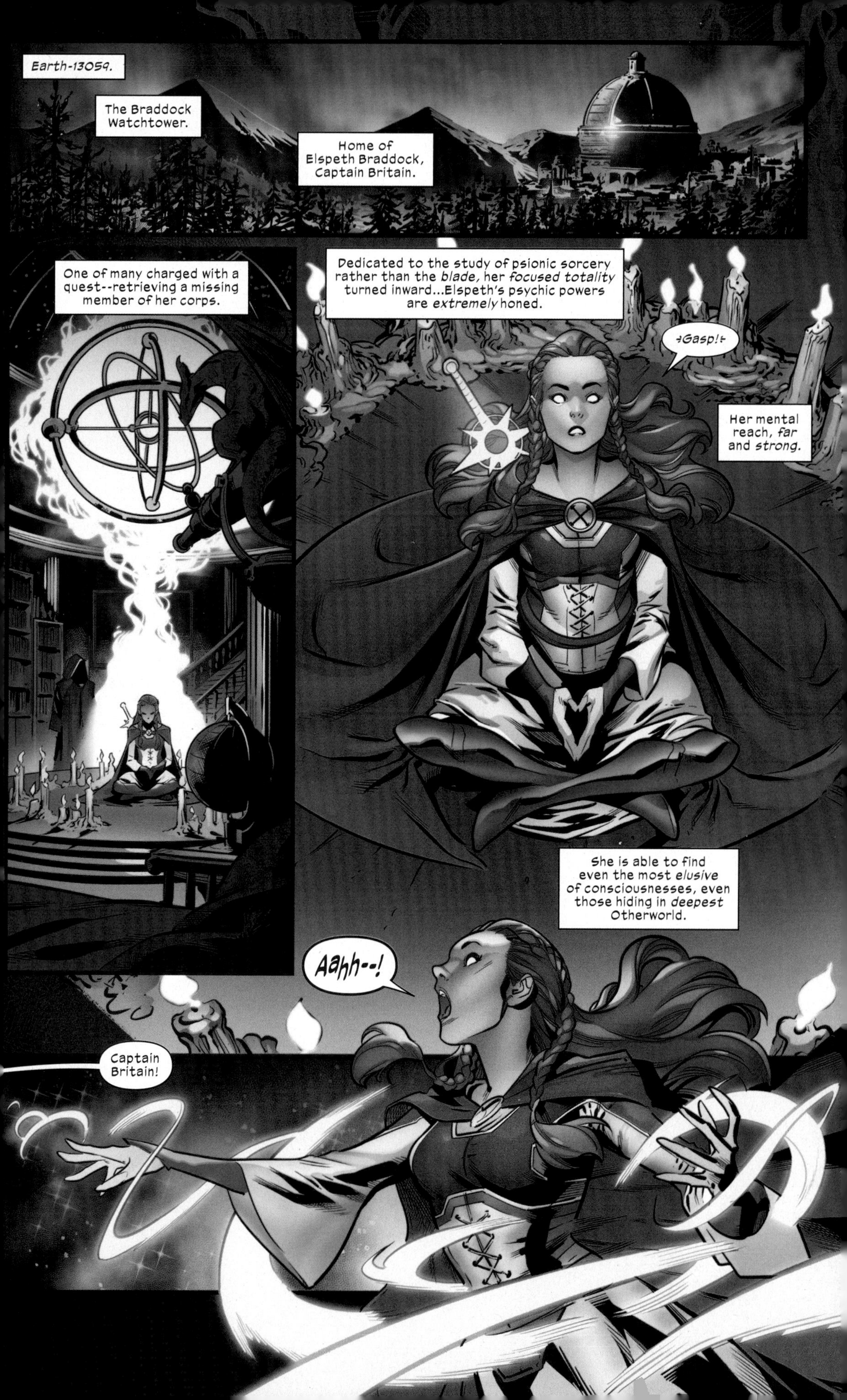

Earth-13059.
The Braddock Watchtower.
Home of Elspeth Braddock, Captain Britain.
One of many charged with a quest--retrieving a missing member of her corps.
Dedicated to the study of psionic sorcery rather than the blade, her focused totality turned inward...Elspeth's psychic powers are extremely honed.
Gasp!
Her mental reach, far and strong.
She is able to find even the most elusive of consciousnesses, even those hiding in deepest Otherworld.
Aahh--!
Captain Britain!

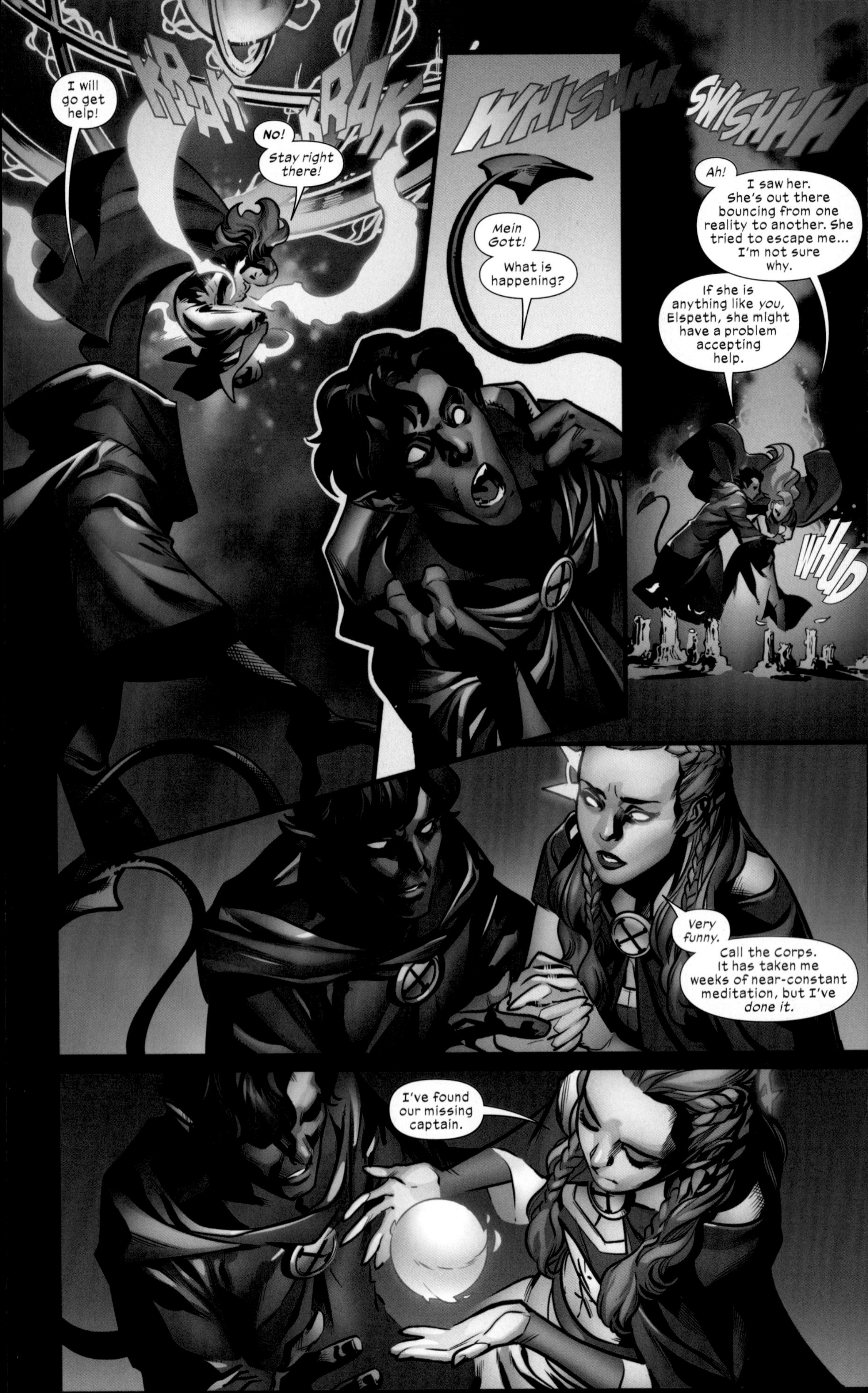

I will go get help!
KRAK
KRAK
No!
Stay right there!
WHISHHH
SWISHHH
Mein Gott!
What is happening?
Ah!
I saw her. She's out there bouncing from one reality to another. She tried to escape me... I'm not sure why.
If she is anything like *you*, Elspeth, she might have a problem accepting help.
WHUD
Very funny.
Call the Corps. It has taken me weeks of near-constant meditation, but I've *done it.*
I've found our missing captain.

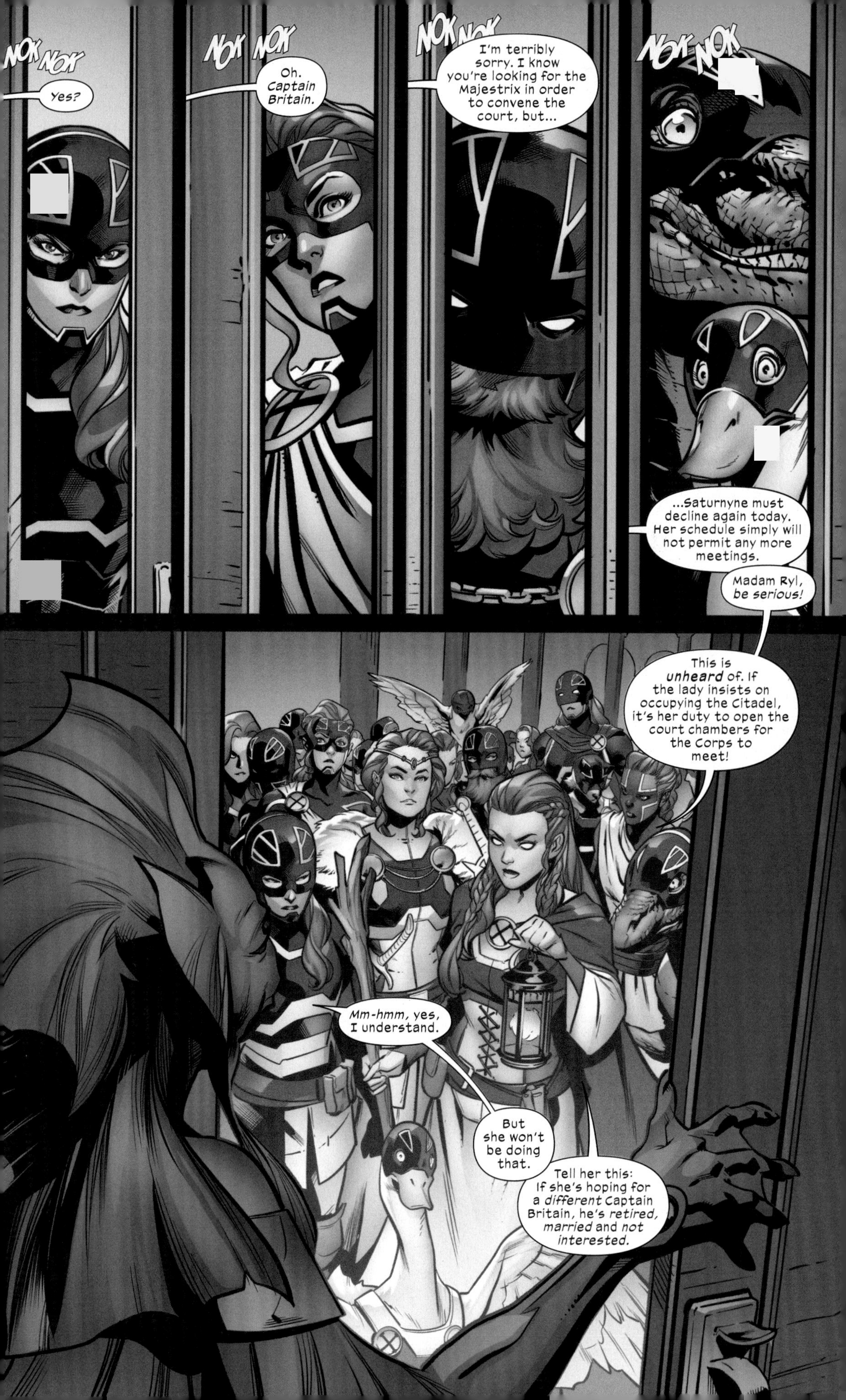

NOK NOK
Yes?
NOK NOK
Oh. Captain Britain.
NOK NOK
I'm terribly sorry. I know you're looking for the Majestrix in order to convene the court, but...
NOK NOK
...Saturnyne must decline again today. Her schedule simply will not permit any more meetings.
Madam Ryl, *be serious!*
This is *unheard* of. If the lady insists on occupying the Citadel, it's her duty to open the court chambers for the Corps to meet!
Mm-hmm, yes, I understand.
But she won't be doing that.
Tell her this: If she's hoping for a *different* Captain Britain, he's *retired, married* and *not interested.*

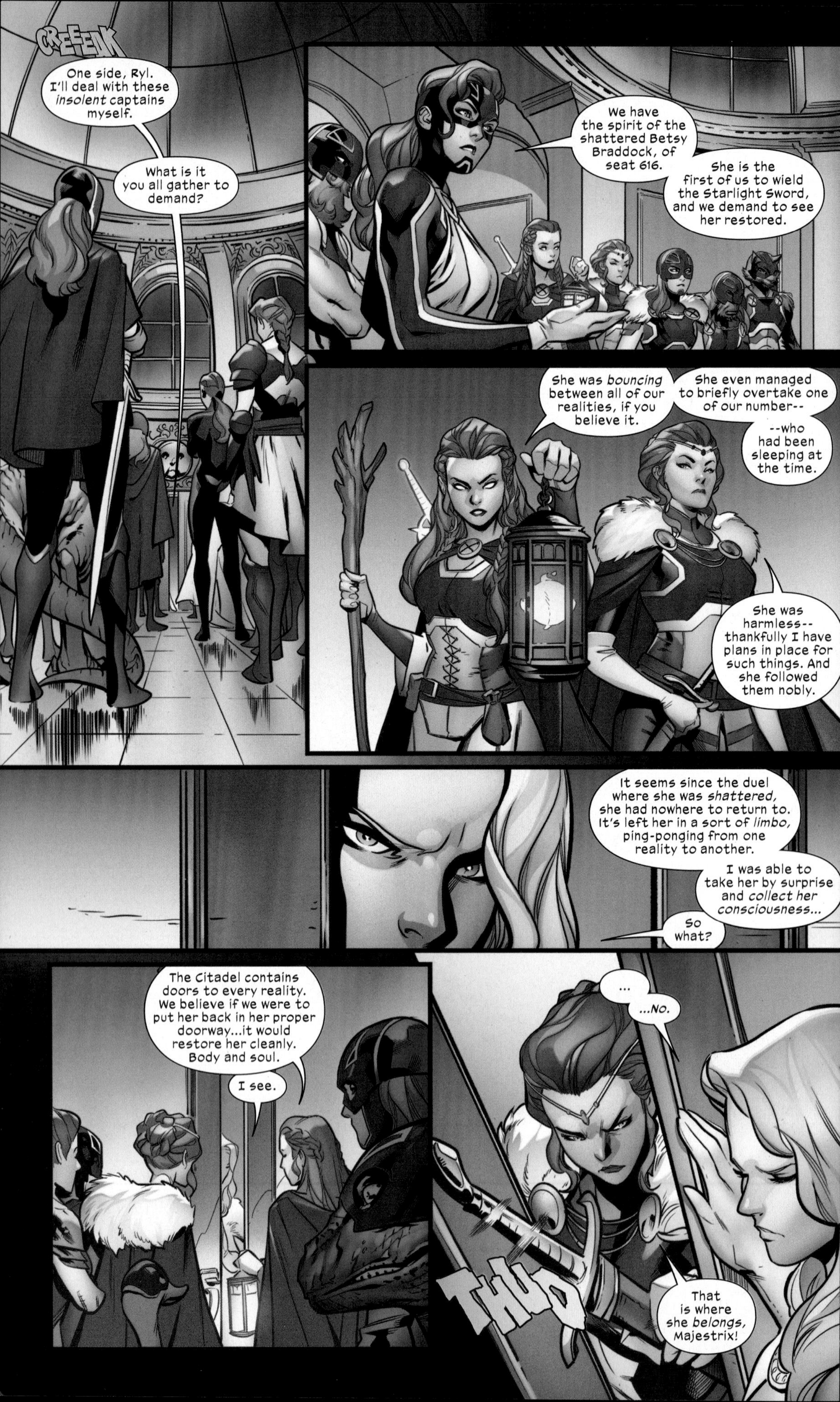
CREEEEK
One side, Ryl. I'll deal with these *insolent* captains myself.
What is it you all gather to demand?
We have the spirit of the shattered Betsy Braddock, of seat 616.
She is the first of us to wield the Starlight Sword, and we demand to see her restored.
She was *bouncing* between all of our realities, if you believe it.
She even managed to briefly overtake one of our number--
--who had been sleeping at the time.
She was harmless--thankfully I have plans in place for such things. And she followed them nobly.
It seems since the duel where she was *shattered,* she had nowhere to return to. It's left her in a sort of *limbo,* ping-ponging from one reality to another.
I was able to take her by surprise and *collect her consciousness...*
So what?
The Citadel contains doors to every reality. We believe if we were to put her back in her proper doorway...it would restore her cleanly. Body and soul.
I see.
...
...NO.
THUD
That is where she *belongs,* Majestrix!

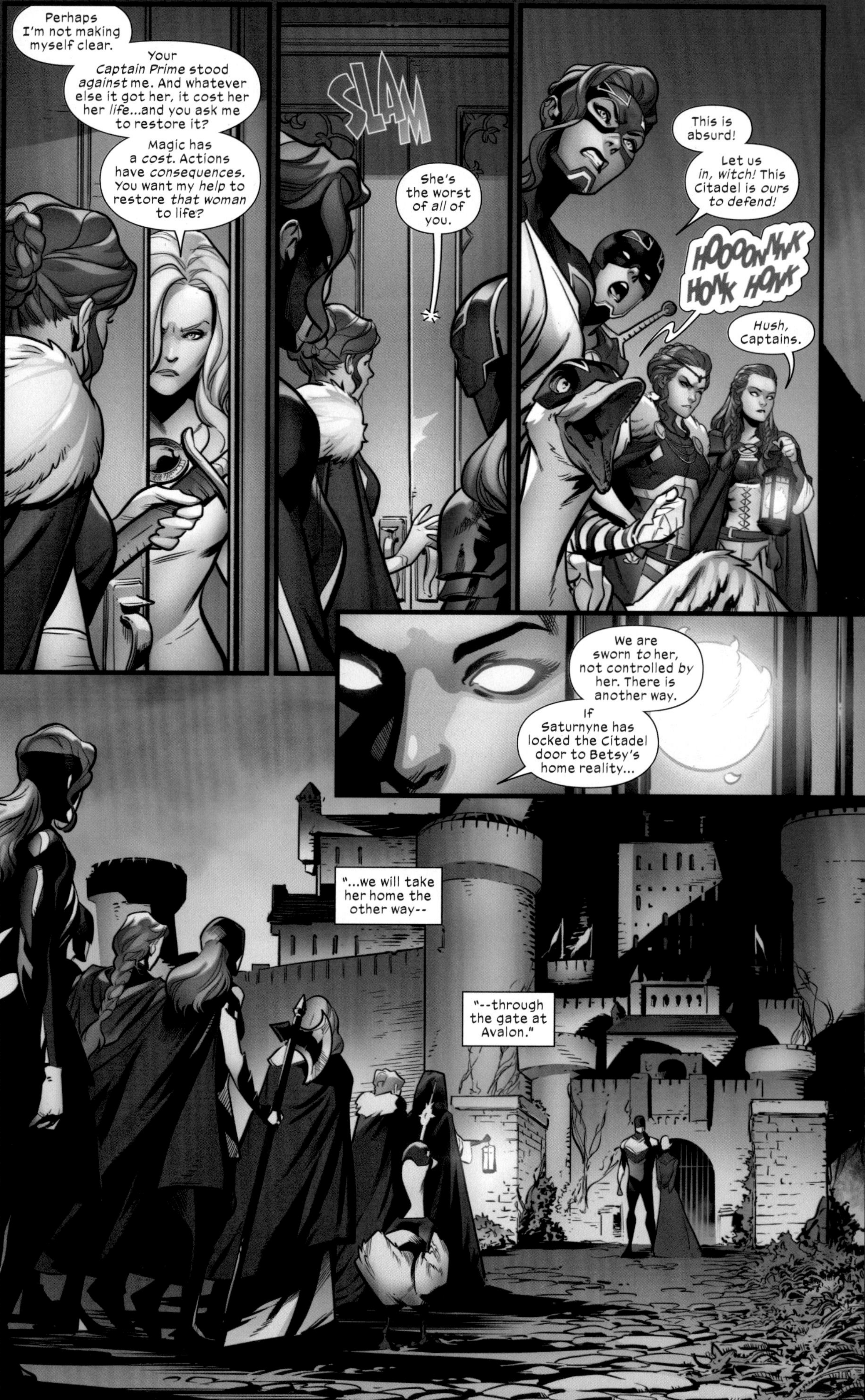
Perhaps I'm not making myself clear.
Your Captain Prime stood against me. And whatever else it got her, it cost her her life...and you ask me to restore it?
Magic has a cost. Actions have consequences. You want my help to restore that woman to life?
SLAM
She's the worst of all of you.
This is absurd!
Let us in, witch! This Citadel is ours to defend!
HOOOONK HONK HONK
Hush, Captains.
We are sworn to her, not controlled by her. There is another way.
If Saturnyne has locked the Citadel door to Betsy's home reality...
"...we will take her home the other way--
"--through the gate at Avalon."

BODY & SOUL

When Captain Britain went missing, EXCALIBUR leaped into action to find her -- and while they thought she was back... the thing inside Betsy's body was not her.

Now Psylocke, the assassin whose body Betsy used to inhabit, is on the case -- and there's no one better for the job.

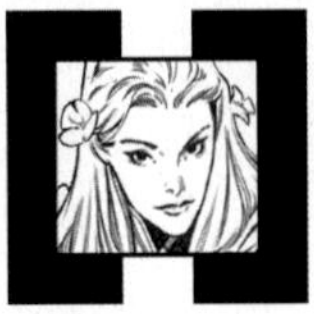
Captain Britain

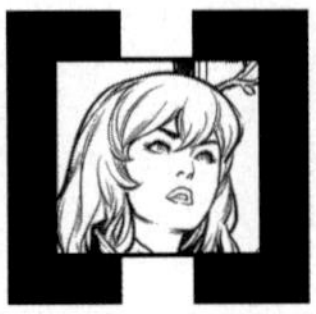
Rogue

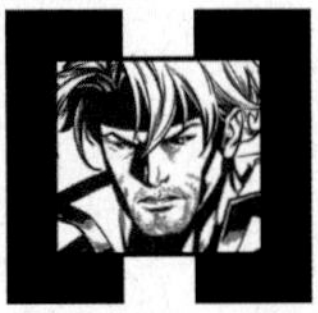
Gambit

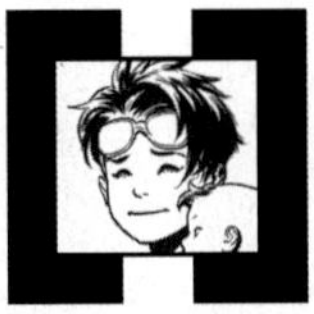
Jubilee

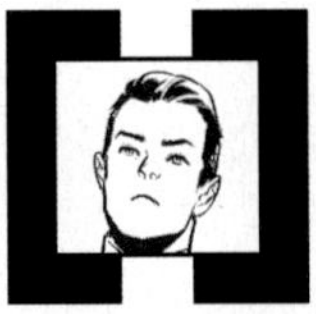
Rictor

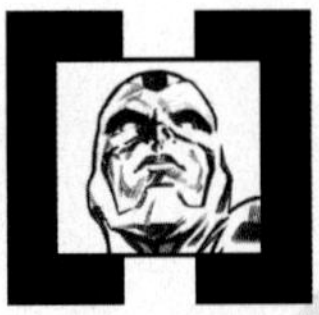
Captain Avalon

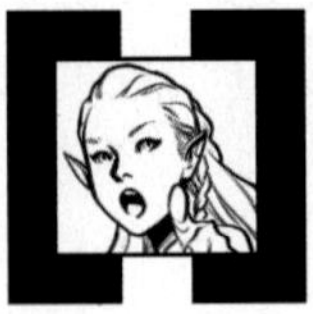
Gloriana

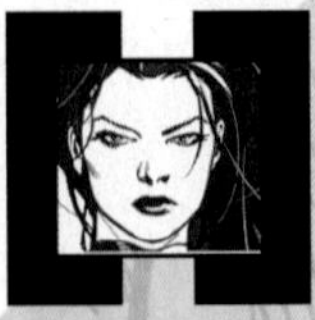
Psylocke

[00_Reign]
[00___ofX]

EXCALIBUR

[X_19]

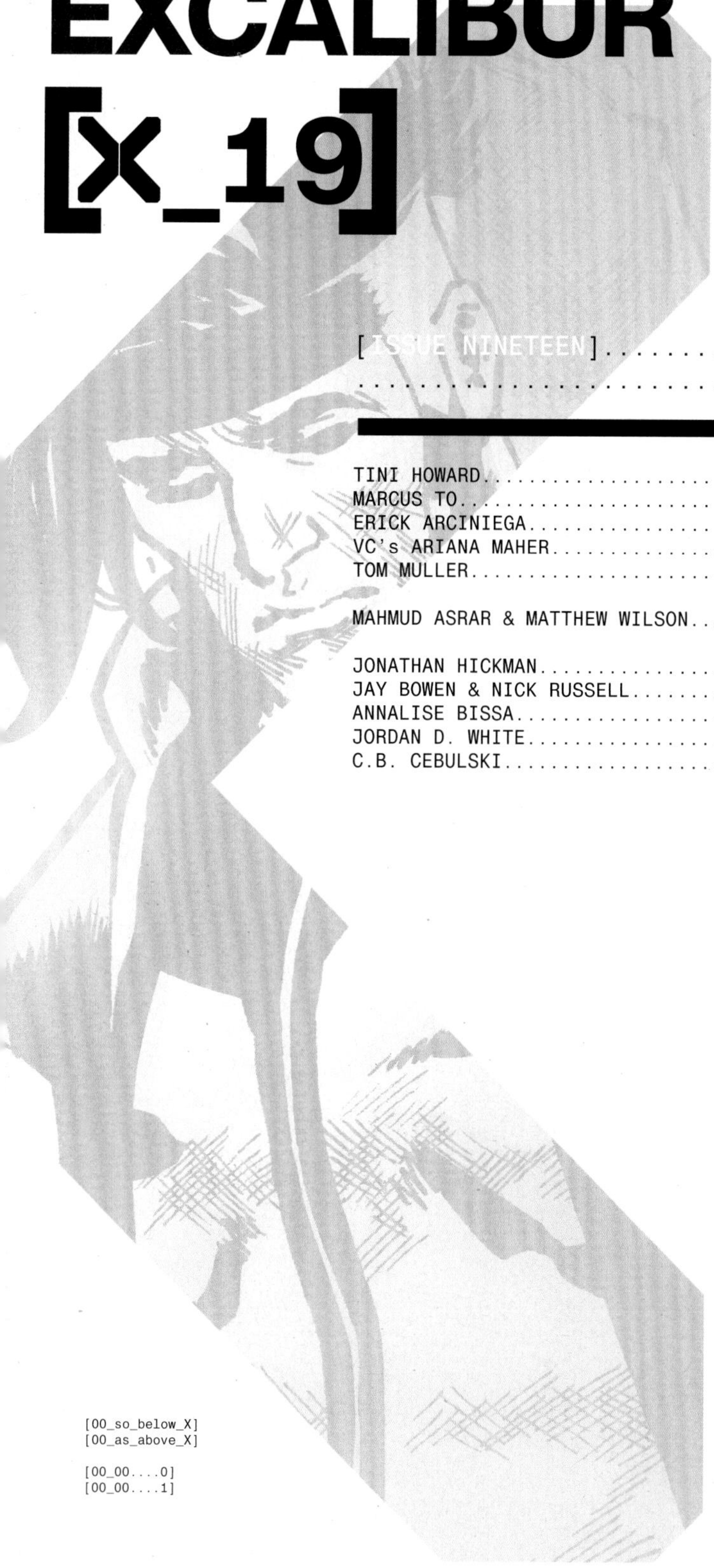

[ISSUE NINETEEN]...............................
...................................WILD VIOLETS

TINI HOWARD..[WRITER]
MARCUS TO..[ARTIST]
ERICK ARCINIEGA...............................[COLOR ARTIST]
VC's ARIANA MAHER................................[LETTERER]
TOM MULLER...[DESIGN]

MAHMUD ASRAR & MATTHEW WILSON...............[COVER ARTISTS]

JONATHAN HICKMAN................................[HEAD OF X]
JAY BOWEN & NICK RUSSELL.......................[PRODUCTION]
ANNALISE BISSA..........................[ASSOCIATE EDITOR]
JORDAN D. WHITE....................................[EDITOR]
C.B. CEBULSKI............................[EDITOR IN CHIEF]

[00_so_below_X]
[00_as_above_X]

[00_00....0]
[00_00....1]

[00_this____]
[00_world___]

[00_and_the_]

[00___other_]

FROM THE GRIMOIRE OF

RITUAL FOR THE REJOINING OF BODY AND SOUL

Directions: ~~North~~ *West-facing? ~~Sunward~~!!! Widdershins.*

Offerings? ~~Incense, fruit,~~ *(Dress her in her clothes?) Don't make it like a funeral—We don't want her to think she's dead.*

Procedure: *Like the others? (Fill this in later, for posterity.)*

MEGGAN
~~ROGUE~~
ME
~~GAMBIT~~
APEX CONDUIT
ROGUE
~~GAMBIT~~
~~ME~~
BETSY??
GAMBIT

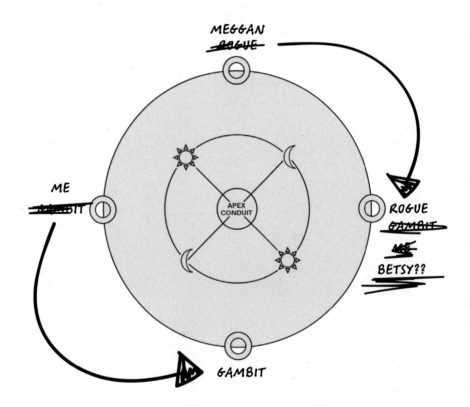

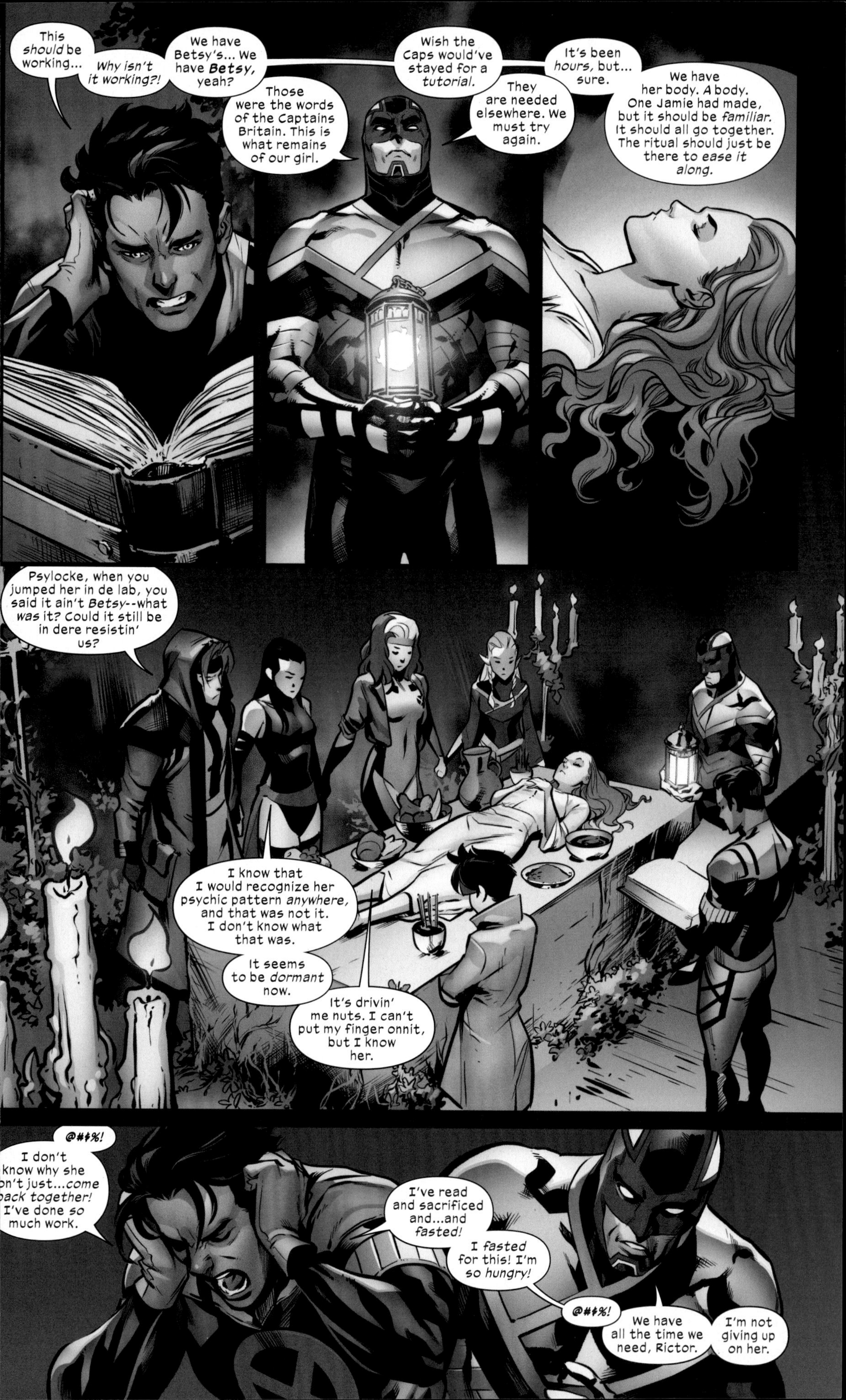

This should be working...
Why isn't it working?!
We have Betsy's... We have Betsy, yeah?
Those were the words of the Captains Britain. This is what remains of our girl.
Wish the Caps would've stayed for a tutorial.
They are needed elsewhere. We must try again.
It's been hours, but... sure.
We have her body. A body. One Jamie had made, but it should be familiar. It should all go together. The ritual should just be there to ease it along.
Psylocke, when you jumped her in de lab, you said it ain't Betsy--what was it? Could it still be in dere resistin' us?
I know that I would recognize her psychic pattern anywhere, and that was not it. I don't know what that was.
It seems to be dormant now.
It's drivin' me nuts. I can't put my finger onnit, but I know her.
@#$%!
I've read and sacrificed and...and fasted!
I fasted for this! I'm so hungry!
@#$%!
We have all the time we need, Rictor.
I'm not giving up on her.

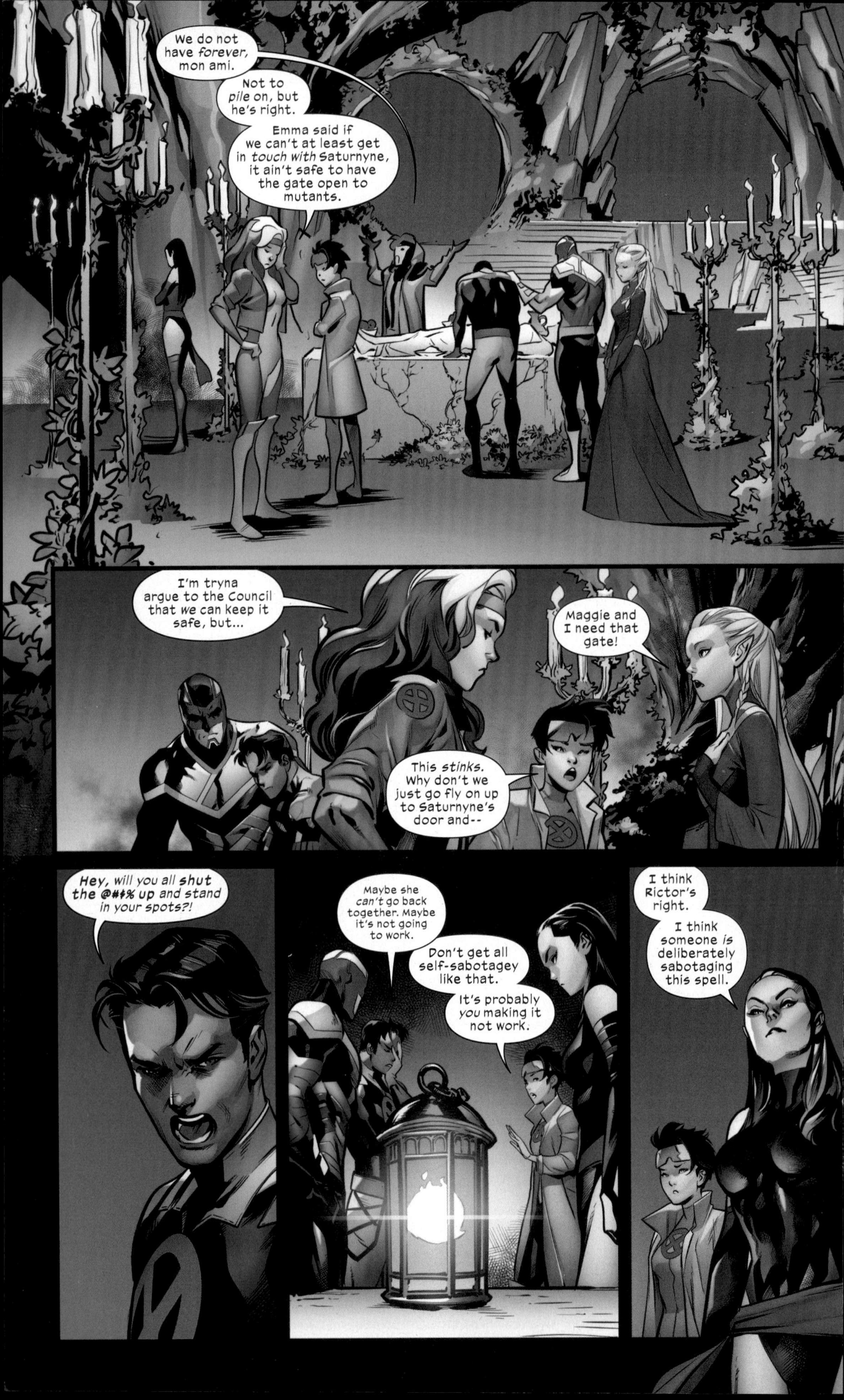

We do not have *forever,* mon ami.
Not to *pile* on, but he's right.
Emma said if we can't at least get in *touch with* Saturnyne, it ain't safe to have the gate open to mutants.
I'm tryna argue to the Council that *we* can keep it safe, but...
Maggie and I need that gate!
This *stinks.* Why don't we just go fly on up to Saturnyne's door and--
Hey, will you all **shut the @#$% up** and stand in your spots?!
Maybe she *can't* go back together. Maybe it's not going to work.
Don't get all self-sabotagey like that.
It's probably *you* making it not work.
I think Rictor's right.
I think someone *is* deliberately sabotaging this spell.

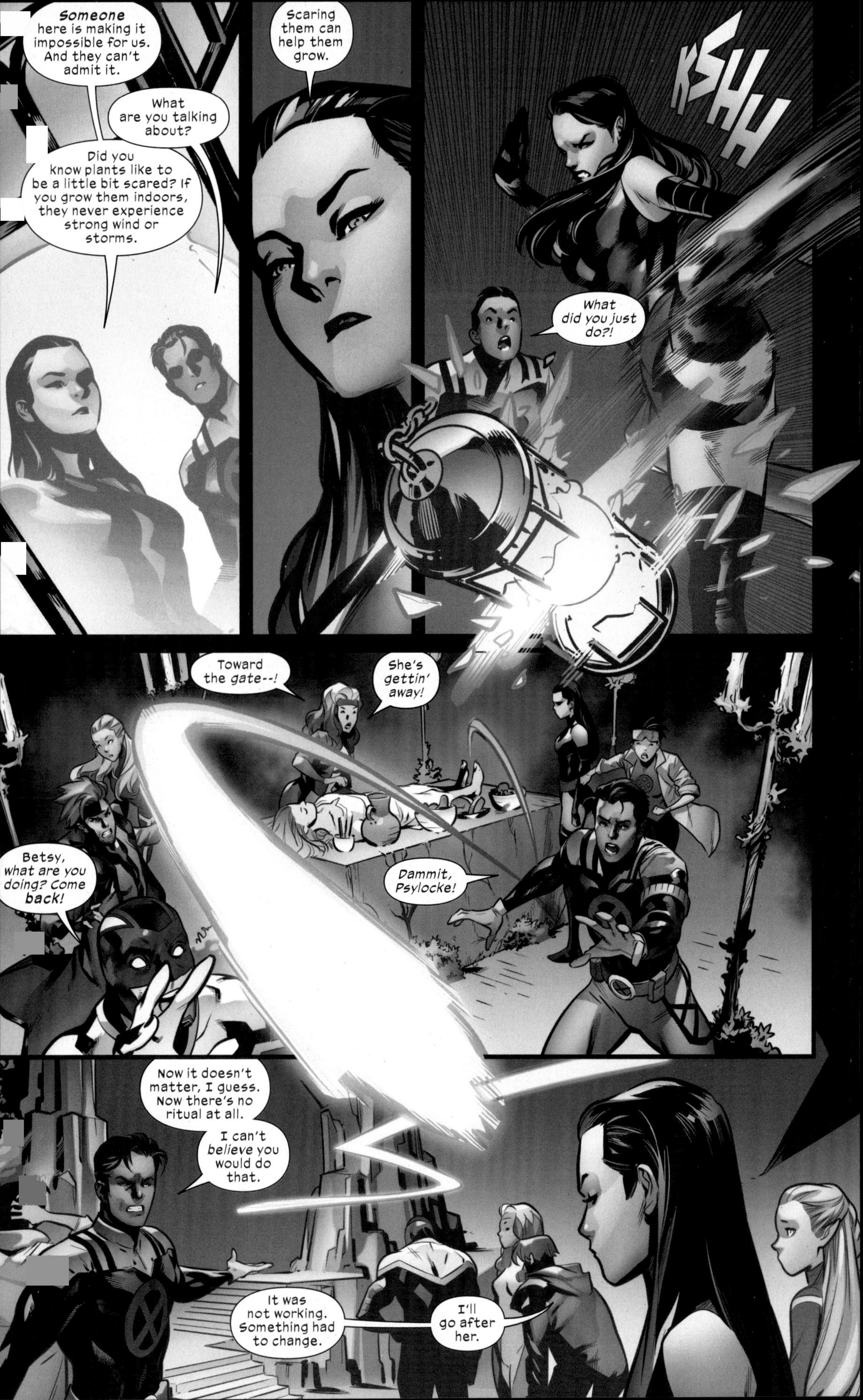

Someone here is making it impossible for us. And they can't admit it.
What are you talking about?
Did you know plants like to be a little bit scared? If you grow them indoors, they never experience strong wind or storms.
Scaring them can help them grow.
KSHH
What did you just do?!
Toward the gate--!
She's gettin' away!
Betsy, what are you doing? Come back!
Dammit, Psylocke!
Now it doesn't matter, I guess. Now there's no ritual at all.
I can't believe you would do that.
It was not working. Something had to change.
I'll go after her.

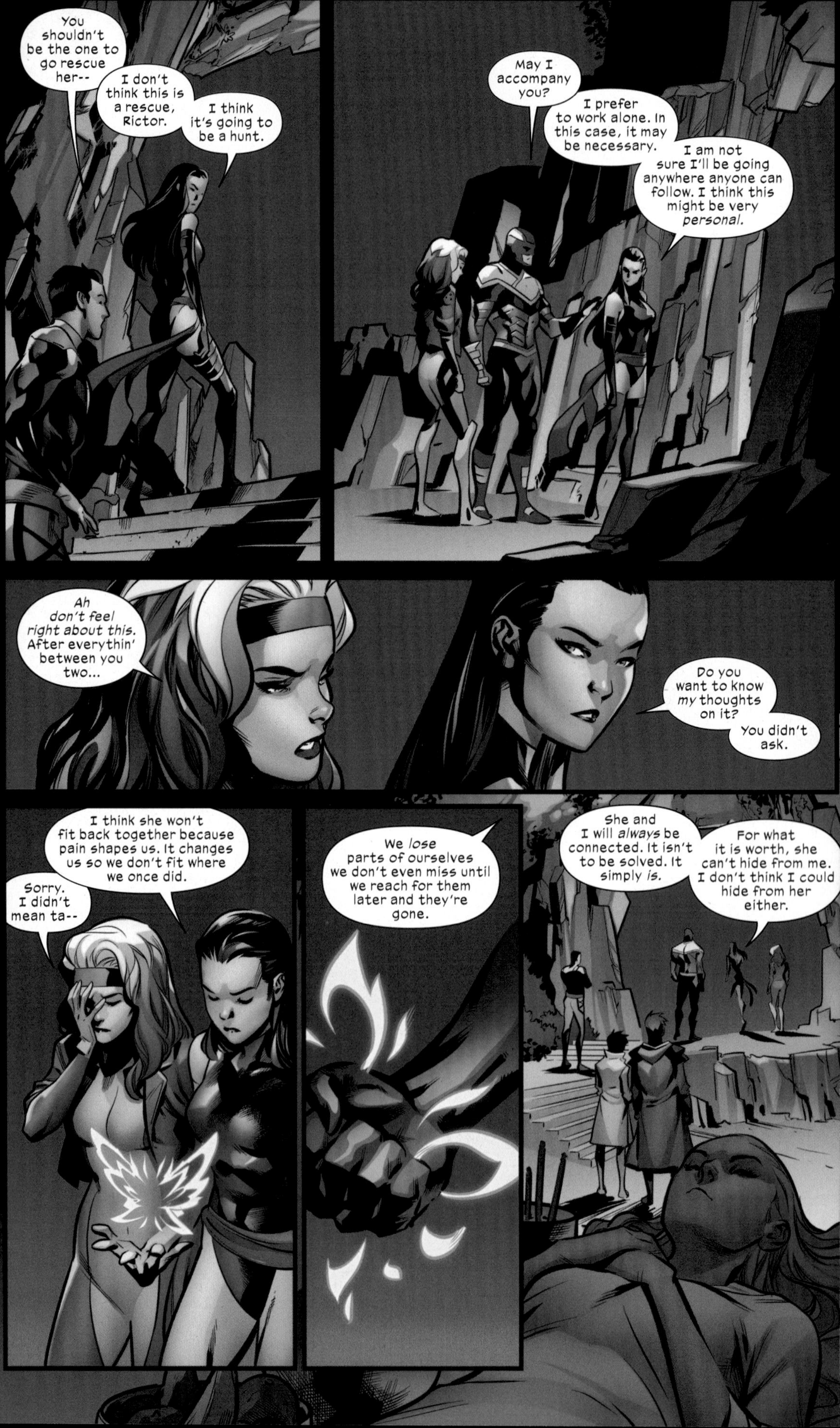
You shouldn't be the one to go rescue her--
I don't think this is a rescue, Rictor.
I think it's going to be a hunt.
May I accompany you?
I prefer to work alone. In this case, it may be necessary.
I am not sure I'll be going anywhere anyone can follow. I think this might be very *personal.*
Ah don't feel right about this. After everythin' between you two...
Do you want to know *my* thoughts on it?
You didn't ask.
Sorry. I didn't mean ta--
I think she won't fit back together because pain shapes us. It changes us so we don't fit where we once did.
We *lose* parts of ourselves we don't even miss until we reach for them later and they're gone.
She and I will *always* be connected. It isn't to be solved. It simply *is.*
For what it is worth, she can't hide from me. I don't think I could hide from her either.

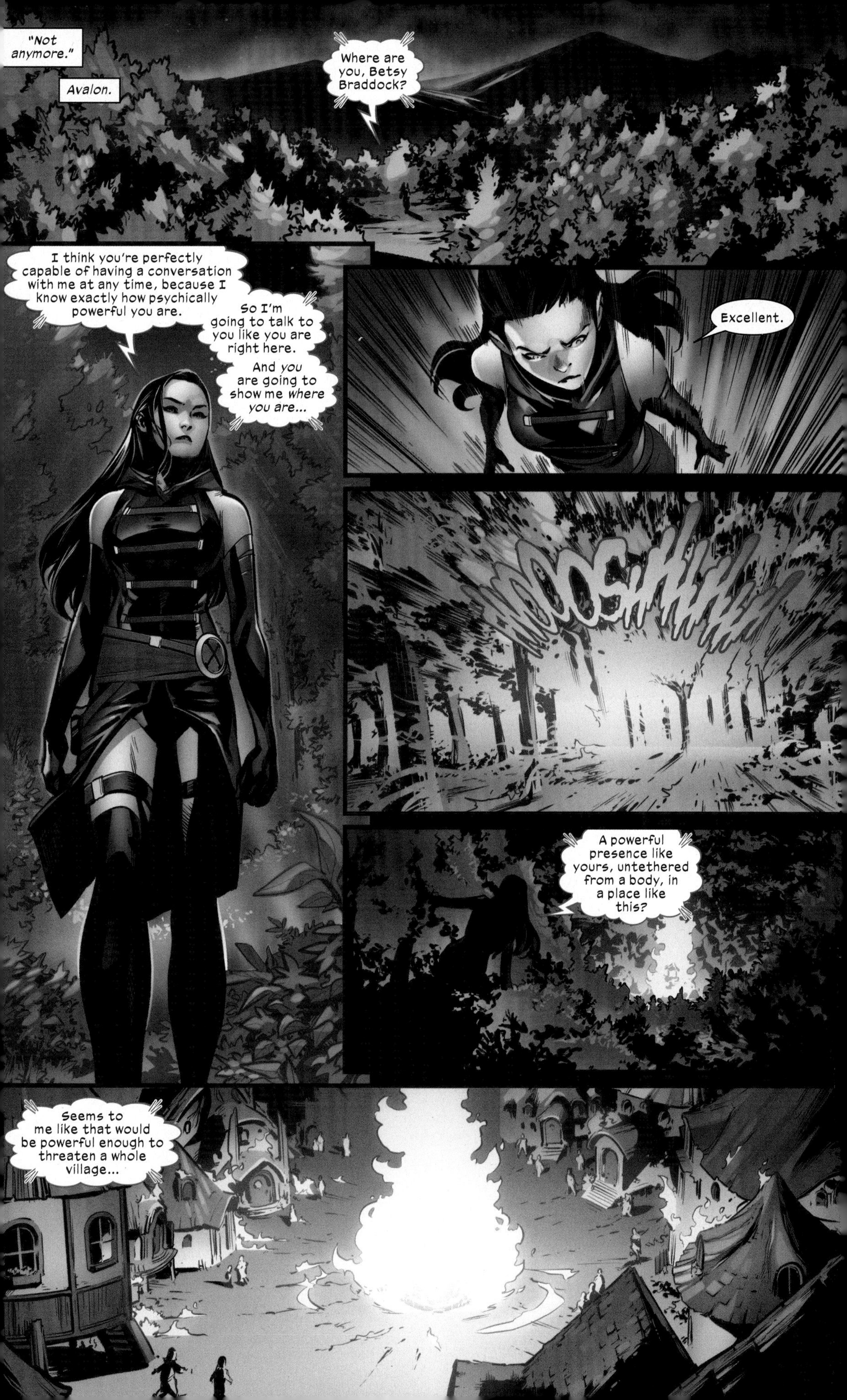
"Not anymore."
Avalon.
Where are you, Betsy Braddock?
I think you're perfectly capable of having a conversation with me at any time, because I know exactly how psychically powerful you are.
So I'm going to talk to you like you are right here.
And *you* are going to show me *where* you are...
Excellent.
WOOSHHH
A powerful presence like yours, untethered from a body, in a place like this?
Seems to me like that would be powerful enough to threaten a whole village...

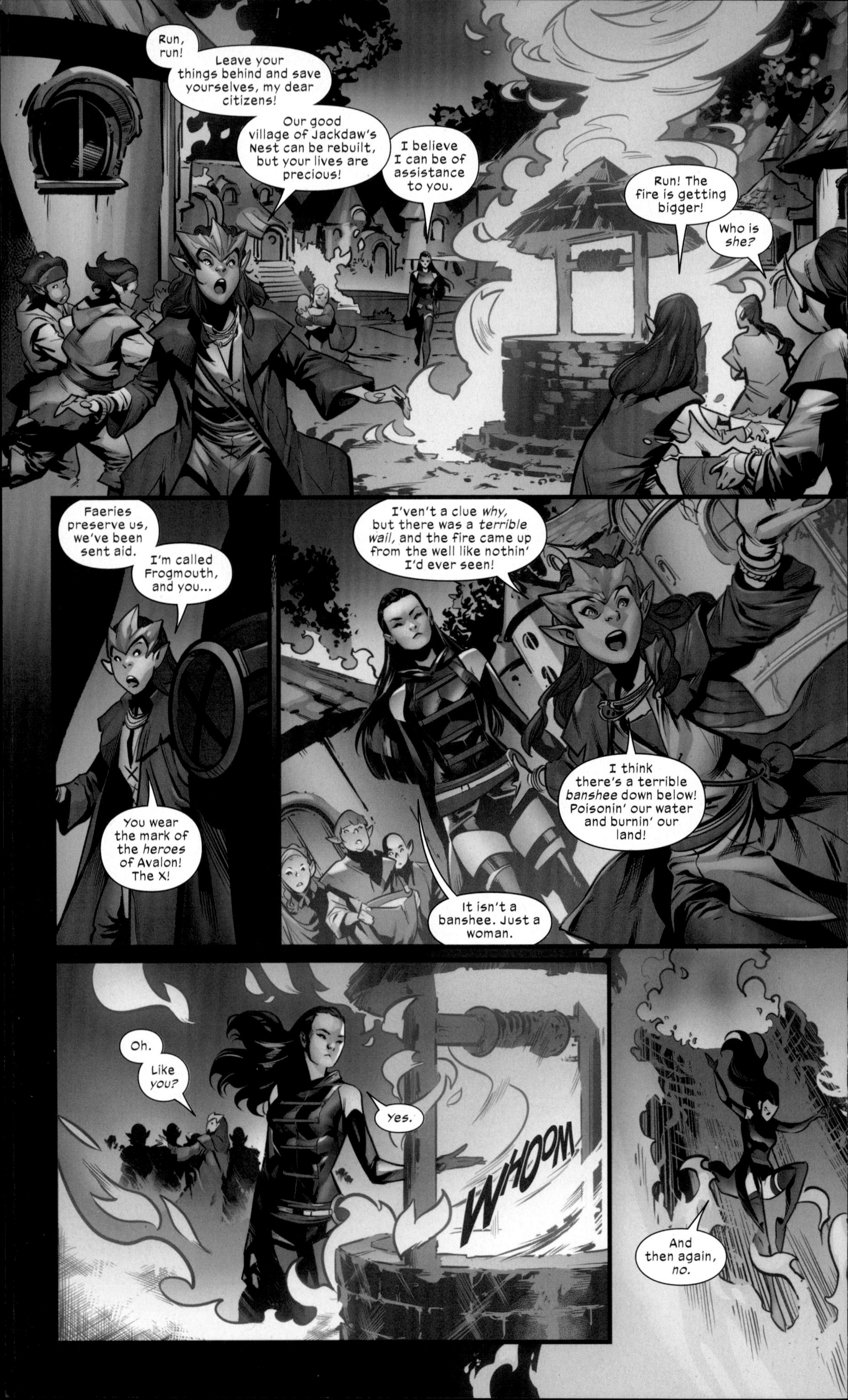
Run, run!
Leave your things behind and save yourselves, my dear citizens!
Our good village of Jackdaw's Nest can be rebuilt, but your lives are precious!
I believe I can be of assistance to you.
Run! The fire is getting bigger!
Who is *she?*
Faeries preserve us, we've been sent aid.
I'm called Frogmouth, and you...
You wear the mark of the *heroes* of Avalon! The X!
I'ven't a clue *why,* but there was a *terrible wail,* and the fire came up from the well like nothin' I'd ever seen!
I think there's a terrible *banshee* down below! Poisonin' our water and burnin' our land!
It isn't a banshee. Just a woman.
Oh.
Like *you?*
Yes.
WHOOM
And then again, *no.*

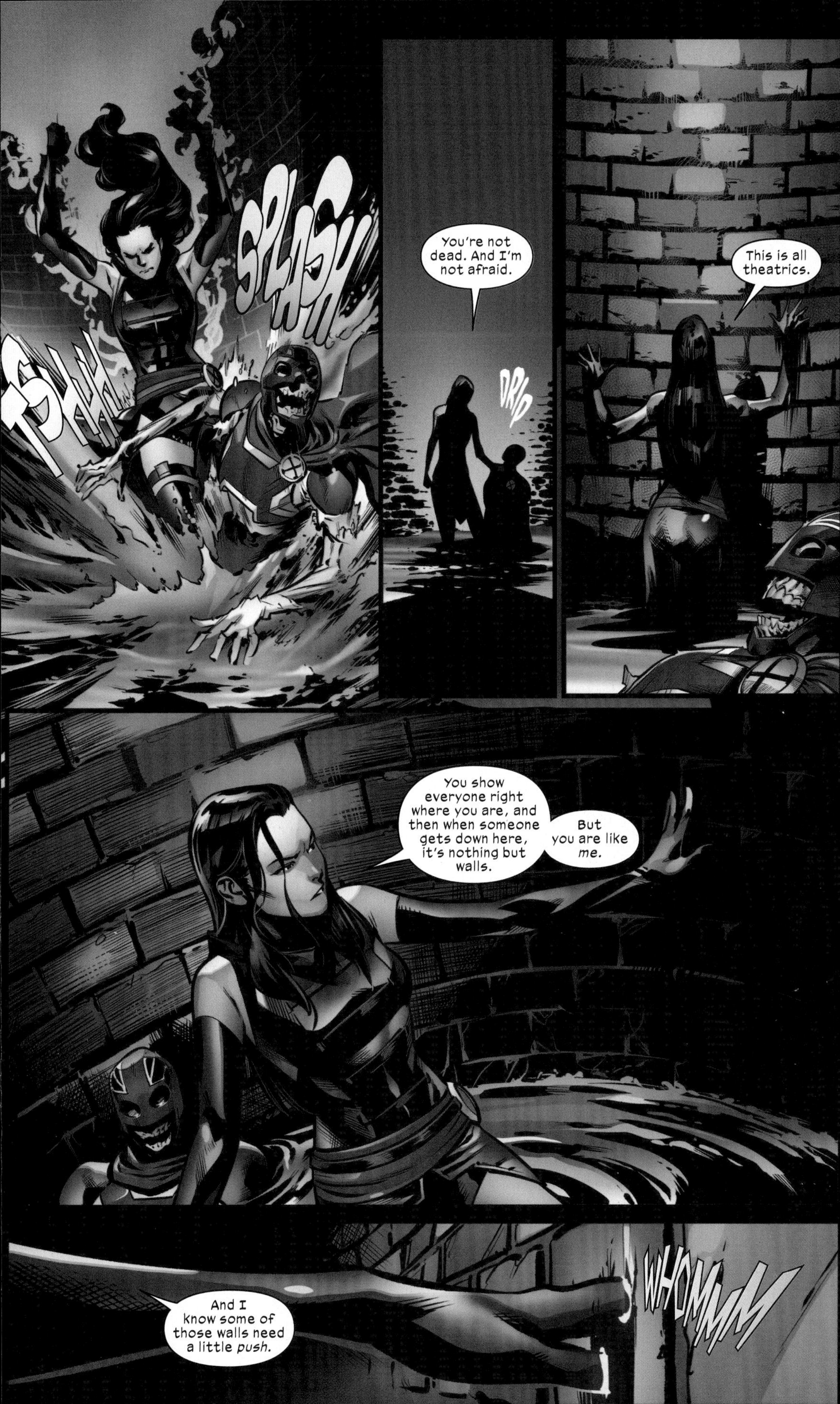
SPLASH
TSHH
You're not dead. And I'm not afraid.
DRIP
This is all theatrics.
You show everyone right where you are, and then when someone gets down here, it's nothing but walls.
But you are like *me.*
And I know some of those walls need a little *push.*
WHOMMM

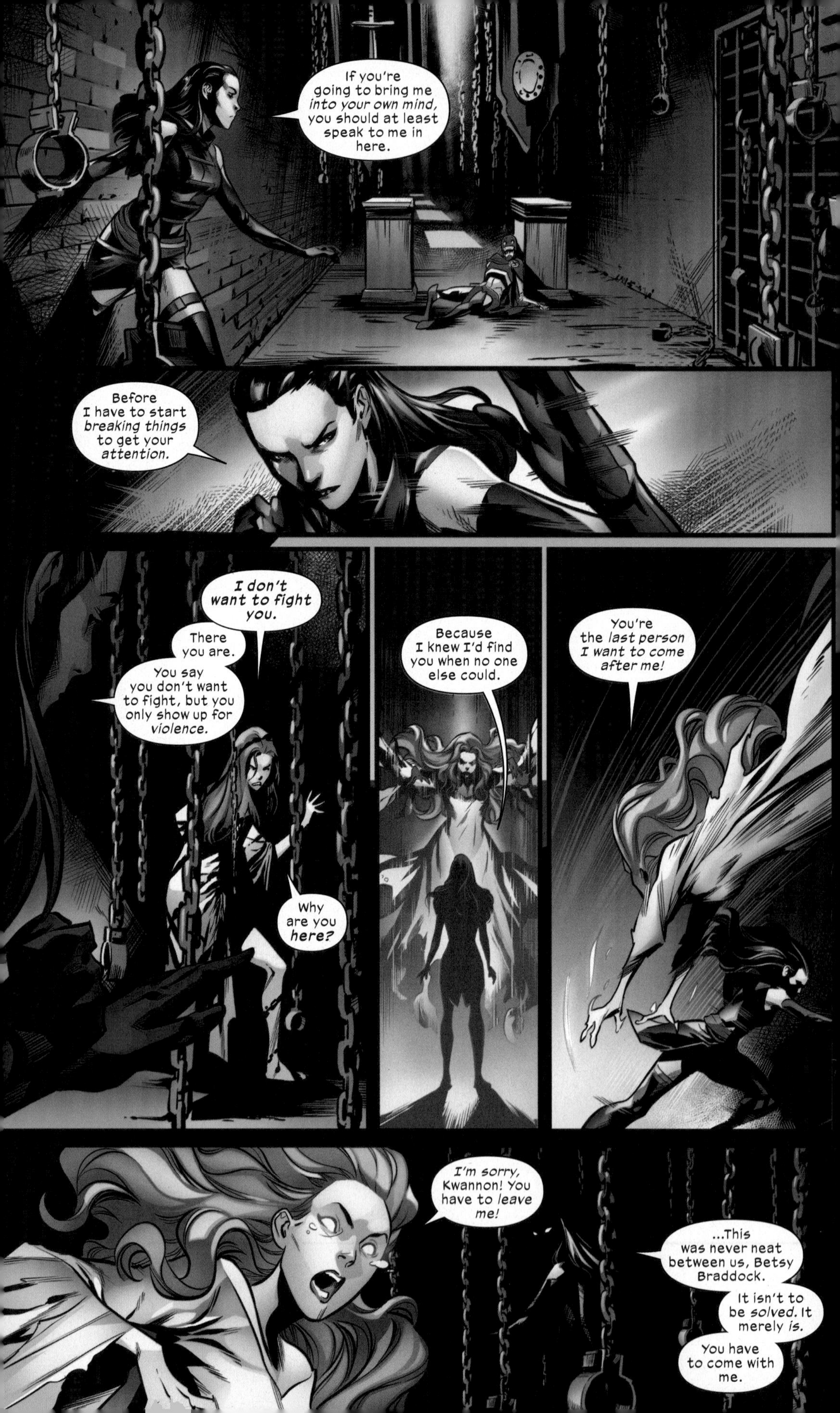
If you're going to bring me *into your own mind,* you should at least speak to me in here.
Before I have to start *breaking things* to get your *attention.*
I don't want to fight you.
There you are.
You say you don't want to fight, but you only show up for *violence.*
Why are you *here?*
Because I knew I'd find you when no one else could.
You're the *last person I want to come after me!*
I'm sorry, Kwannon! You have to *leave* me!
...This was never neat between us, Betsy Braddock.
It isn't to be *solved.* It merely *is.*
You have to come with me.

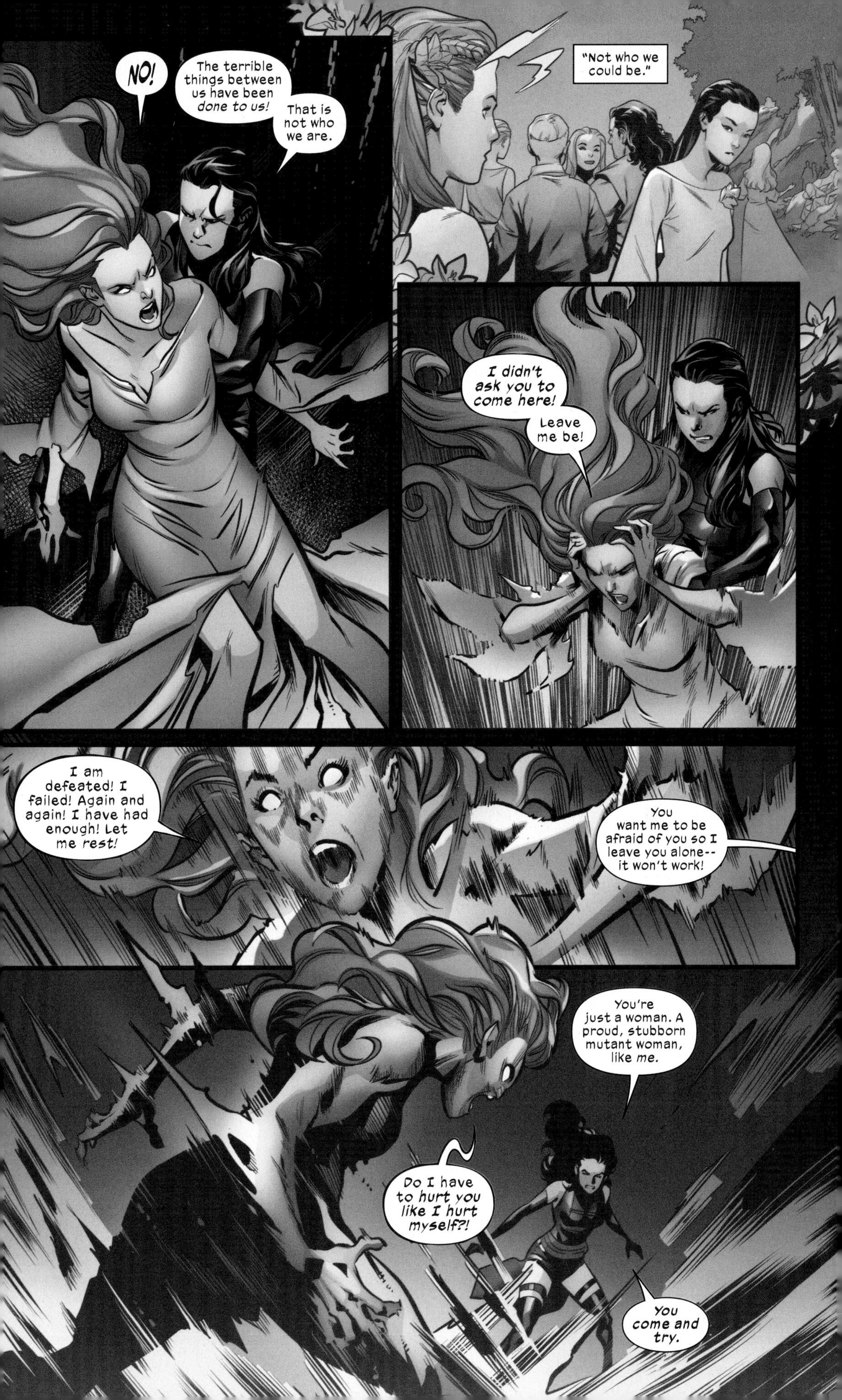
NO!
The terrible things between us have been done to us!
That is not who we are.
"Not who we could be."
I didn't ask you to come here!
Leave me be!
I am defeated! I failed! Again and again! I have had enough! Let me rest!
You want me to be afraid of you so I leave you alone-- it won't work!
You're just a woman. A proud, stubborn mutant woman, like me.
Do I have to hurt you like I hurt myself?!
You come and try.

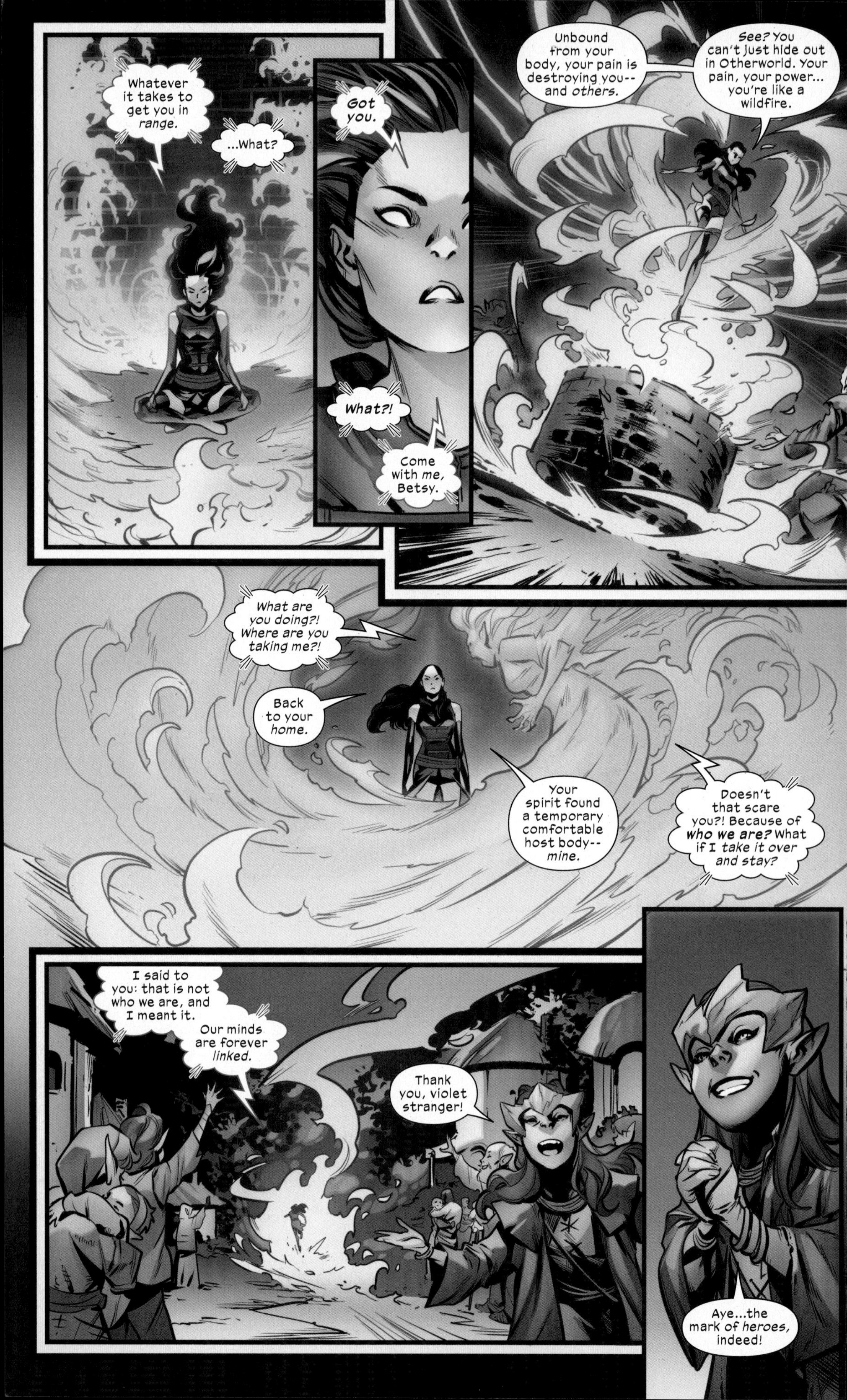
Whatever it takes to get you in *range*.
...What?
Got you.
What?!
Come with *me*, Betsy.
Unbound from your body, your pain is destroying you-- and *others*.
See? You can't just hide out in Otherworld. Your pain, your power... you're like a wildfire.
What are you doing?! Where are you taking me?!
Back to your *home.*
Your spirit found a temporary comfortable host body-- *mine.*
Doesn't that scare you?! Because of ***who we are?*** What if I *take it over and stay?*
I said to you: that is not who we are, and I meant it.
Our minds are forever *linked.*
Thank you, violet stranger!
Aye...the mark of *heroes,* indeed!

THE BALLAD OF THE VIOLET STRANGER

Hark! Hear the tale of the Violet Stranger!
Hero of Jackdaw's Nest,
Who came when the fires threatened our village
And left us truly blest.

When a ghostly form cried out in the square
And arrived in a burning light,
It lit our thatch and our well afire
And made day from darkest night.

O, our Nest did burn, our eggs did cook,
Our hatchlings wailed in fear!
Eyes stung by smoke, our throats did choke
--then the Violet Stranger appeared.

Ho, through the haze of the burning homestead,
The Violet Stranger came,
Spoke no hello, but drew her sword
And descended into the flames.

Some say when she was down in the well,
She was forced to slay a beast.
And some say when she was down in the well,
A great evil was released .

But I heard it was just a woman,
A lonely sort of ghost.
And the Stranger was to her a friend,
And occasionally -- host.

When she left, the fire went with her.
Aye, the ghost, her pain was gone. (Yip-pee!)
In her hand -- the blade of Captain Britain!
Hero of Avalon!

[softly, leaning in]
So, who is she to the Captain?
There, the line between them blurs.
Is the Violet Stranger the Captain's shadow?
Or is Captain Britain hers?

Hey!

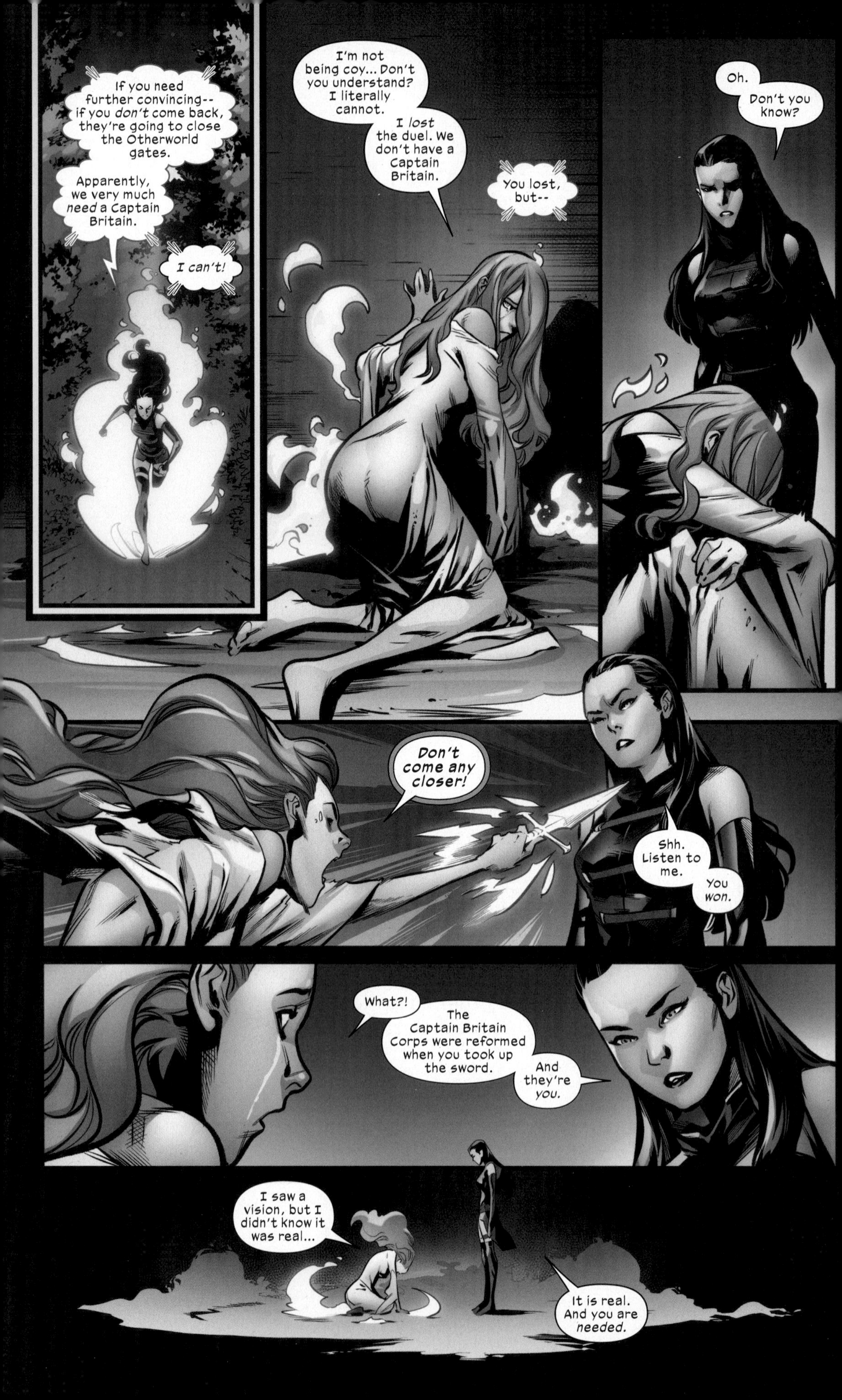

If you need further convincing--if you *don't* come back, they're going to close the Otherworld gates.
Apparently, we very much *need* a Captain Britain.
I can't!
I'm not being coy... Don't you understand? I literally cannot.
I *lost* the duel. We don't have a Captain Britain.
You lost, but--
Oh.
Don't you know?
Don't come any closer!
Shh. Listen to me.
You *won.*
What?!
The Captain Britain Corps were reformed when you took up the sword.
And they're *you.*
I saw a vision, but I didn't know it was real...
It is real. And you are *needed.*

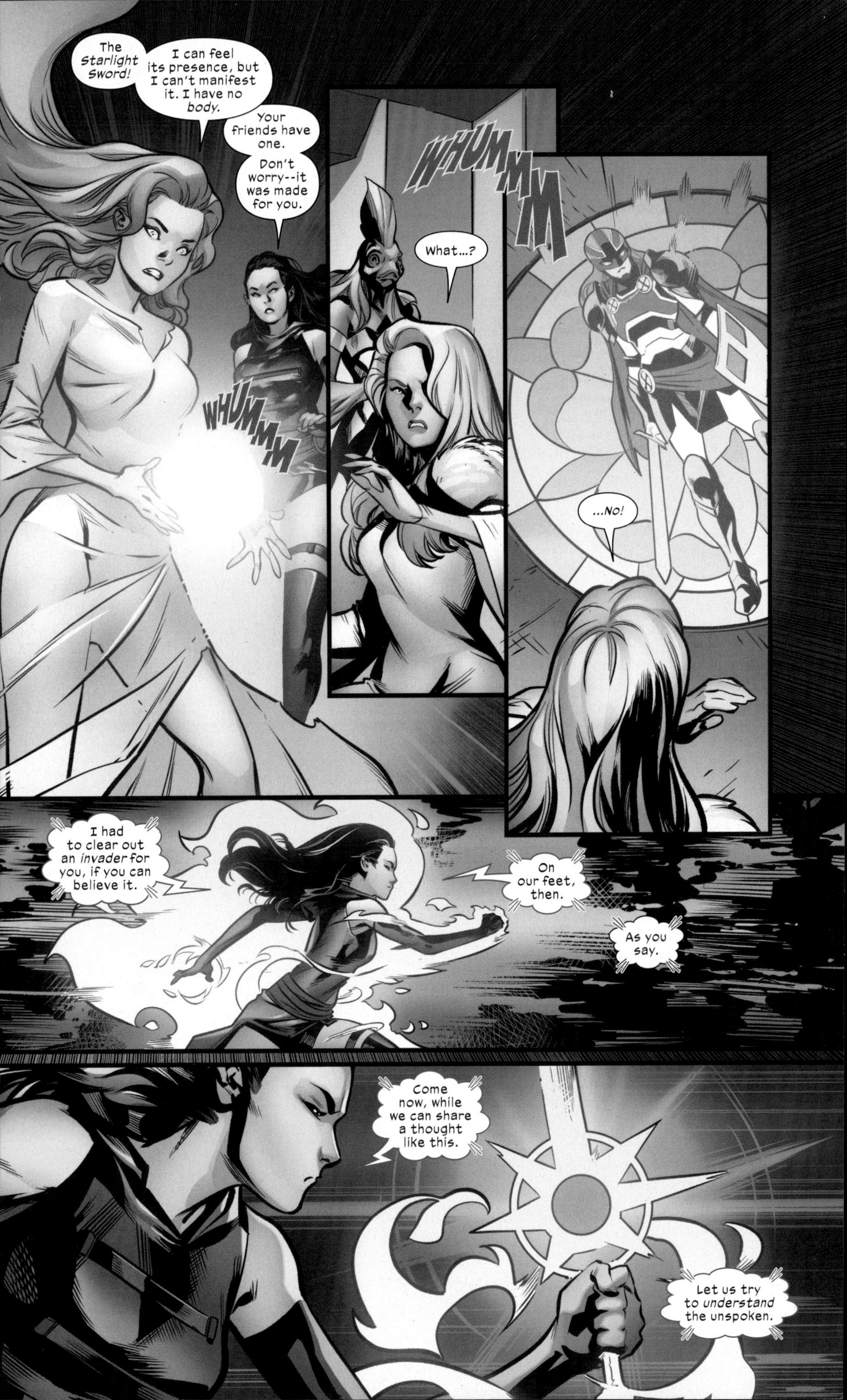
The Starlight Sword!
I can feel its presence, but I can't manifest it. I have no body.
Your friends have one.
Don't worry--it was made for you.
WHUMMM
WHUMMMM
What...?
...NO!
I had to clear out an invader for you, if you can believe it.
On our feet, then.
As you say.
Come now, while we can share a thought like this.
Let us try to understand the unspoken.

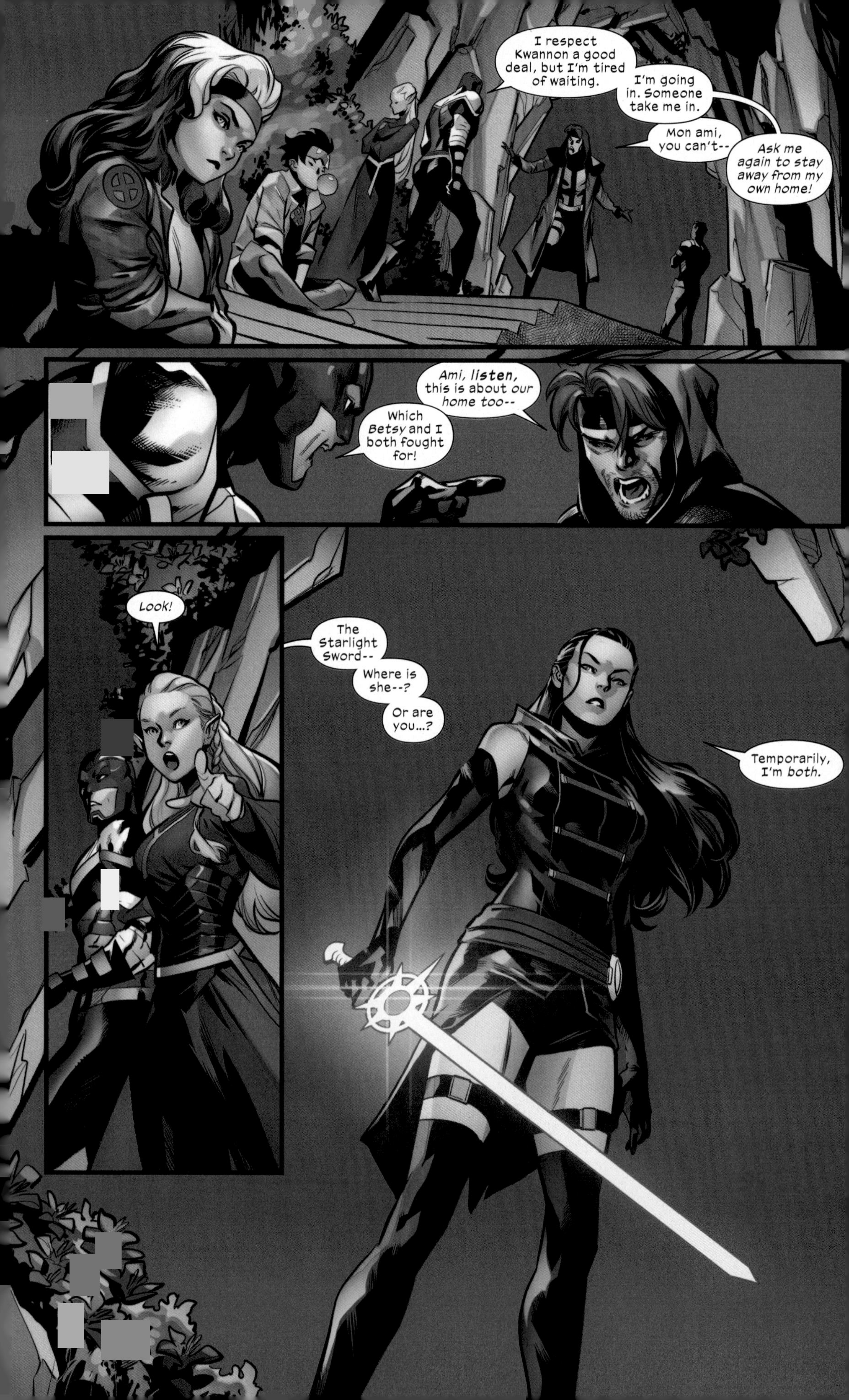

I respect Kwannon a good deal, but I'm tired of waiting.
I'm going in. Someone take me in.
Mon ami, you can't--
Ask me again to stay away from my own home!
Ami, listen, this is about our home too--
Which Betsy and I both fought for!
Look!
The Starlight Sword--
Where is she--?
Or are you...?
Temporarily, I'm both.

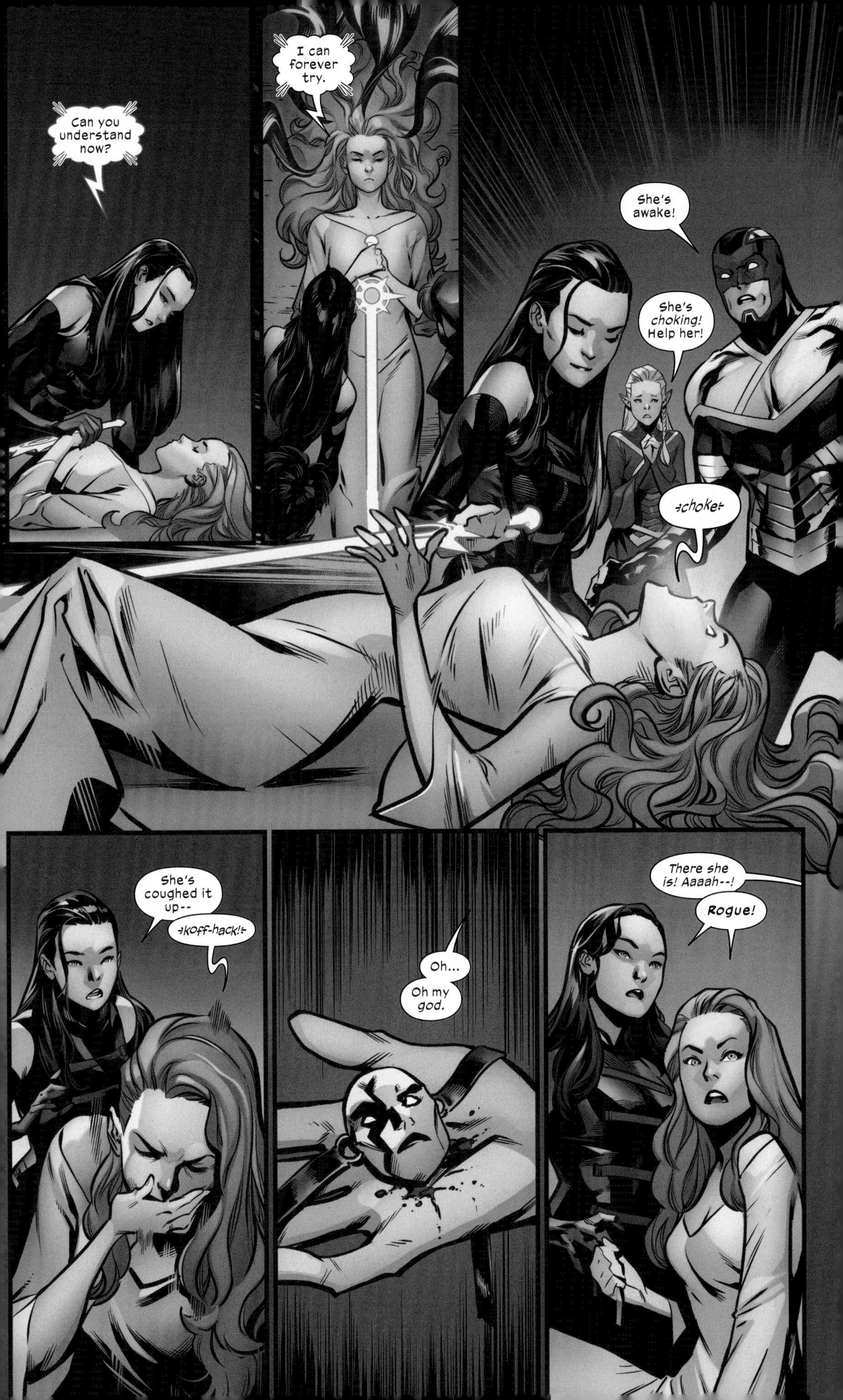
Can you understand now?
I can forever try.
She's awake!
She's choking! Help her!
choke
She's coughed it up--
koff-hack!
Oh...
Oh my god.
There she is! Aaaah--!
Rogue!

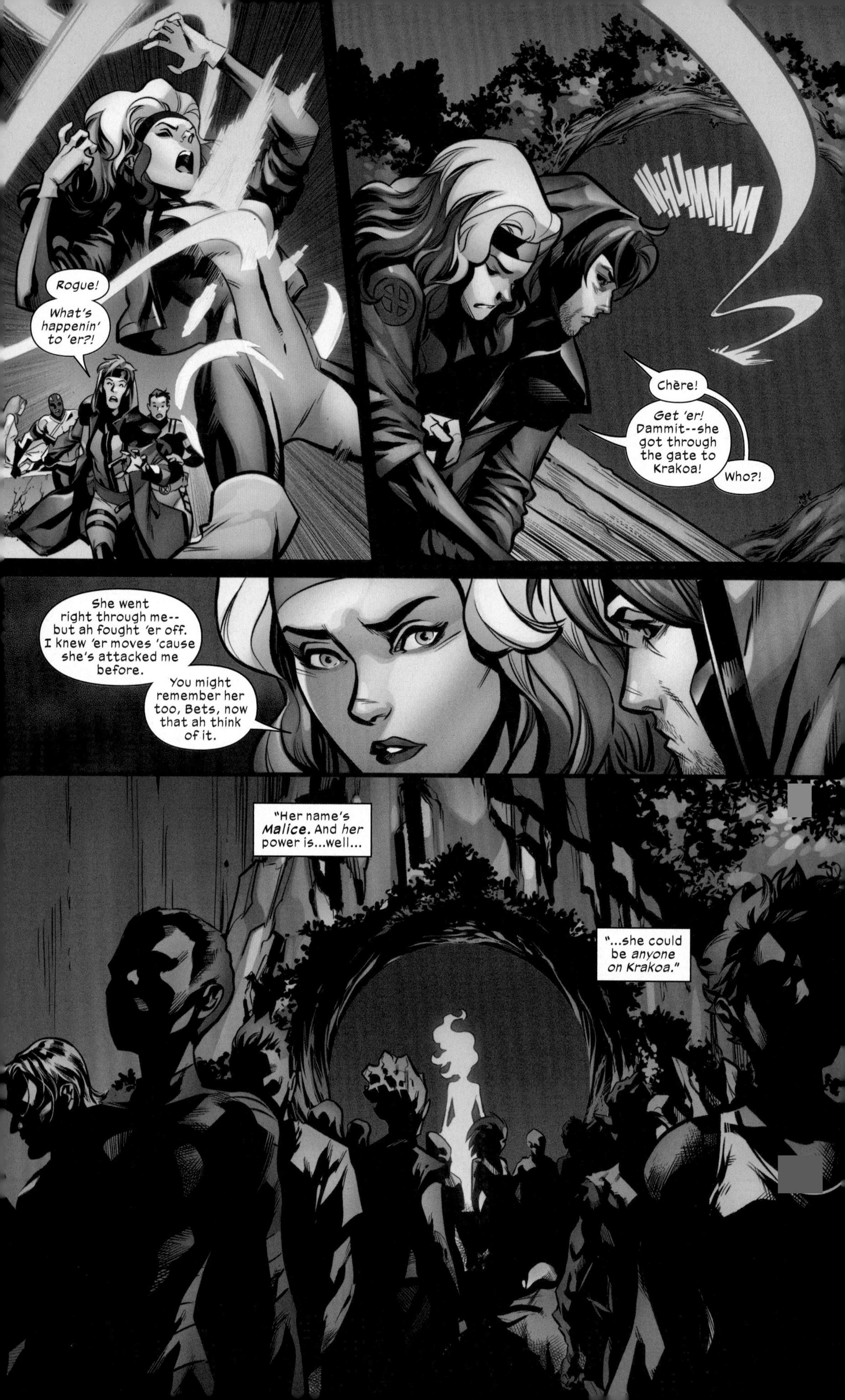

Rogue!
What's happenin' to 'er?!
WHUMMM
Chère!
Get 'er! Dammit--she got through the gate to Krakoa!
Who?!
She went right through me--but ah fought 'er off. I knew 'er moves 'cause she's attacked me before.
You might remember her too, Bets, now that ah think of it.
"Her name's *Malice*. And *her* power is...well...
"...she could be *anyone* on Krakoa."

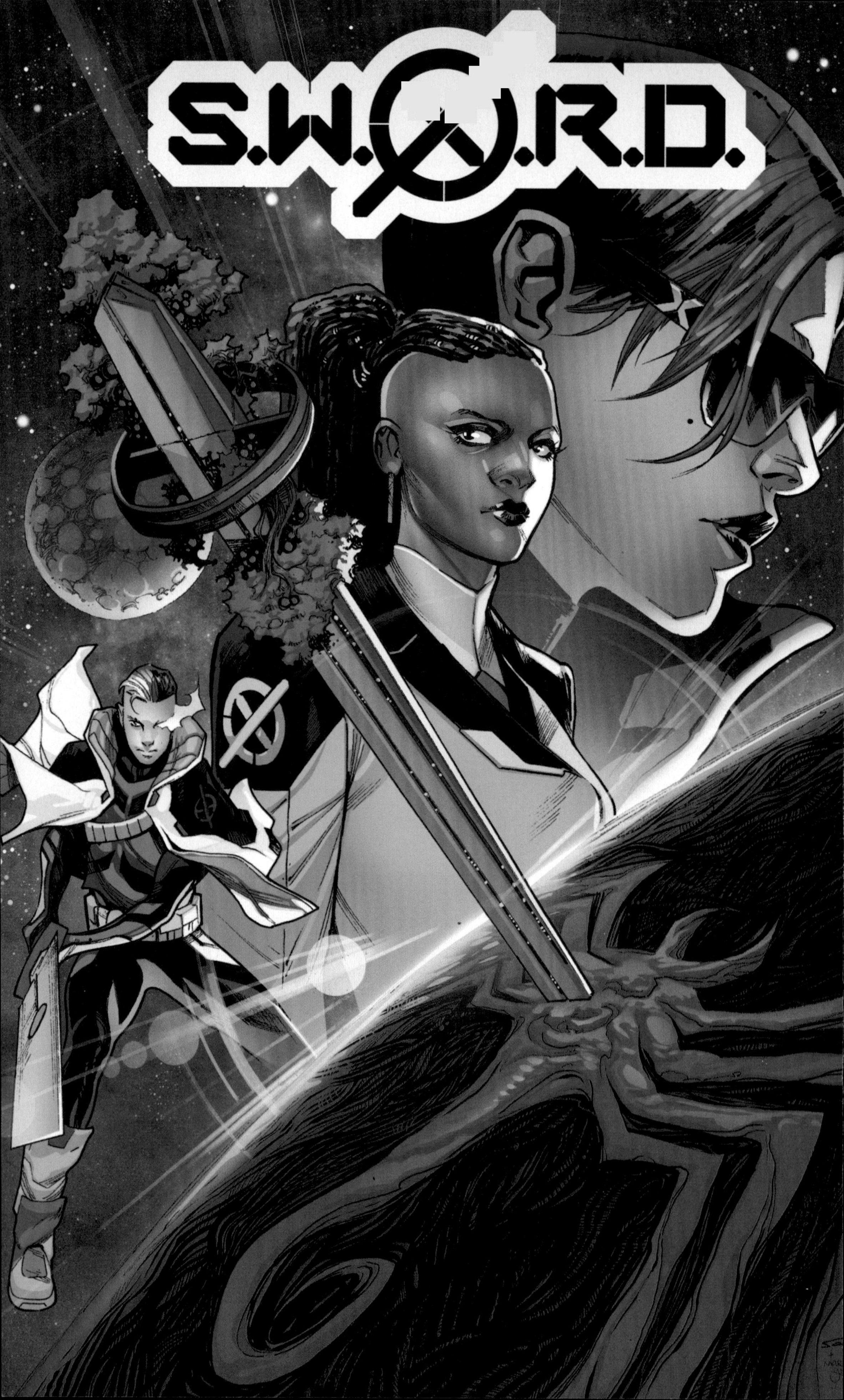
S.W.O.R.D.

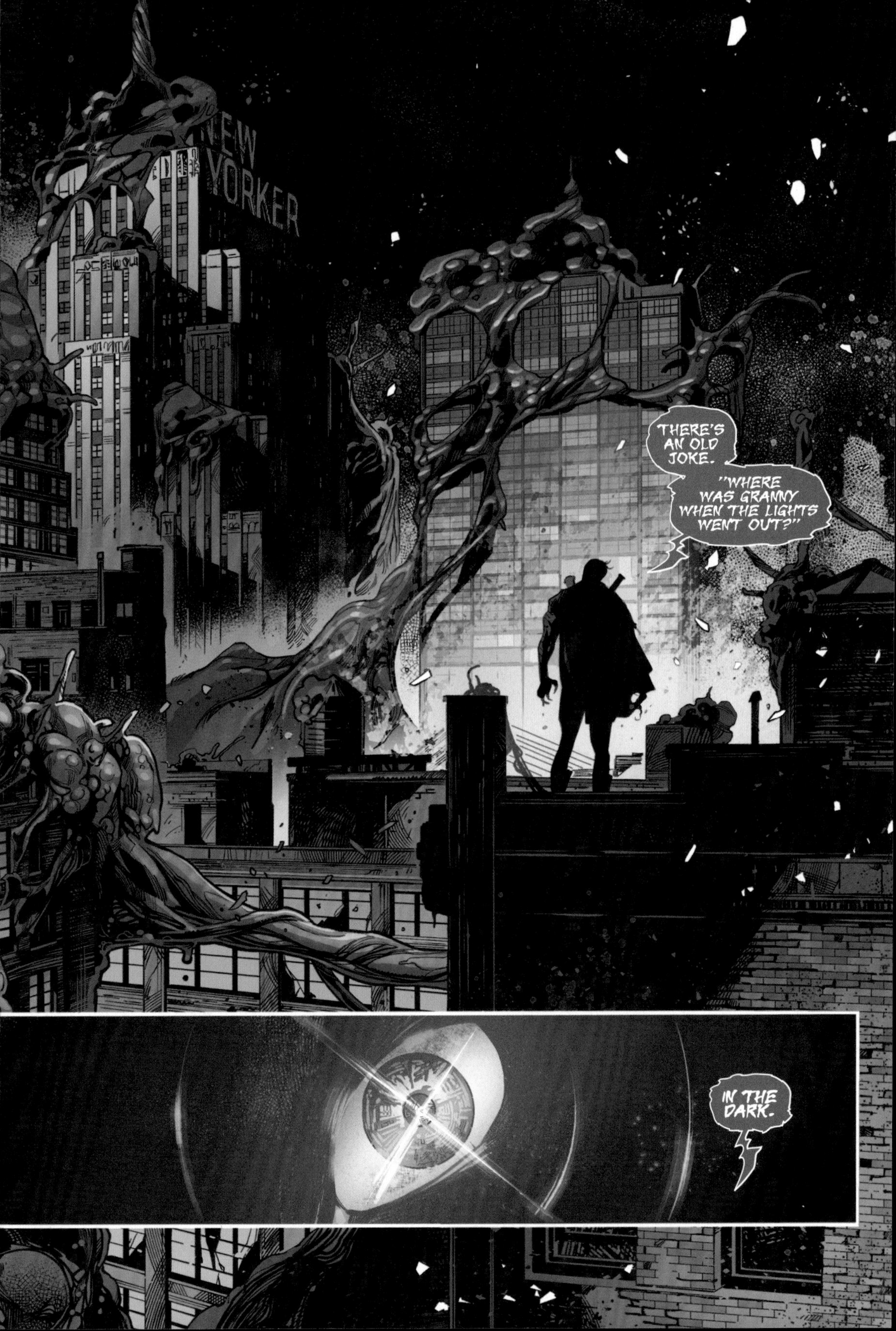
NEW YORKER
THERE'S AN OLD JOKE.
"WHERE WAS GRANNY WHEN THE LIGHTS WENT OUT?"
IN THE DARK.

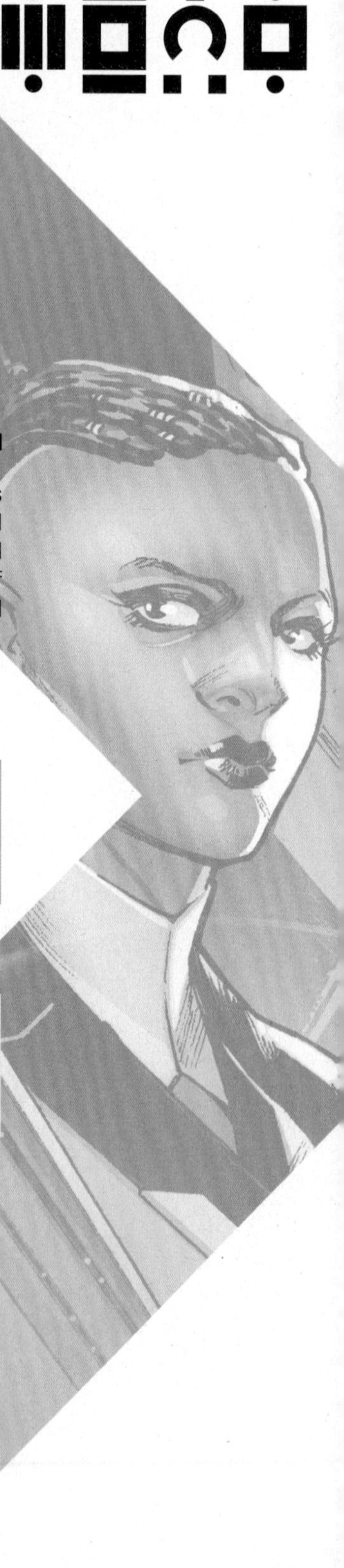

LIQUID LATEX FROM OUTER SPACE

In a stunning display of crisis mismanagement, Earth's human heroes -- despite advance warning of the threat and the assistance of both the X-Men and the Quiet Council -- have been unable to prevent Knull, Symbiote God of the Void, from establishing dominion over the planet. All communication with Earth has now been lost.

S.W.O.R.D. is attempting to clean up the mess.

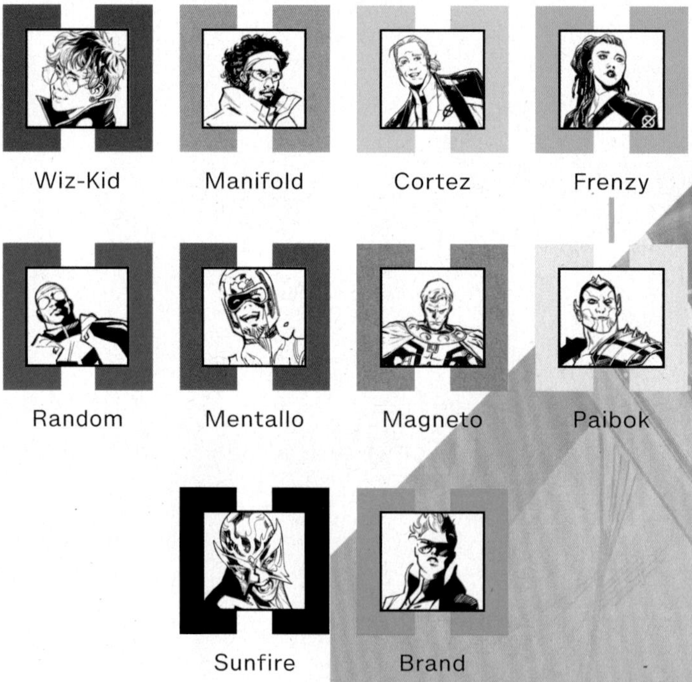
Wiz-Kid
Manifold
Cortez
Frenzy
Random
Mentallo
Magneto
Paibok
Sunfire
Brand

[00__king]
[00_black]

S.W.O.R.D.

[X_02]

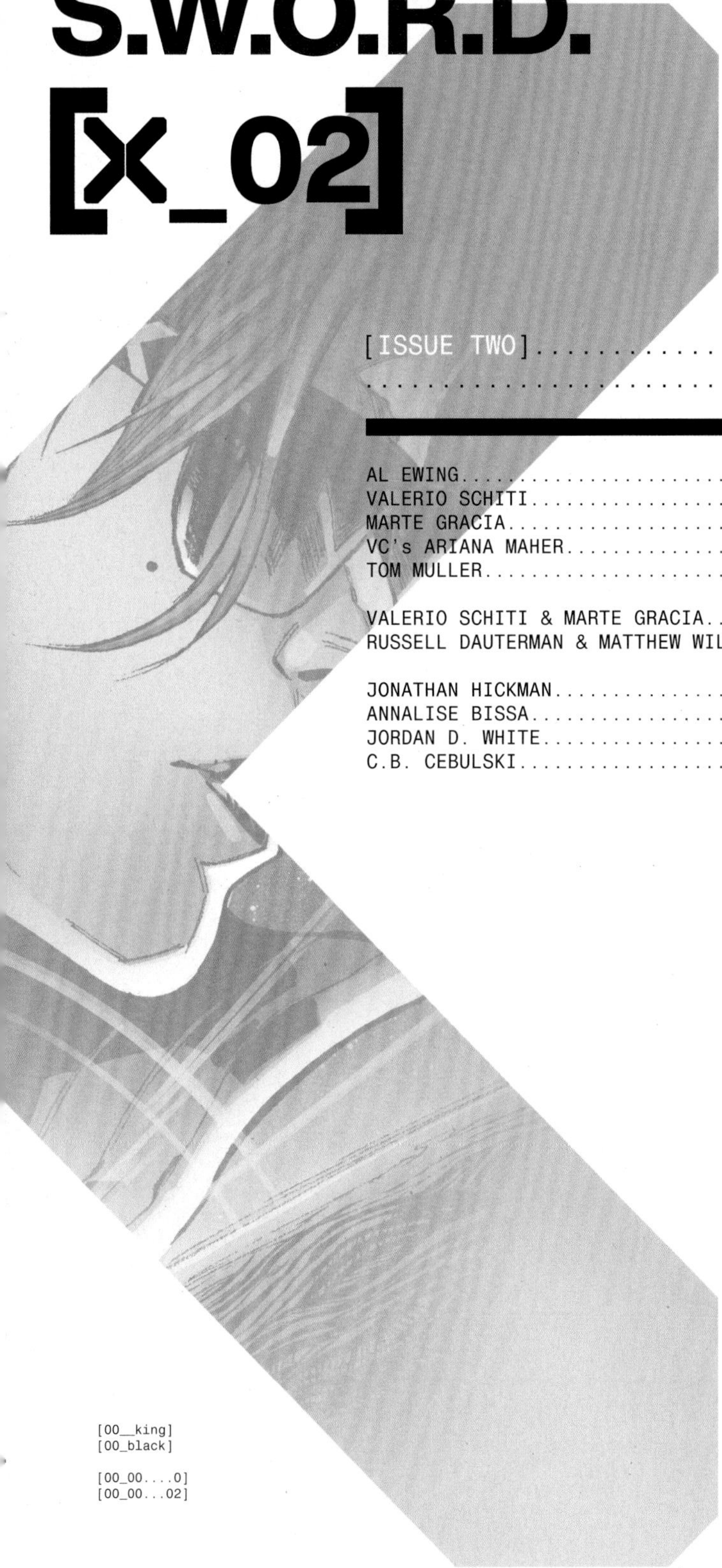

[ISSUE TWO].................................
..................................IN THE DARK

AL EWING..[WRITER]
VALERIO SCHITI....................................[ARTIST]
MARTE GRACIA..............................[COLOR ARTIST]
VC's ARIANA MAHER..................[LETTERER & PRODUCTION]
TOM MULLER..[DESIGN]

VALERIO SCHITI & MARTE GRACIA...............[COVER ARTISTS]
RUSSELL DAUTERMAN & MATTHEW WILSON..[VARIANT COVER ARTISTS]

JONATHAN HICKMAN...............................[HEAD OF X]
ANNALISE BISSA..........................[ASSOCIATE EDITOR]
JORDAN D. WHITE...................................[EDITOR]
C.B. CEBULSKI.............................[EDITOR IN CHIEF]

[00__king]
[00_black]

[00_00....0]
[00_00...02]

[00_knull_]
[00______]

[00______]

[00______X]

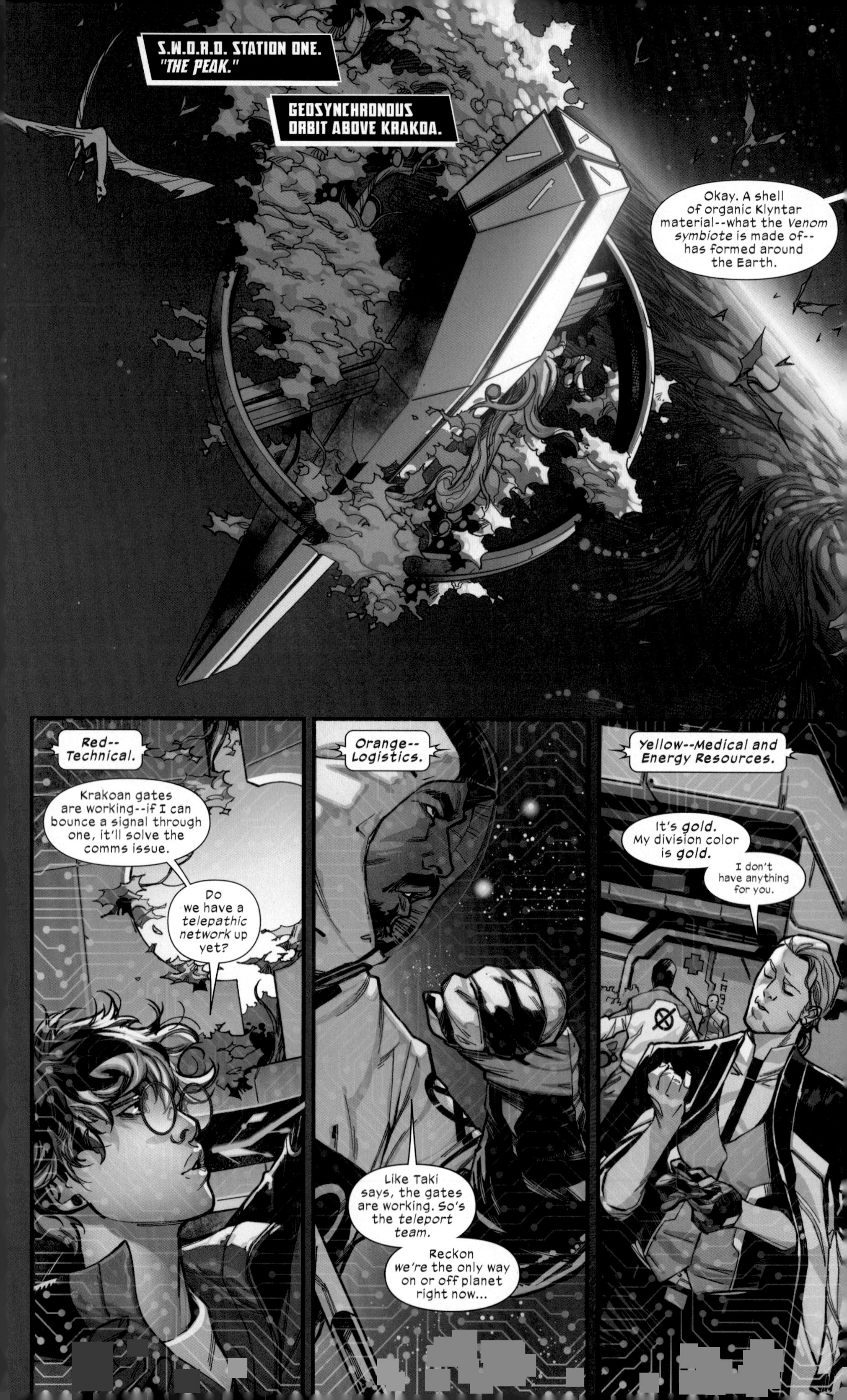
S.W.O.R.D. STATION ONE. "THE PEAK."
GEOSYNCHRONOUS ORBIT ABOVE KRAKOA.
Okay. A shell of organic Klyntar material--what the *Venom symbiote* is made of--has formed around the Earth.
Red--Technical.
Krakoan gates are working--if I can bounce a signal through one, it'll solve the comms issue.
Do we have a *telepathic network* up yet?
Orange--Logistics.
Like Taki says, the gates are working. So's the *teleport* team.
Reckon *we're* the only way on or off planet right now...
Yellow--Medical and Energy Resources.
It's *gold.* My division color is *gold.*
I don't have anything for you.

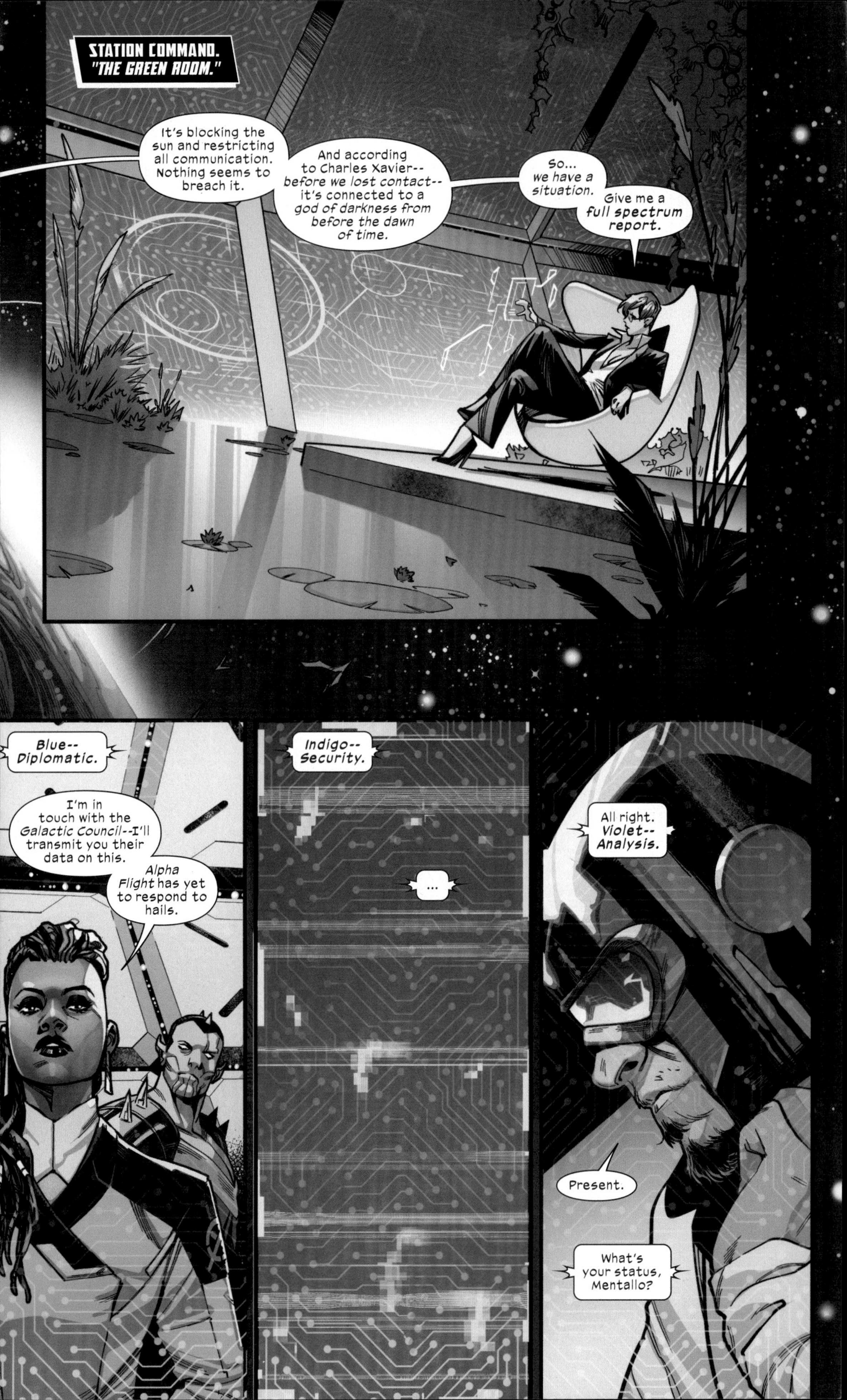
STATION COMMAND. "THE GREEN ROOM."
It's blocking the sun and restricting all communication. Nothing seems to breach it.
And according to Charles Xavier--before we lost contact--it's connected to a god of darkness from before the dawn of time.
So... we have a situation.
Give me a full spectrum report.
Blue--Diplomatic.
I'm in touch with the Galactic Council--I'll transmit you their data on this.
Alpha Flight has yet to respond to hails.
Indigo--Security.
...
All right. Violet--Analysis.
Present.
What's your status, Mentallo?

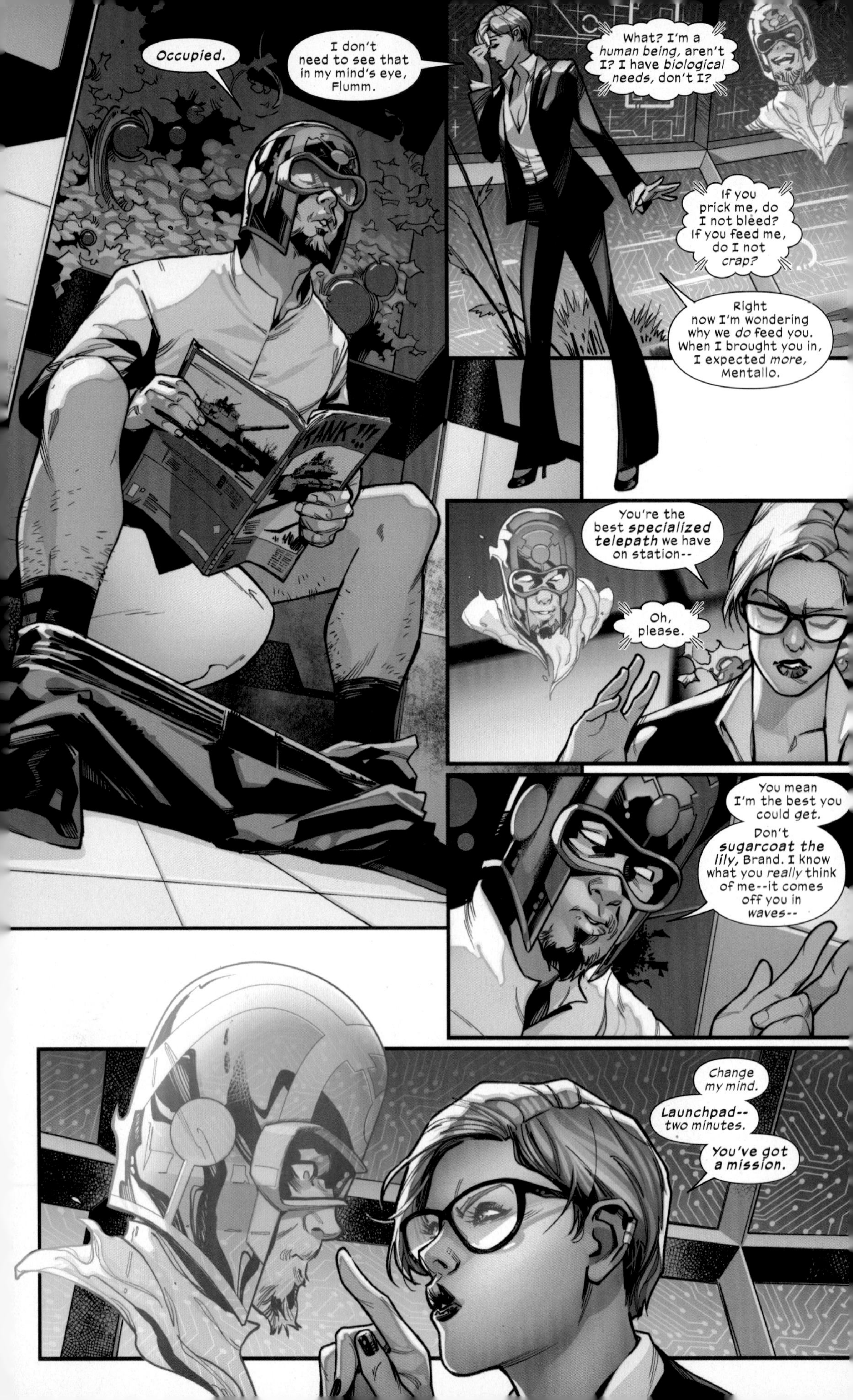
Occupied.
I don't need to see that in my mind's eye, Flumm.
What? I'm a *human being*, aren't I? I have *biological needs*, don't I?
If you prick me, do I not bleed? If you feed me, do I not *crap?*
Right now I'm wondering why we *do* feed you. When I brought you in, I expected *more*, Mentallo.
TANK!!!
You're the best ***specialized telepath*** we have on station--
Oh, please.
You mean I'm the best you could *get*.
Don't ***sugarcoat the lily,*** Brand. I know what you *really* think of me--it comes off you in *waves*--
Change my mind.
Launchpad-- two minutes.
You've got a mission.

PERSONNEL NOTES :: MARVIN FLUMM/MENTALLO

ABIGAIL BRAND :: *E-7-14 11/20* :: *GSTC 0245*

I'm letting Marvin Flumm think he's the best telepath I can get.

He's a criminal to the core. That's not some moral statement from atop my lofty high ground -- just the truth. If Flumm weren't a telepath, he'd be a con artist or a second-story man -- the mind-reading just gets him invited to a fancier class of heist. He's never cared who sends the invite, either -- he has no ideology of his own, no credo or belief beyond what puts the most zeros in the Swiss account. Which makes him deeply despicable or deeply useful, depending how cynical I feel on a given day.

To a man like that, the mutant nation is the latest in a long line of hustles. Amnesty is an easy out. Resurrection is an ace in the hole. Mutant rights are a grift, just like last time.

A man like that has no loyalty to Krakoa. In a land with no use for money, he's got an undivided loyalty to the money. So as long as I have the money -- and I do, thanks to Nick Fury's black-budget bank card -- he'll take my orders over the Quiet Council's. There's no other telepath I could say that about.

Marvin Flumm is the best telepath I could get.

(Regarding his last foray into mutant rights -- he's going to keep bringing up "the you-know-what" until Wiz-Kid builds him a new one. Leaning into the midlife crisis might get more out of him.)

—

DEEP SECRET :: ABOVE EYES ONLY

Private note: Speaking of telepathy -- all personnel currently speak English, Krakoan and Galactic Standard via telepathic download. Any other language can be learned in seconds via similar methods. That eliminates the need for translator implants -- especially the old-style beta-era implants, the ones you had to code yourself like you had nothing better to do. In these troubled economic times, you can pick up a pack of twenty for fifty creds or a fuel cell -- assuming anybody remembers them at all.

I remember. In fact, I've got one in my neck loaded up with a cypher that changes twice daily and a pack of nineteen just like it in the usual spot.

I need to start making a list of people I trust.

People who speak my language.

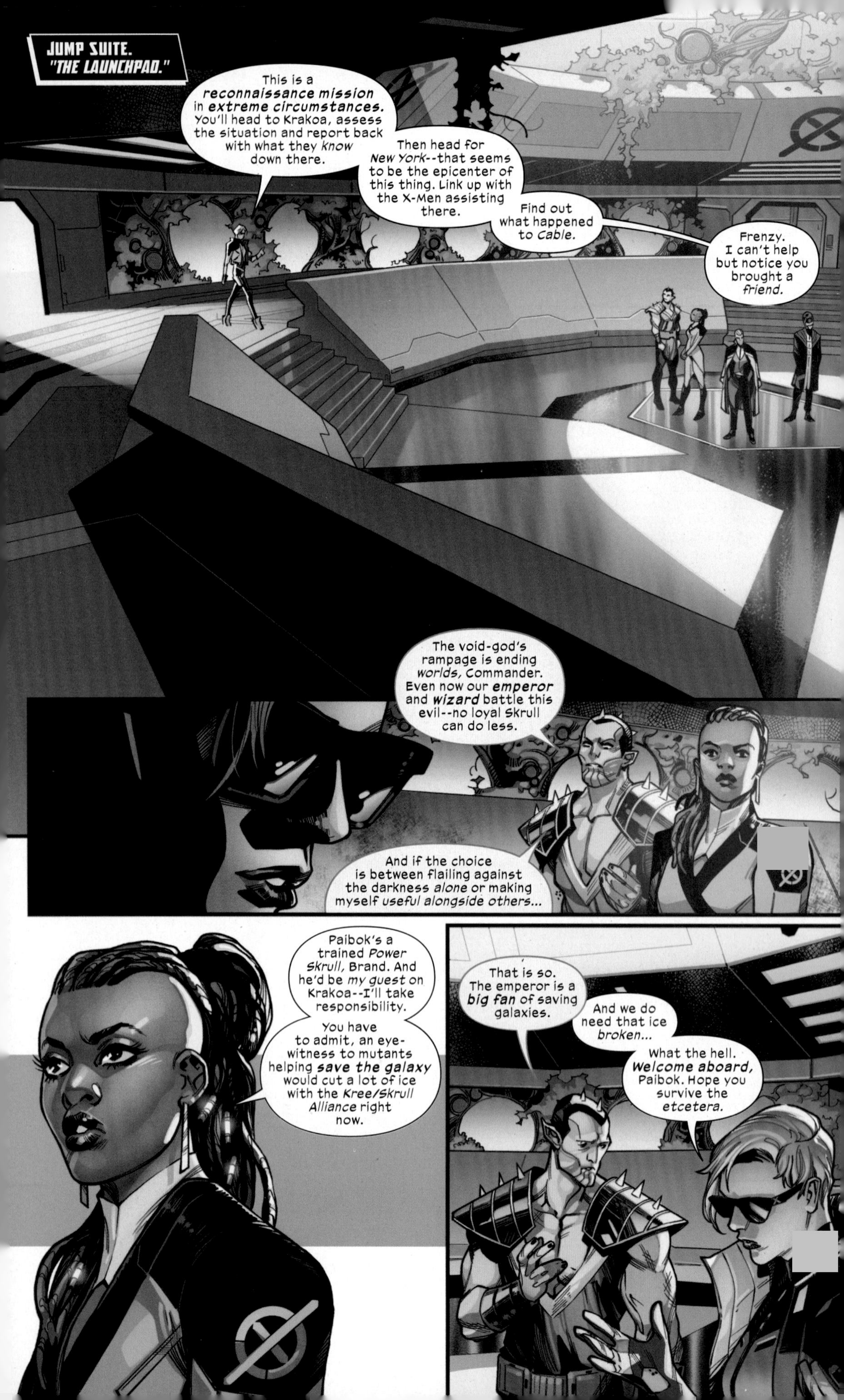
JUMP SUITE. "THE LAUNCHPAD."
This is a reconnaissance mission in extreme circumstances. You'll head to Krakoa, assess the situation and report back with what they know down there.
Then head for New York--that seems to be the epicenter of this thing. Link up with the X-Men assisting there.
Find out what happened to Cable.
Frenzy. I can't help but notice you brought a friend.
The void-god's rampage is ending worlds, Commander. Even now our emperor and wizard battle this evil--no loyal Skrull can do less.
And if the choice is between flailing against the darkness alone or making myself useful alongside others...
Paibok's a trained Power Skrull, Brand. And he'd be my guest on Krakoa--I'll take responsibility.
You have to admit, an eye-witness to mutants helping save the galaxy would cut a lot of ice with the Kree/Skrull Alliance right now.
That is so. The emperor is a big fan of saving galaxies.
And we do need that ice broken...
What the hell. Welcome aboard, Paibok. Hope you survive the etcetera.

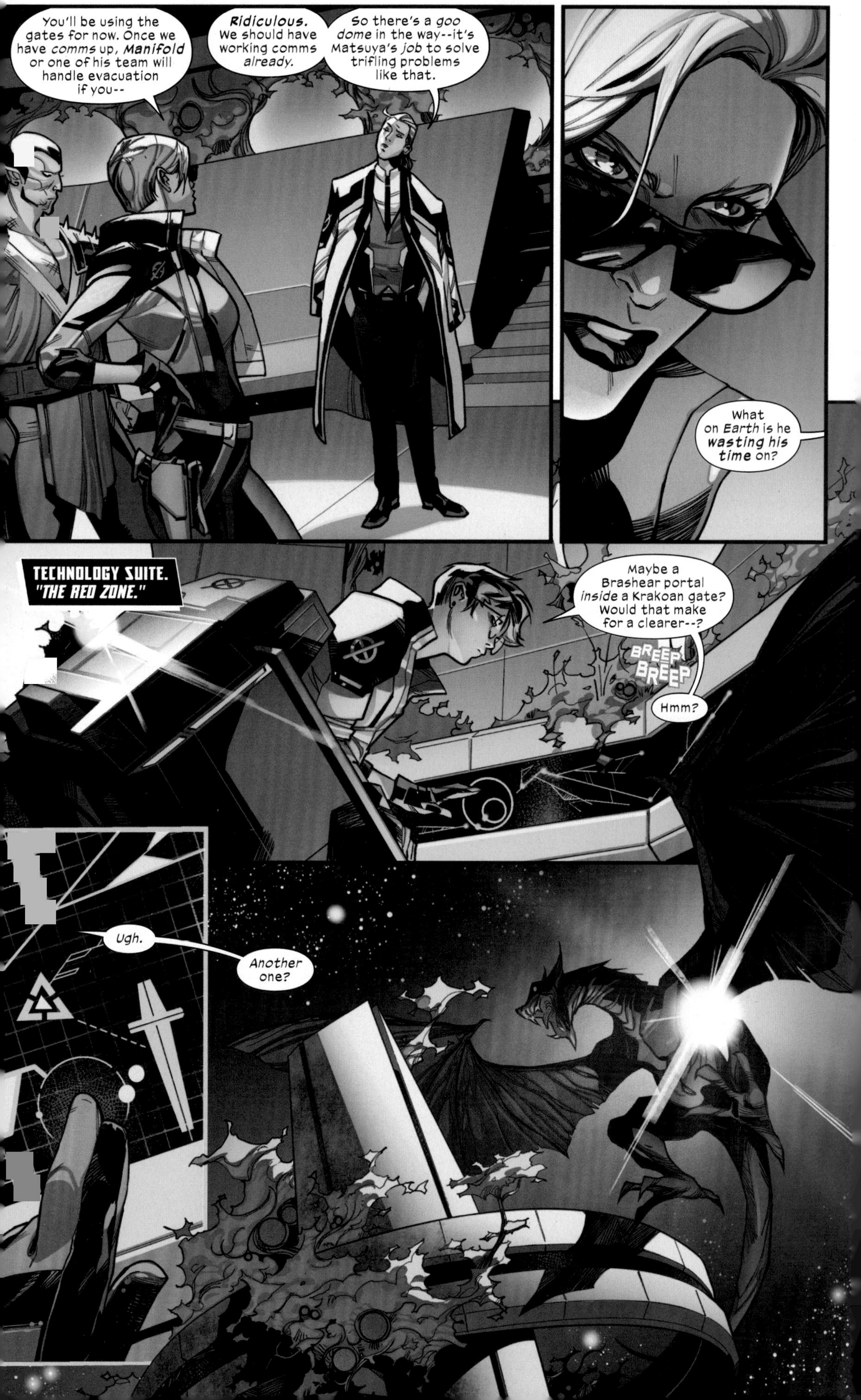

You'll be using the gates for now. Once we have *comms* up, ***Manifold*** or one of his team will handle evacuation if you--
Ridiculous. We should have working comms *already.*
So there's a *goo dome* in the way--it's Matsuya's *job* to solve trifling problems like that.
What on *Earth* is he ***wasting his time*** on?
TECHNOLOGY SUITE. "THE RED ZONE."
Maybe a Brashear portal *inside* a Krakoan gate? Would that make for a clearer--?
BREEP BREEP
Hmm?
Ugh.
Another one?

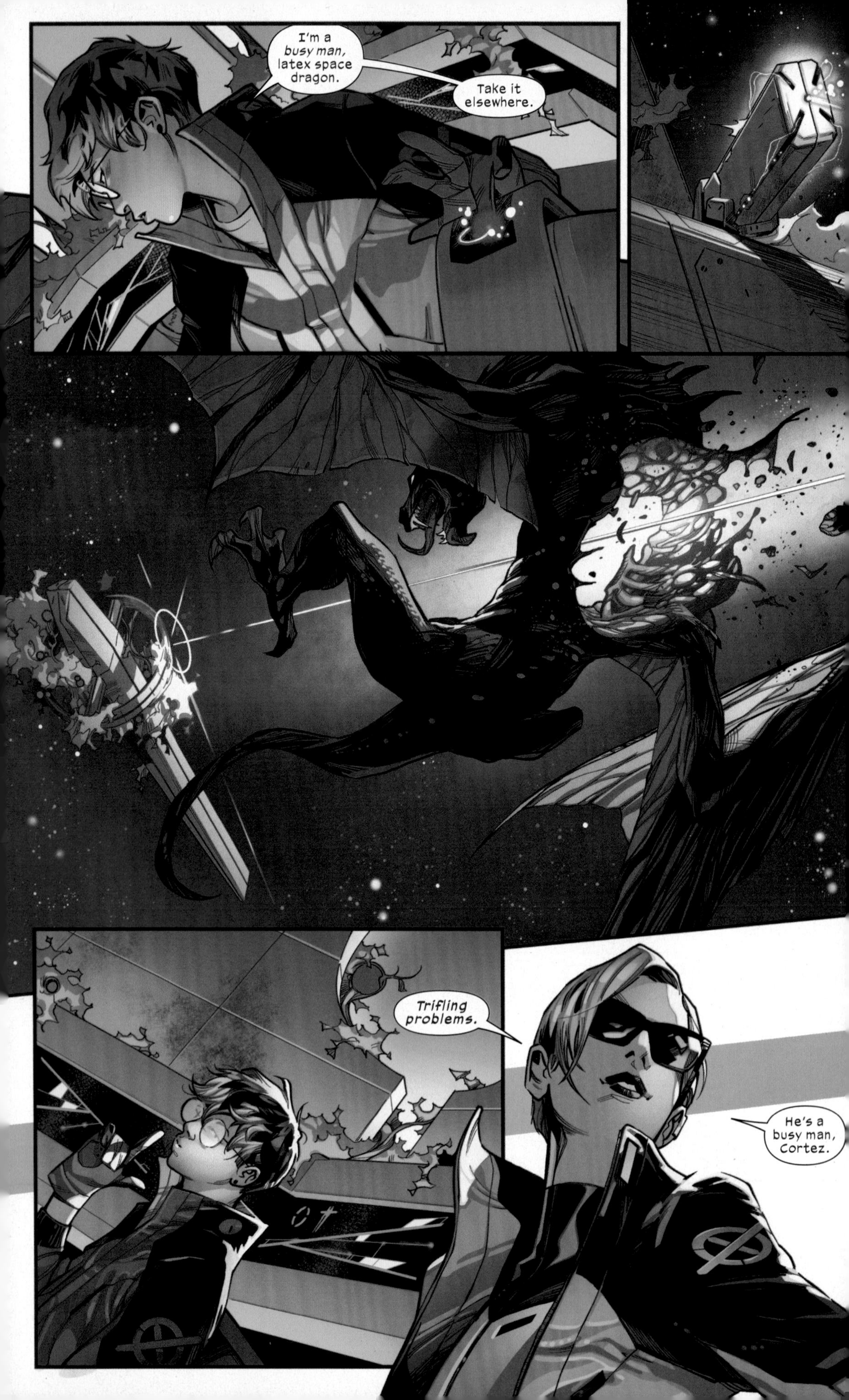
I'm a *busy man,* latex space dragon.
Take it elsewhere.
Trifling problems.
He's a busy man, Cortez.

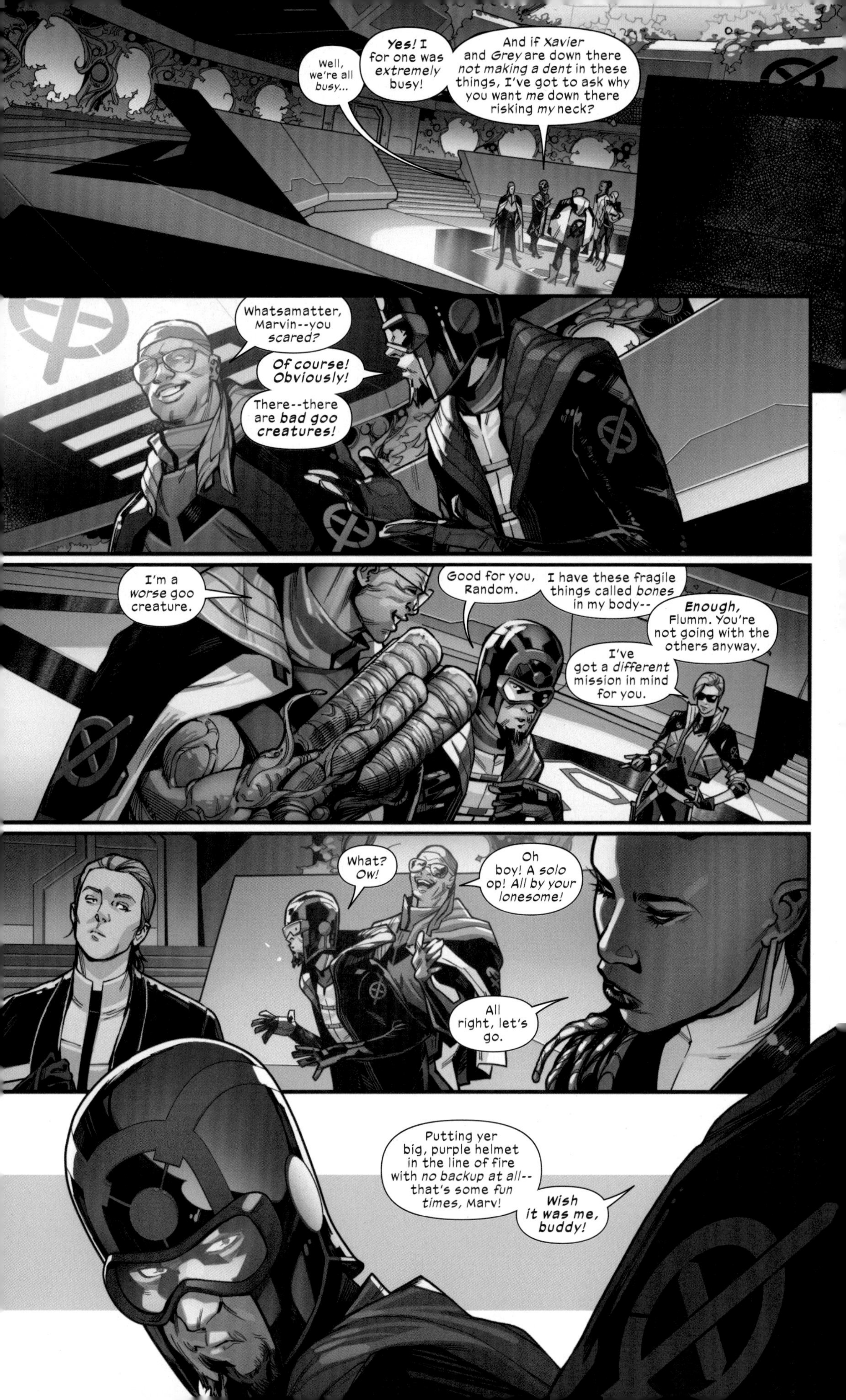
Well, we're all busy...
Yes! I for one was extremely busy!
And if Xavier and Grey are down there not making a dent in these things, I've got to ask why you want me down there risking my neck?
Whatsamatter, Marvin--you scared?
Of course! Obviously!
There--there are bad goo creatures!
I'm a worse goo creature.
Good for you, Random.
I have these fragile things called bones in my body--
Enough, Flumm. You're not going with the others anyway.
I've got a different mission in mind for you.
What? Ow!
Oh boy! A solo op! All by your lonesome!
All right, let's go.
Putting yer big, purple helmet in the line of fire with no backup at all--that's some fun times, Marv!
Wish it was me, buddy!

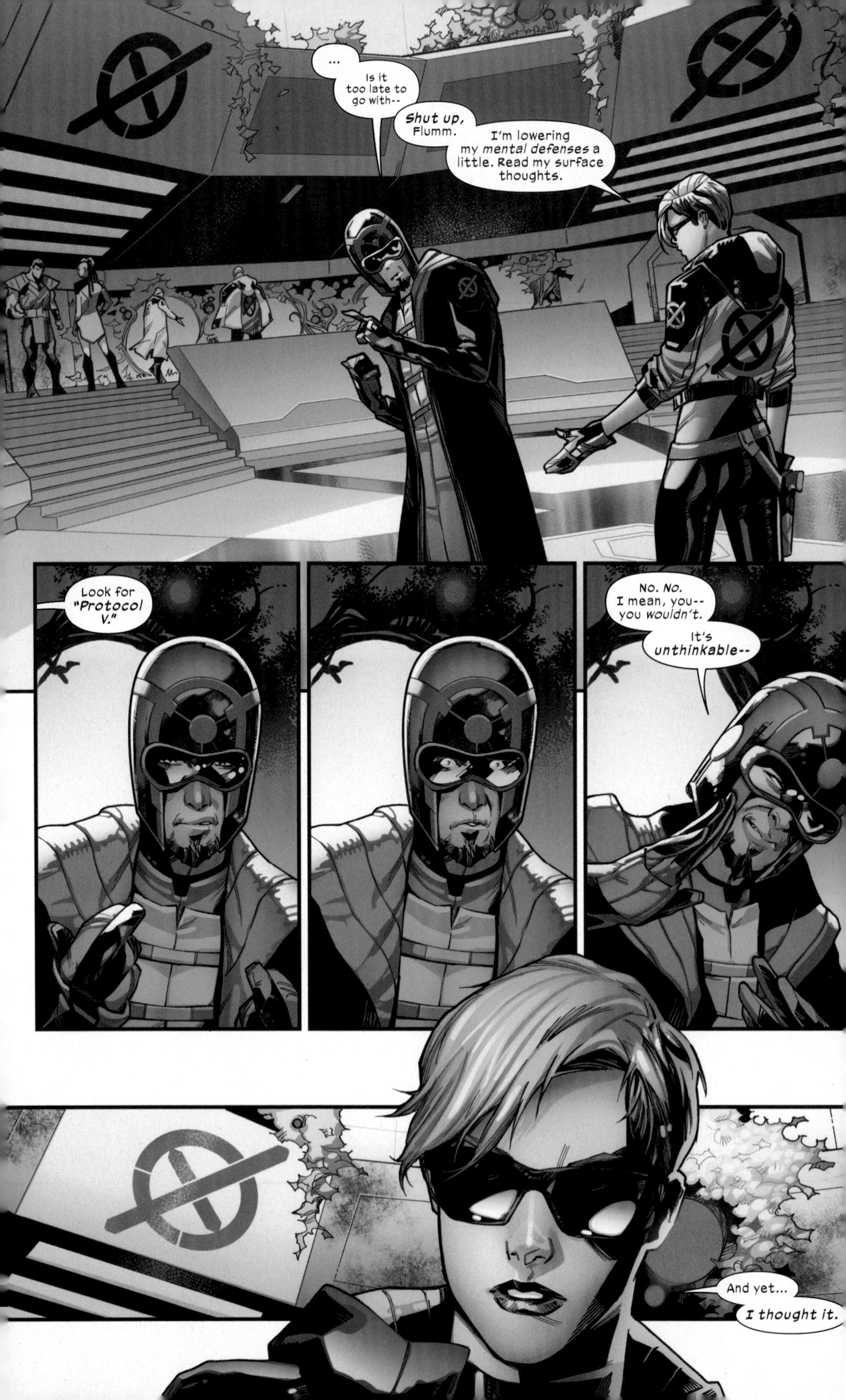
...
Is it too late to go with--
Shut up, Flumm.
I'm lowering my mental defenses a little. Read my surface thoughts.
Look for "Protocol V."
No. No. I mean, you-- you wouldn't.
It's unthinkable--
And yet...
I thought it.

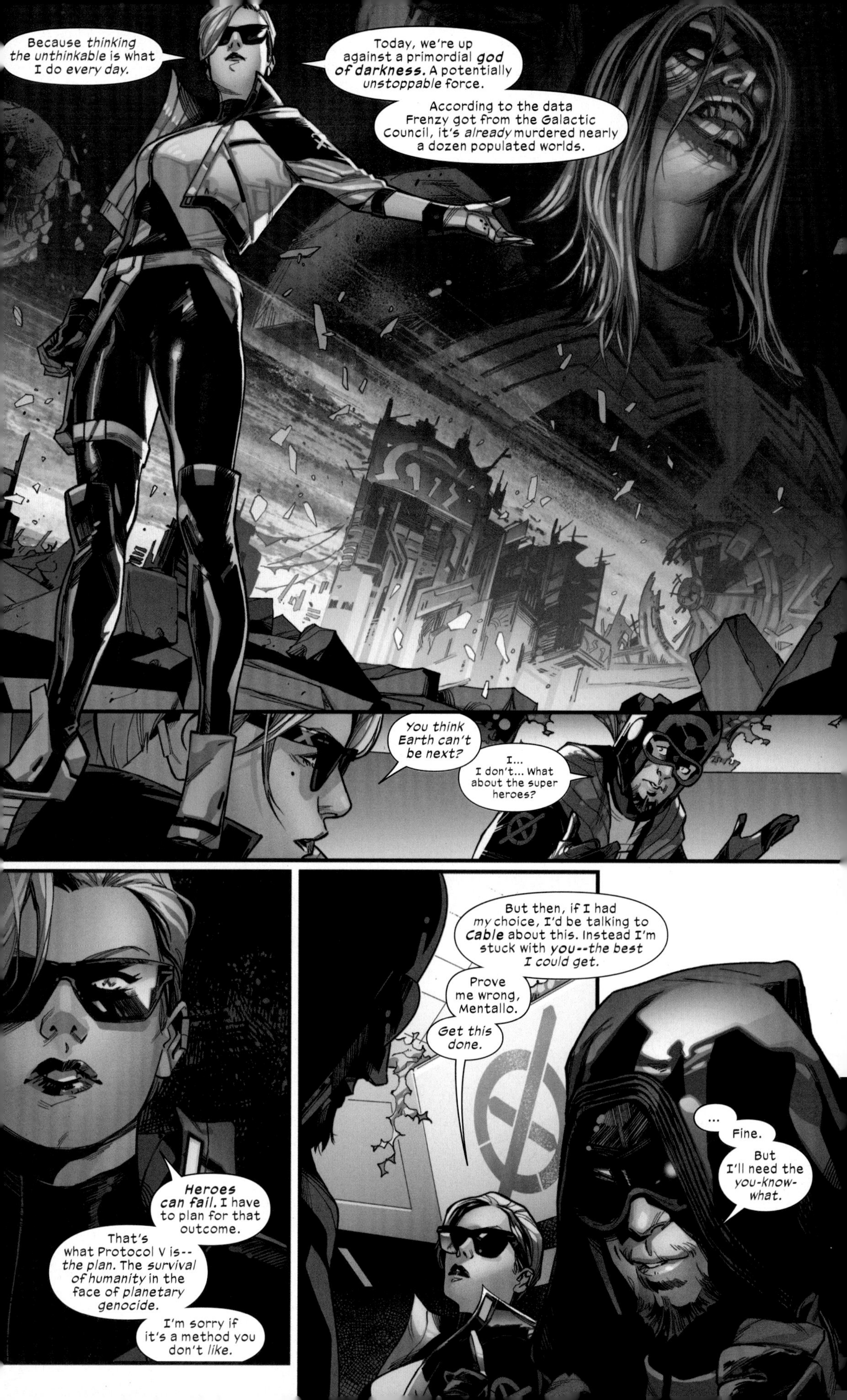
Because thinking the unthinkable is what I do every day.
Today, we're up against a primordial god of darkness. A potentially unstoppable force.
According to the data Frenzy got from the Galactic Council, it's already murdered nearly a dozen populated worlds.
You think Earth can't be next?
I... I don't... What about the super heroes?
Heroes can fail. I have to plan for that outcome.
That's what Protocol V is-- the plan. The survival of humanity in the face of planetary genocide.
I'm sorry if it's a method you don't like.
But then, if I had my choice, I'd be talking to Cable about this. Instead I'm stuck with you--the best I could get.
Prove me wrong, Mentallo.
Get this done.
...
Fine.
But I'll need the you-know-what.

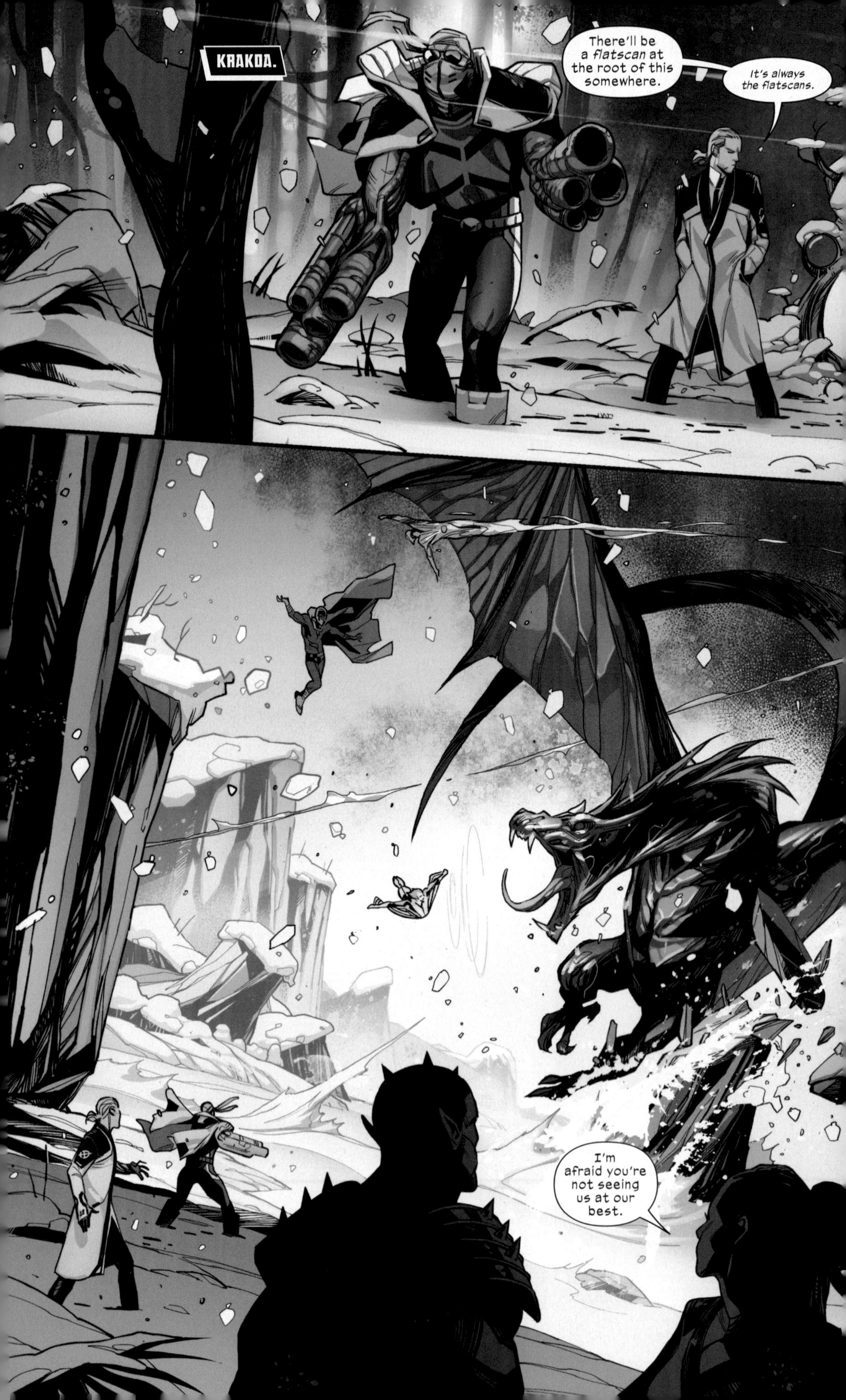
KRAKOA.
There'll be a flatscan at the root of this somewhere.
It's always the flatscans.
I'm afraid you're not seeing us at our best.

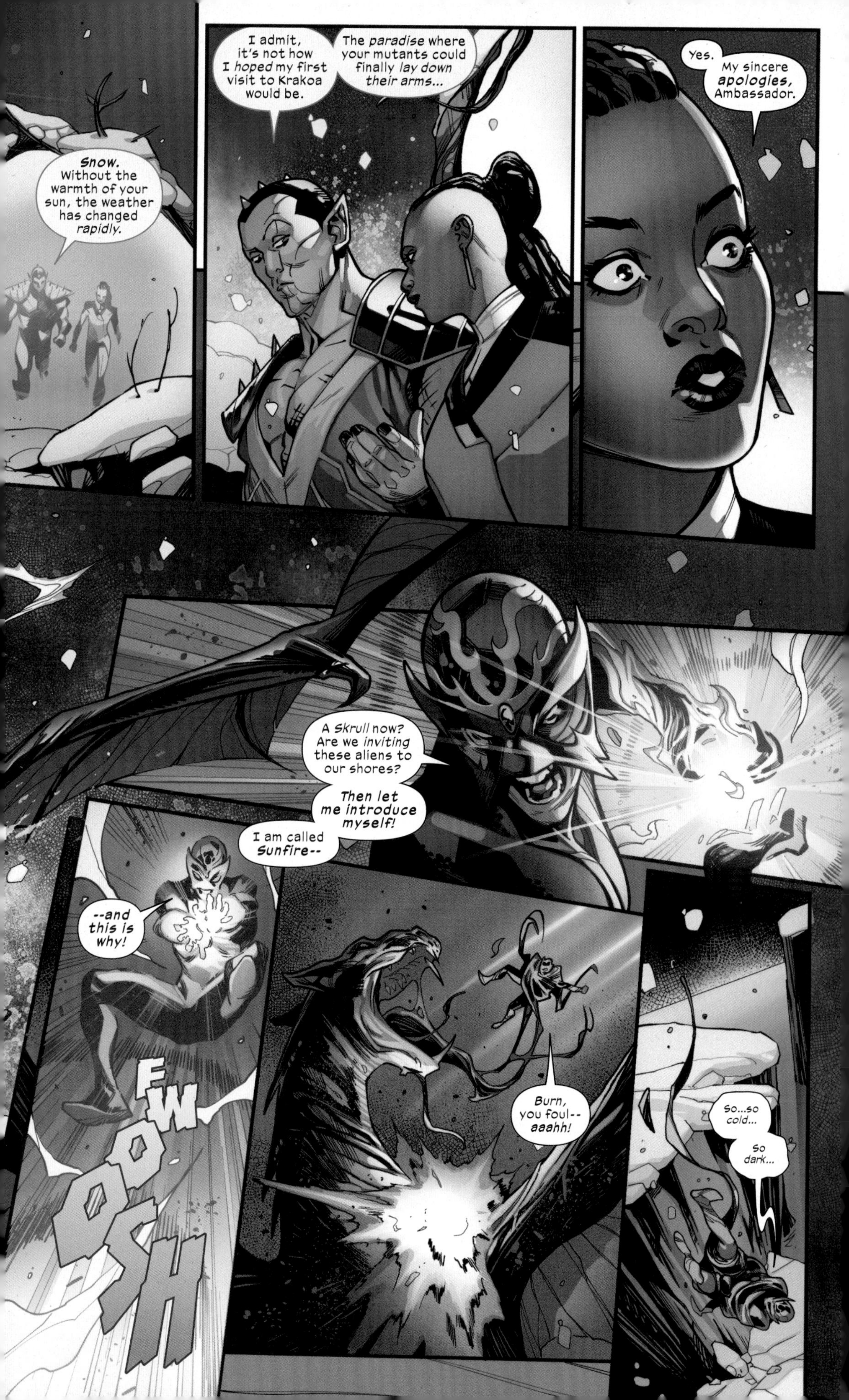

Snow. Without the warmth of your sun, the weather has changed rapidly.
I admit, it's not how I hoped my first visit to Krakoa would be.
The paradise where your mutants could finally lay down their arms...
Yes. My sincere apologies, Ambassador.
A Skrull now? Are we inviting these aliens to our shores?
Then let me introduce myself!
I am called Sunfire--
--and this is why!
FWOOOSH
Burn, you foul--aaahh!
So...so cold...
So dark...

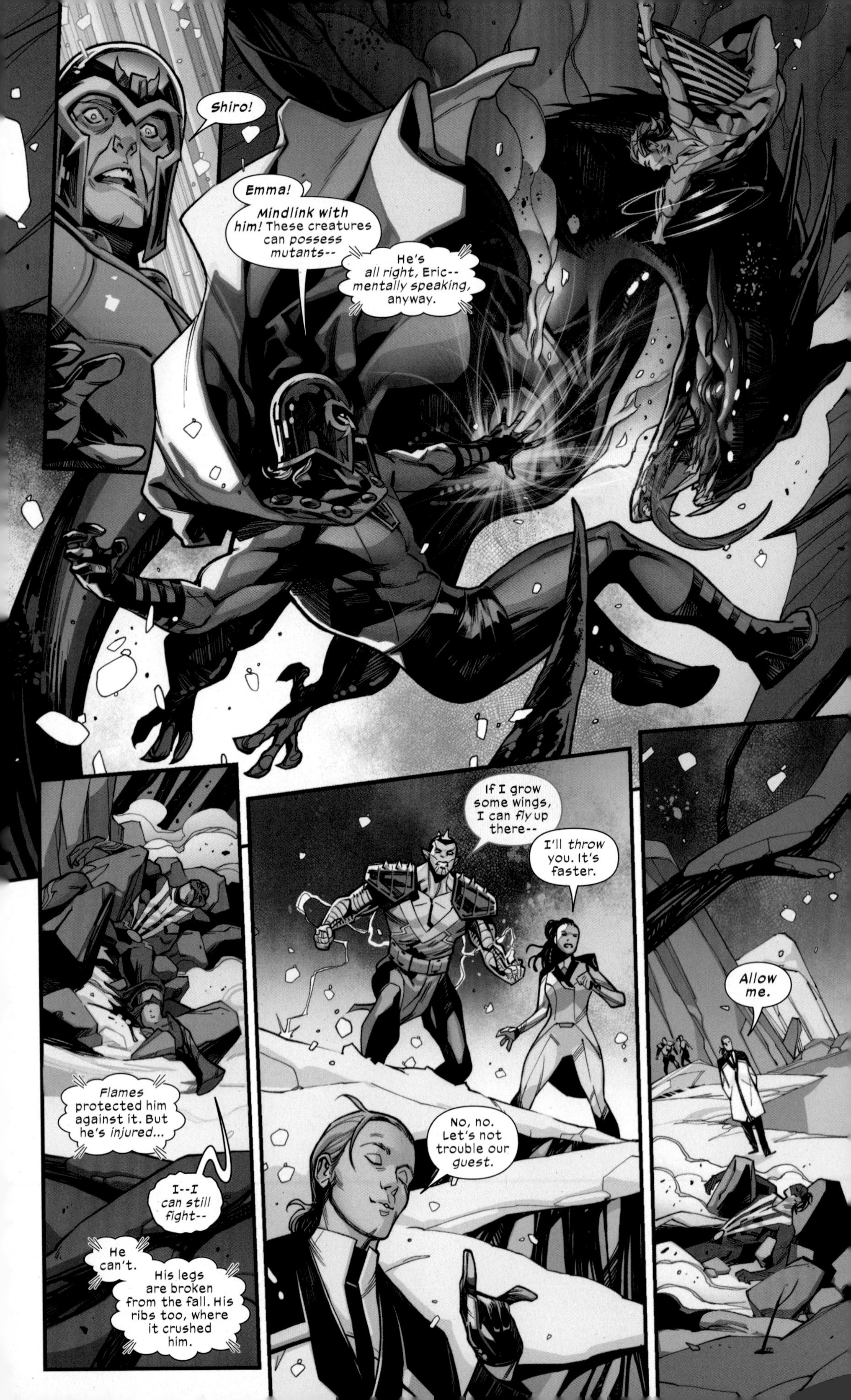

Shiro!
Emma!
Mindlink with him! These creatures can possess mutants--
He's all right, Eric-- mentally speaking, anyway.
Flames protected him against it. But he's injured...
I--I can still fight--
He can't.
His legs are broken from the fall. His ribs too, where it crushed him.
If I grow some wings, I can fly up there--
I'll throw you. It's faster.
No, no. Let's not trouble our guest.
Allow me.

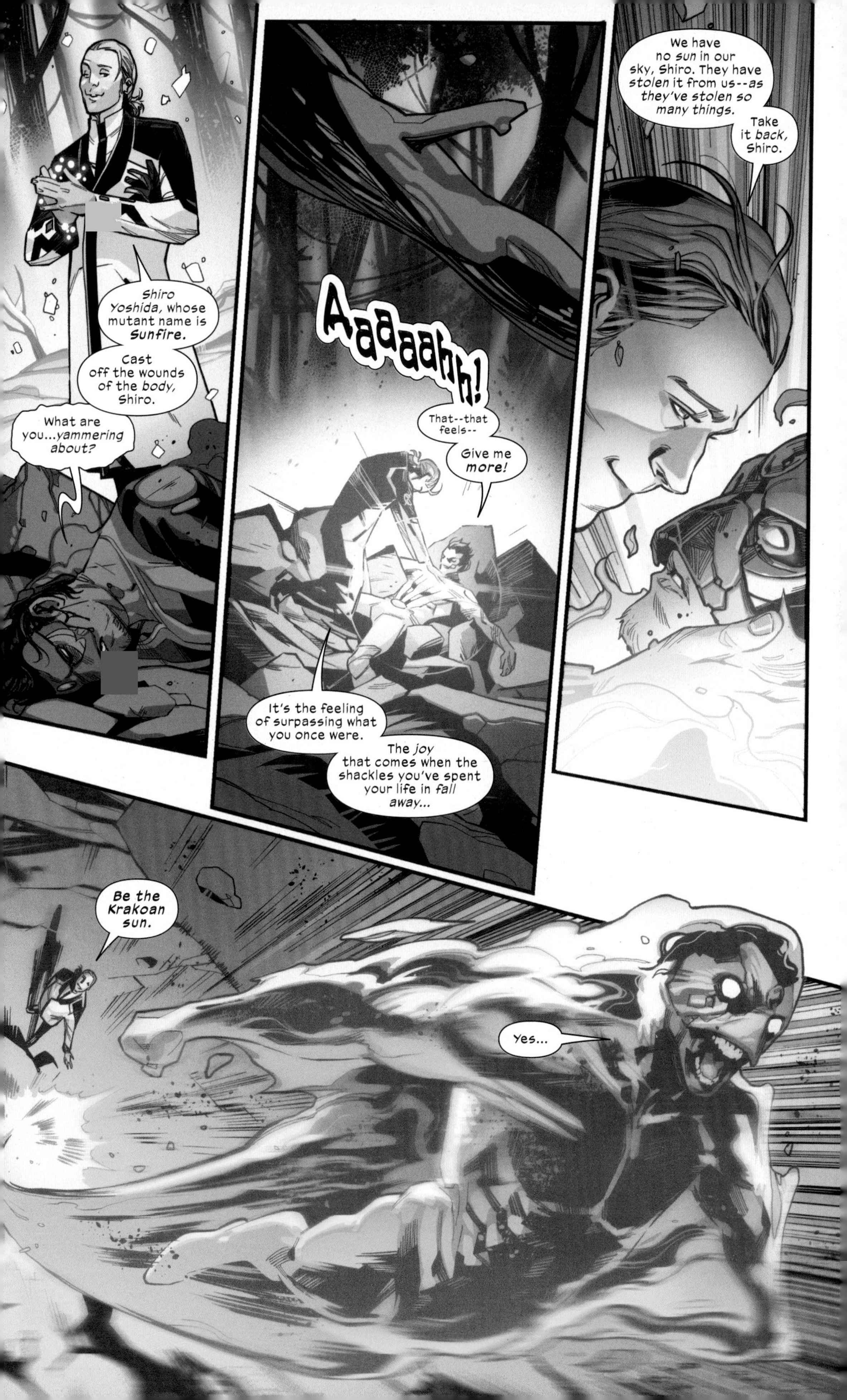
Shiro Yoshida, whose mutant name is Sunfire.
Cast off the wounds of the body, Shiro.
What are you...yammering about?
Aaaaaahh!
That--that feels--
Give me more!
It's the feeling of surpassing what you once were.
The joy that comes when the shackles you've spent your life in fall away...
We have no sun in our sky, Shiro. They have stolen it from us--as they've stolen so many things.
Take it back, Shiro.
Be the Krakoan sun.
Yes...

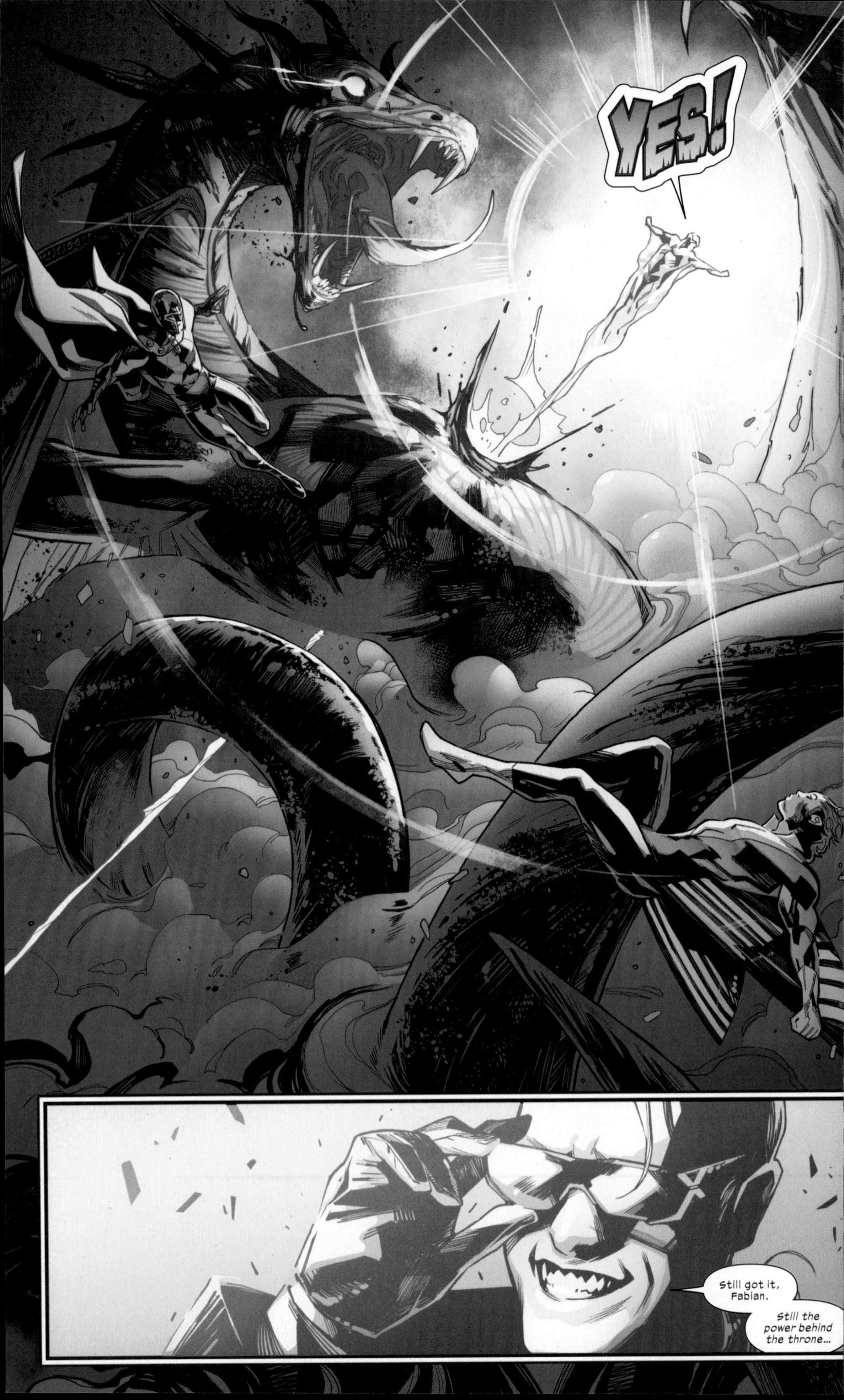
YES!
Still got it, Fabian.
Still the power behind the throne...

PERSONNEL NOTES :: FABIAN CORTEZ/*NO NAME GIVEN*

ABIGAIL BRAND :: E-7-15 11/24 :: GSTC 1078

Fabian Cortez has the exact power set required for the vital exploration and retrieval missions we're conducting in higher space. We need him on board.

Unfortunately, he's a treacherous sack of yuppie pus who'll stab any back or kiss any behind for a taste of power. I can fob him off with some meaningless title for now, but that won't salve his ambition forever, and it's possible some of the egos on the Council might fall for his shtick before I can create a long-term solution.

—

POTENTIAL REPLACEMENTS	PROBLEMS/ISSUES
Michael Nowlan/*No Name Given*	Unlike Cortez, Nowlan is unable to control the addictive nature of his power amplification. Also, Nowlan is unwilling to cooperate with Krakoan authority after learning that as a baseline human, his ex-wife **Susan Nowlan** cannot be resurrected.
Brian Dunlop/Boost	Boost amplifies powers by merging bodily with other mutants; as such, he cannot amplify more than one mutant at a time. *Note: still a very useful power. Consider for security team or* [redacted].
Absolon Mercator/Mister M	Unavailable. Whereabouts unknown.
[redacted]	Primary loyalty is most likely [redacted]. That said, she fits all other criteria, with the added bonus that [redacted] Snarkwar [redacted].

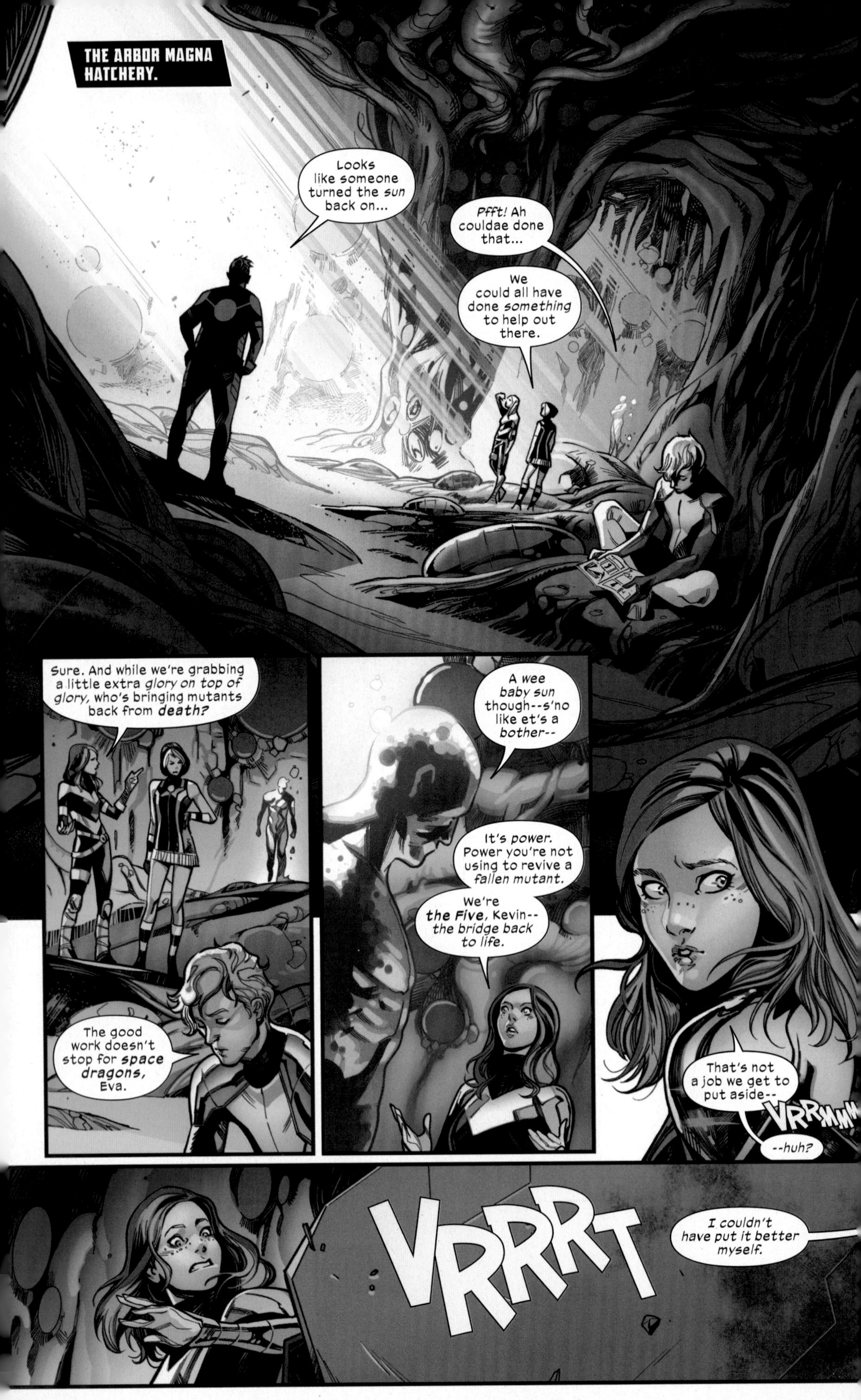
THE ARBOR MAGNA HATCHERY.
Looks like someone turned the *sun* back on...
Pffft! Ah couldae done that...
We could all have done *something* to help out there.
Sure. And while we're grabbing a little extra *glory on top of glory,* who's bringing mutants back from *death?*
The good work doesn't stop for *space dragons,* Eva.
A *wee baby sun* though--s'no like et's a *bother*--
It's *power.* Power you're not using to revive a *fallen mutant.*
We're *the Five,* Kevin--the bridge back to life.
That's not a job we get to put aside--
VRRMMM
--huh?
VRRRT
I couldn't have put it better myself.

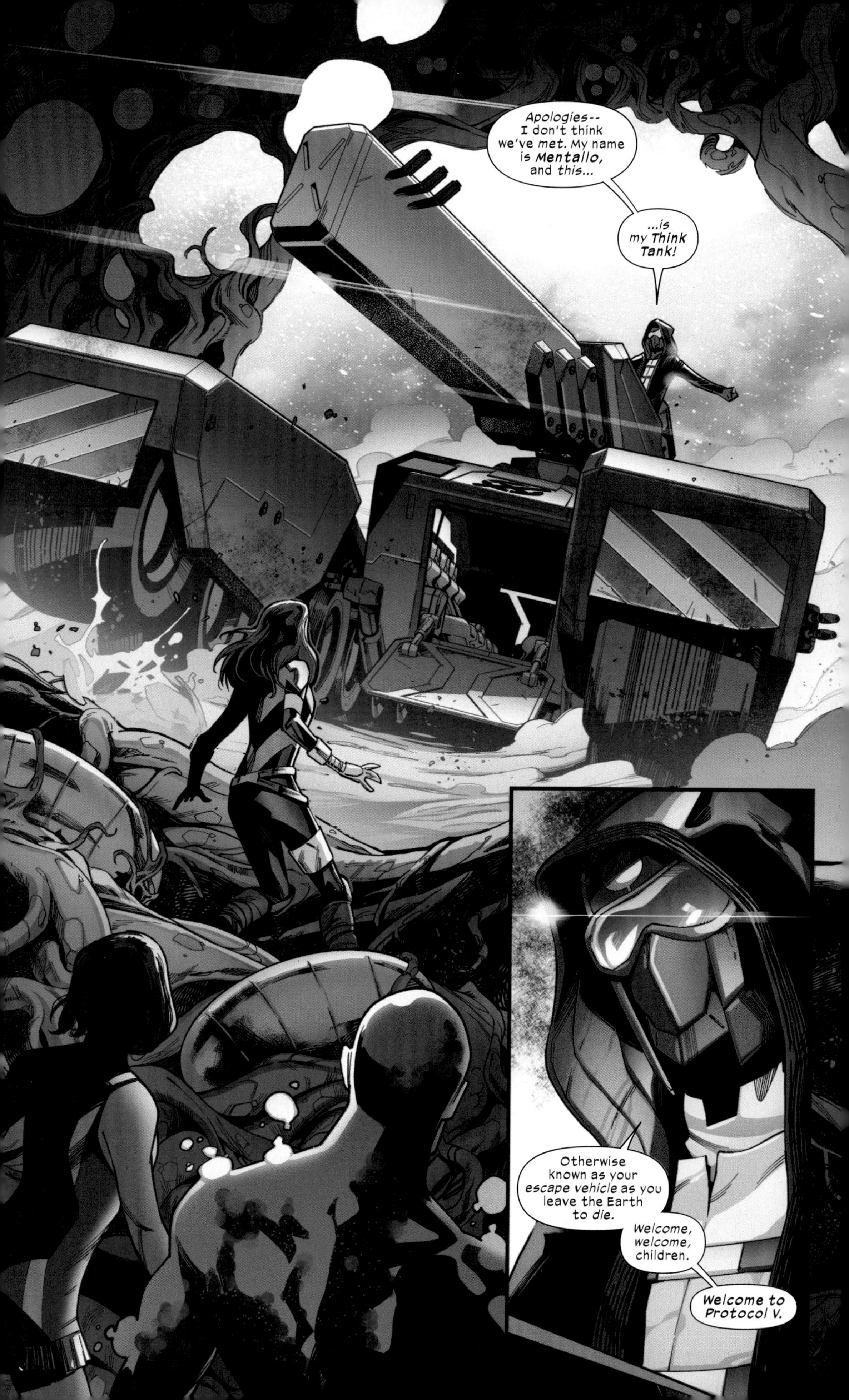
Apologies-- I don't think we've met. My name is Mentallo, and this...
...is my Think Tank!
Otherwise known as your escape vehicle as you leave the Earth to die.
Welcome, welcome, children.
Welcome to Protocol V.

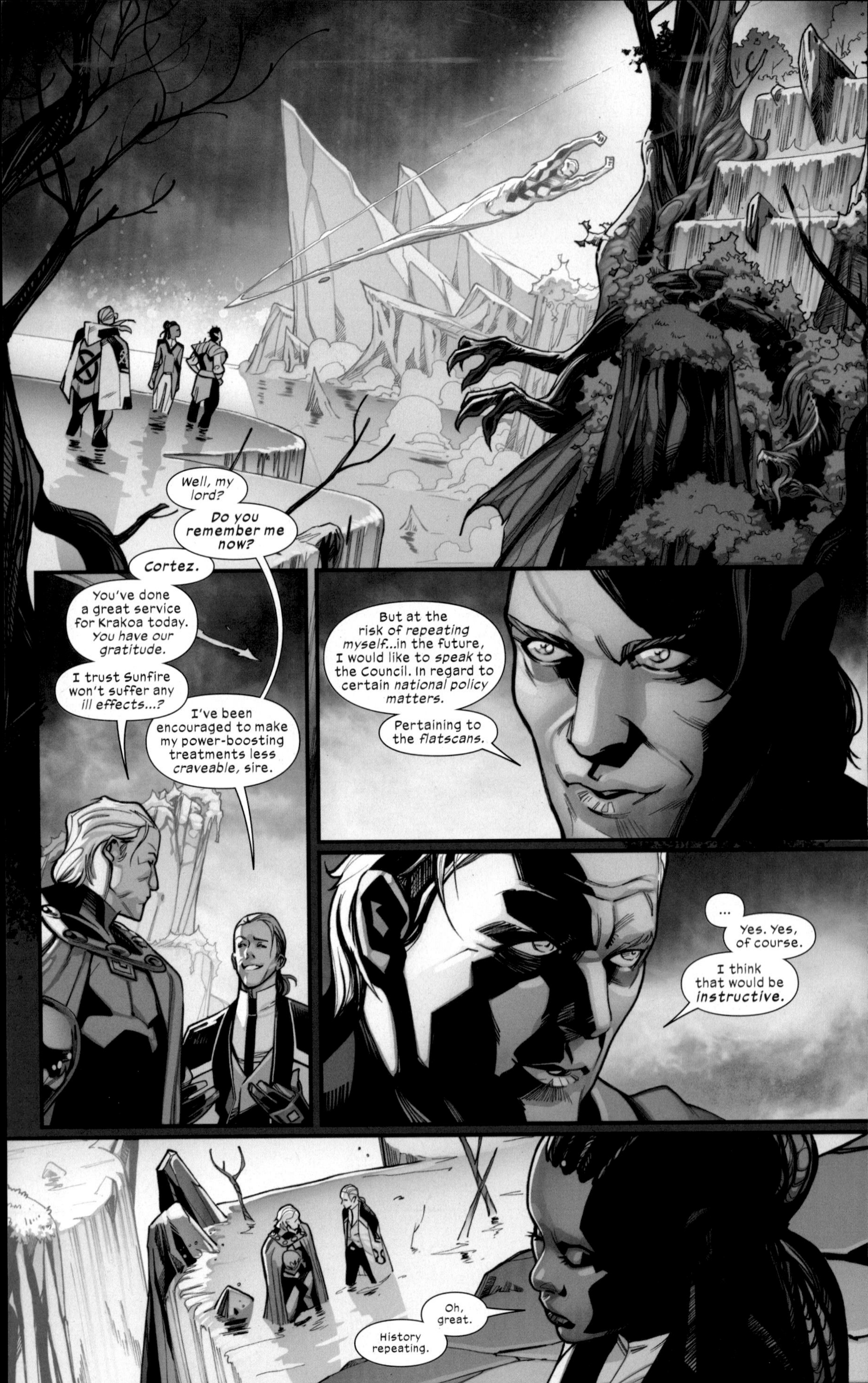
Well, my lord?
Do you remember me now?
Cortez.
You've done a great service for Krakoa today. You have our gratitude.
I trust Sunfire won't suffer any ill effects...?
I've been encouraged to make my power-boosting treatments less craveable, sire.
But at the risk of repeating myself...in the future, I would like to speak to the Council. In regard to certain national policy matters.
Pertaining to the flatscans.
...
Yes. Yes, of course.
I think that would be instructive.
Oh, great.
History repeating.

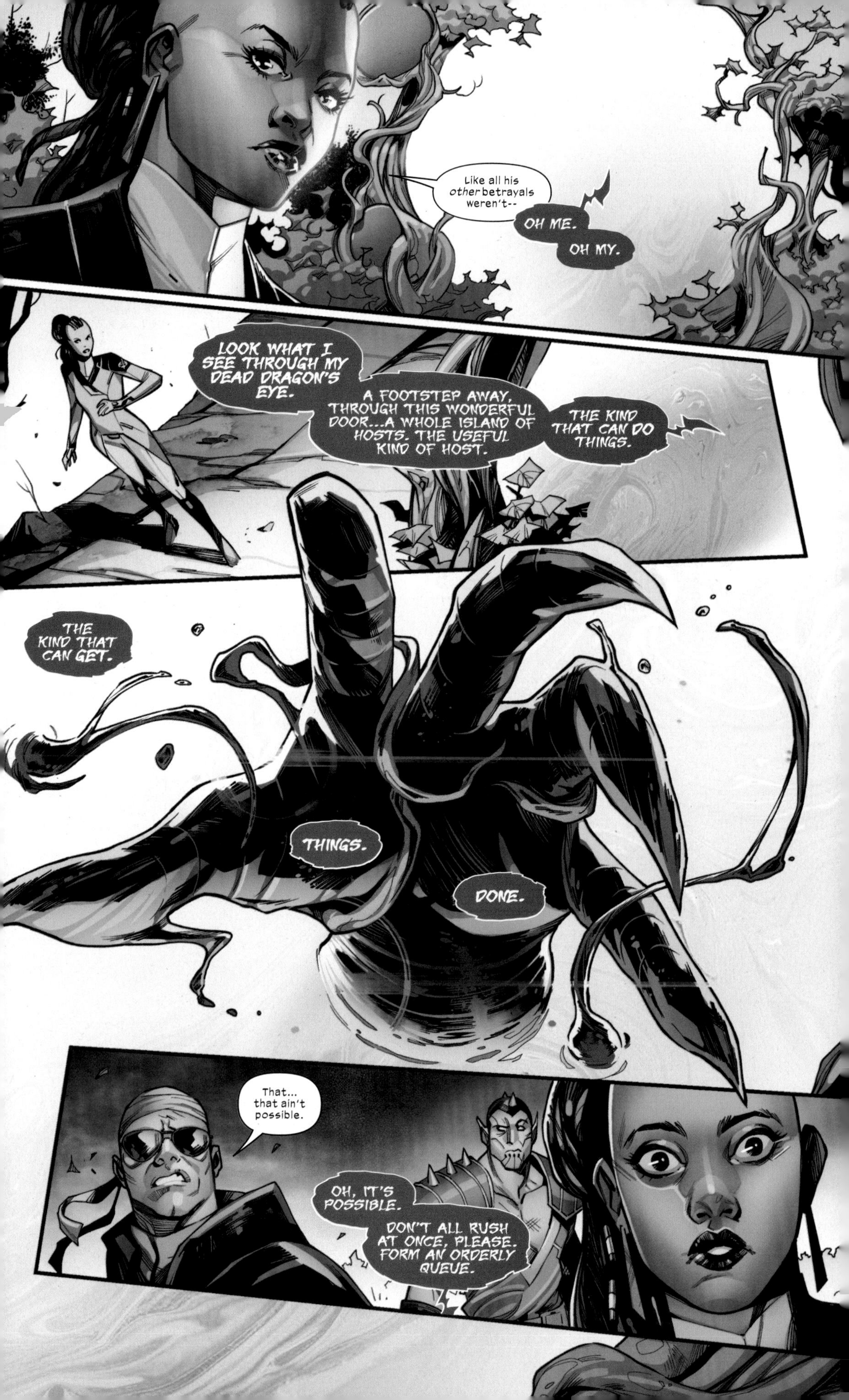
Like all his *other* betrayals weren't--
OH ME.
OH MY.
LOOK WHAT I SEE THROUGH MY DEAD DRAGON'S EYE.
A FOOTSTEP AWAY, THROUGH THIS WONDERFUL DOOR...A WHOLE ISLAND OF HOSTS. THE USEFUL KIND OF HOST.
THE KIND THAT CAN DO THINGS.
THE KIND THAT CAN GET.
THINGS.
DONE.
That... that ain't possible.
OH, IT'S POSSIBLE.
DON'T ALL RUSH AT ONCE, PLEASE. FORM AN ORDERLY QUEUE.

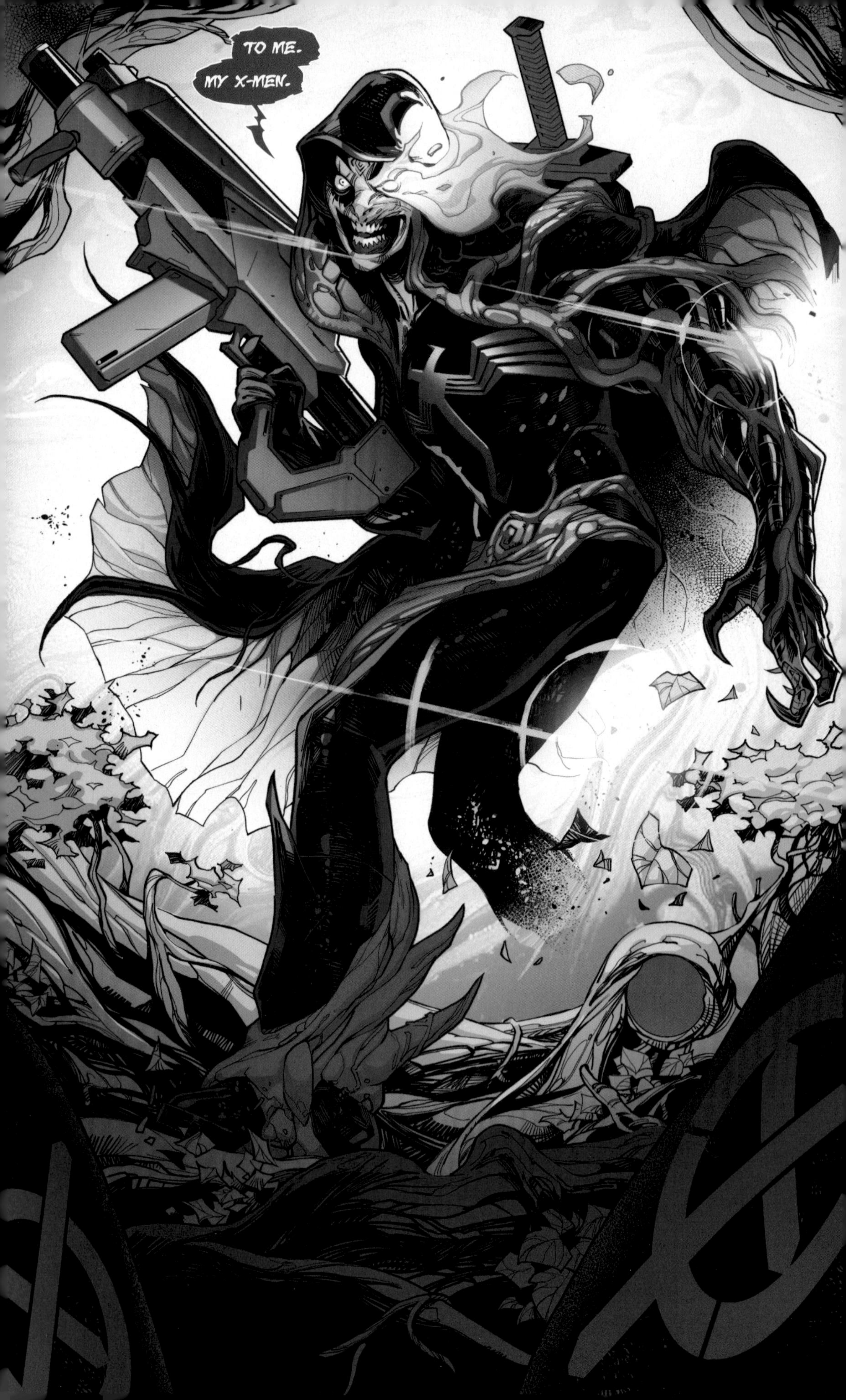
TO ME.
MY X-MEN.

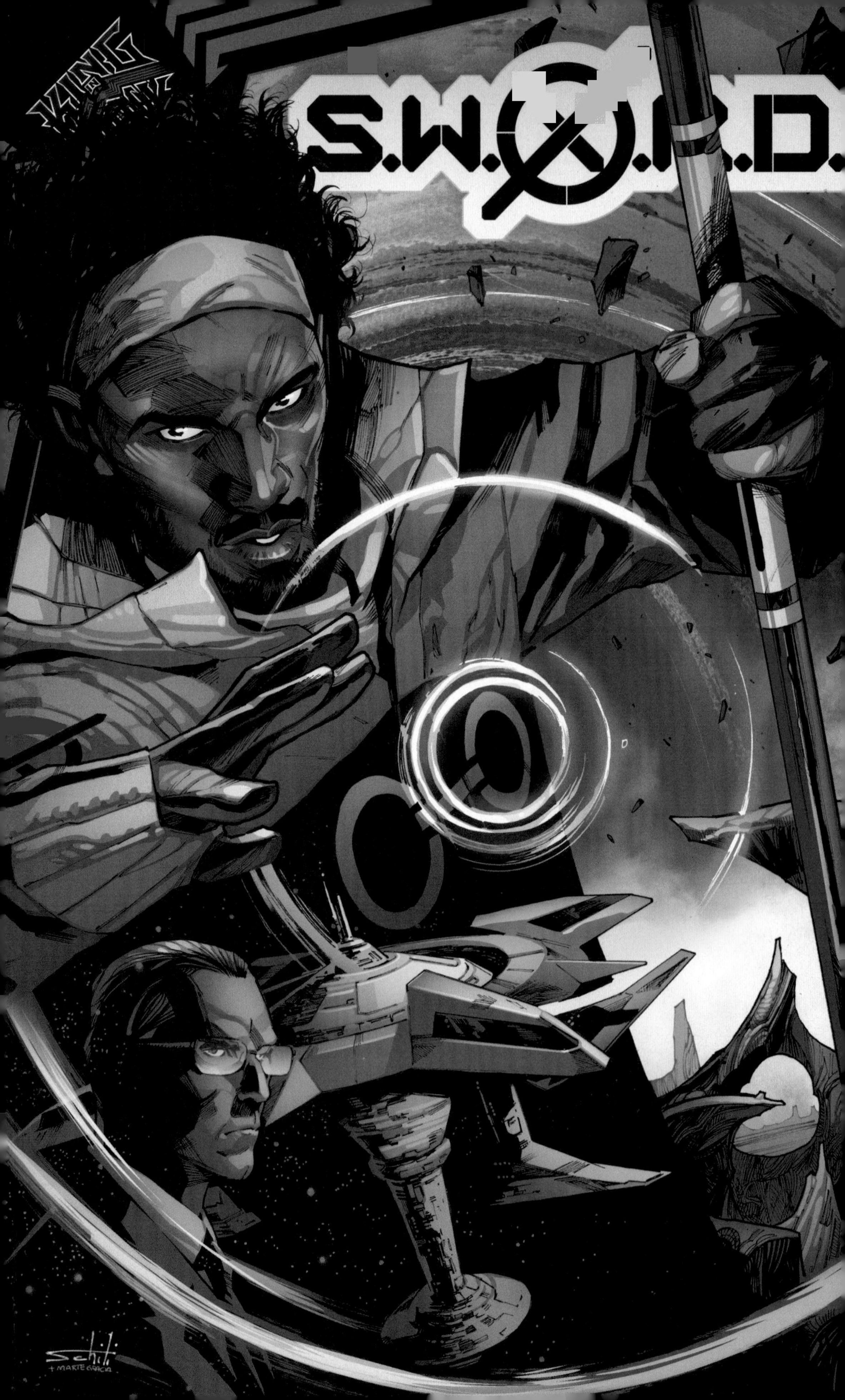
S.W.O.R.D.
Schiti
+ MARTE GRACIA

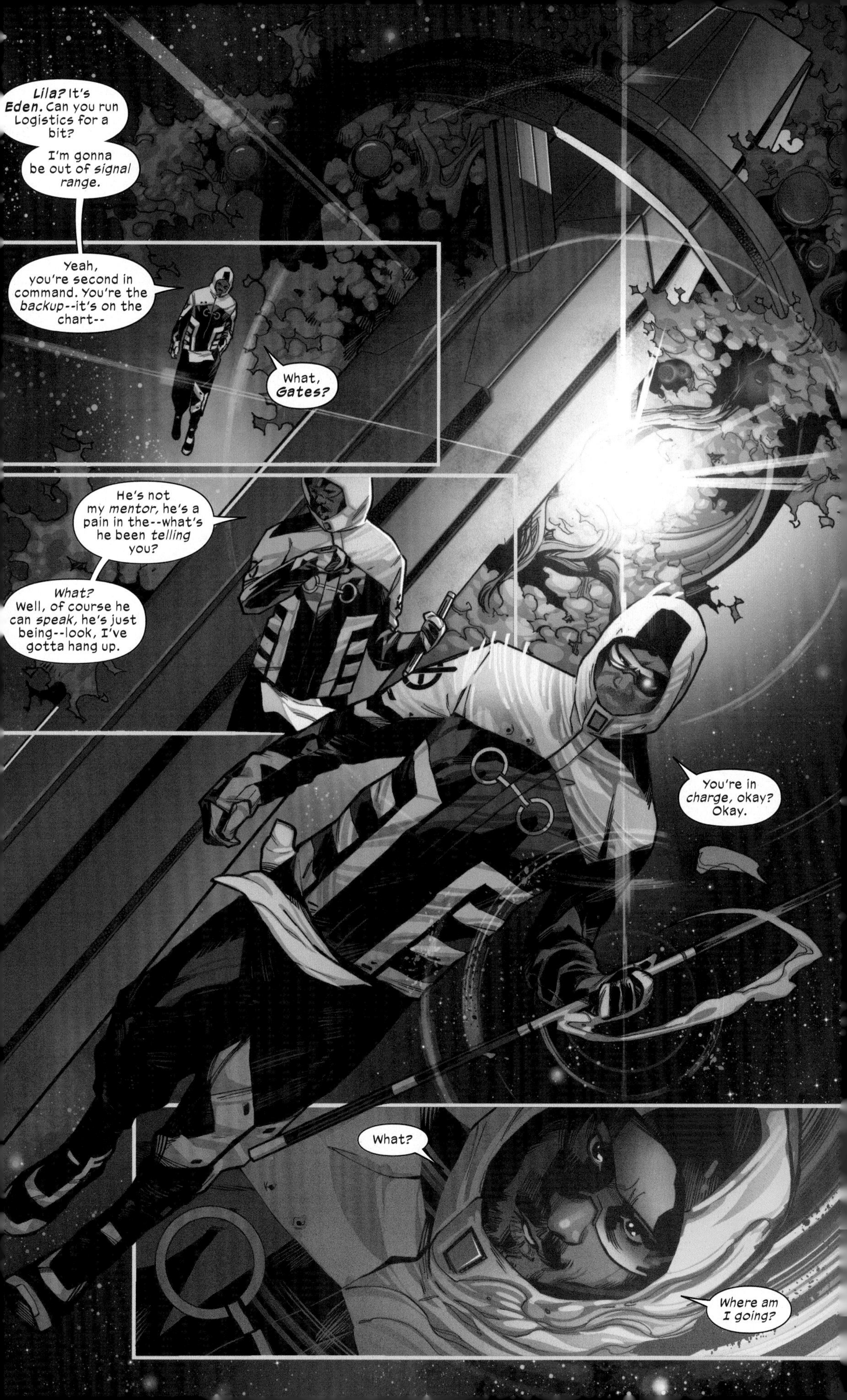
Lila? It's Eden. Can you run Logistics for a bit?
I'm gonna be out of signal range.
Yeah, you're second in command. You're the backup--it's on the chart--
What, Gates?
He's not my mentor, he's a pain in the--what's he been telling you?
What? Well, of course he can speak, he's just being--look, I've gotta hang up.
You're in charge, okay? Okay.
What?
Where am I going?

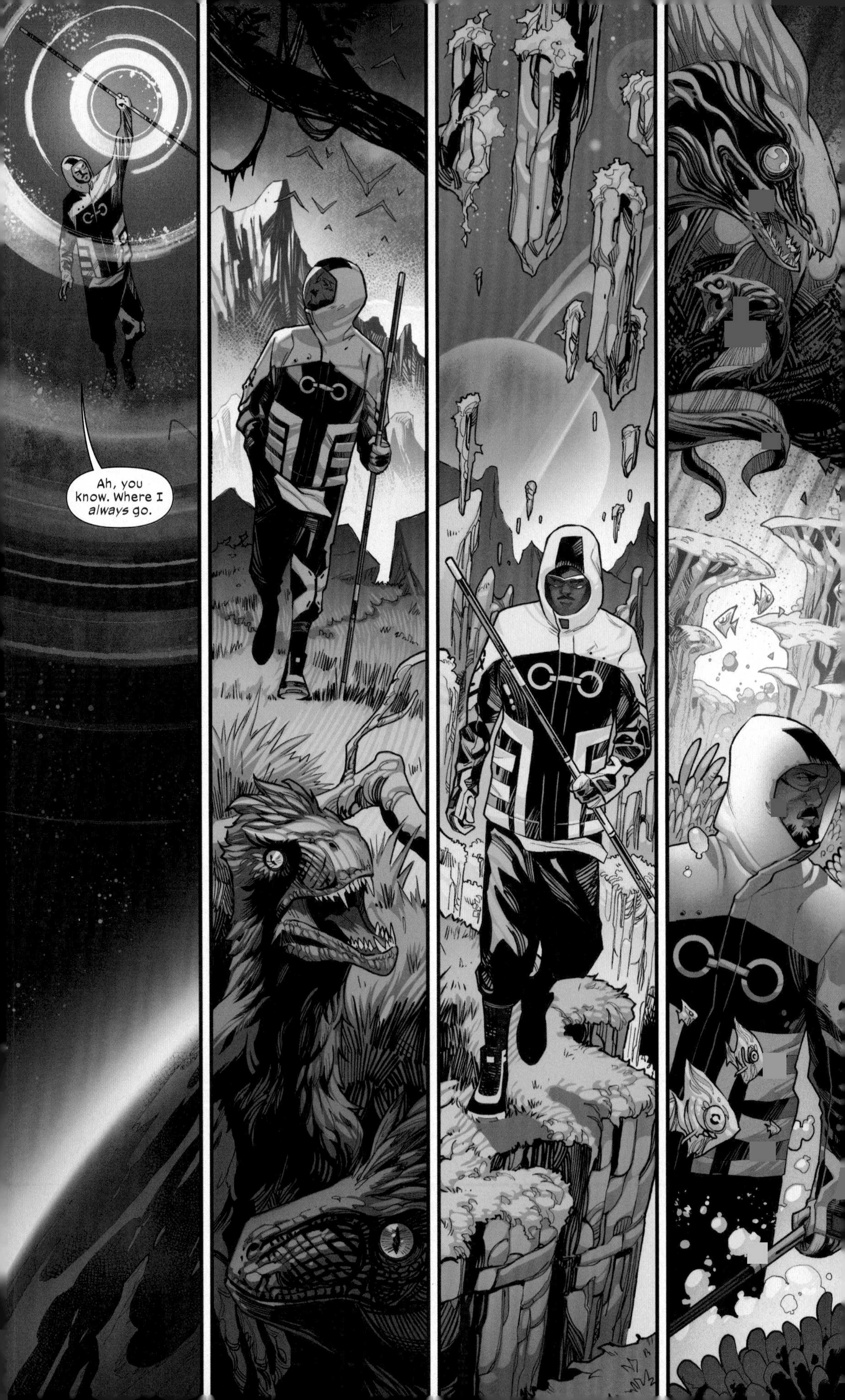
Ah, you know. Where I *always* go.

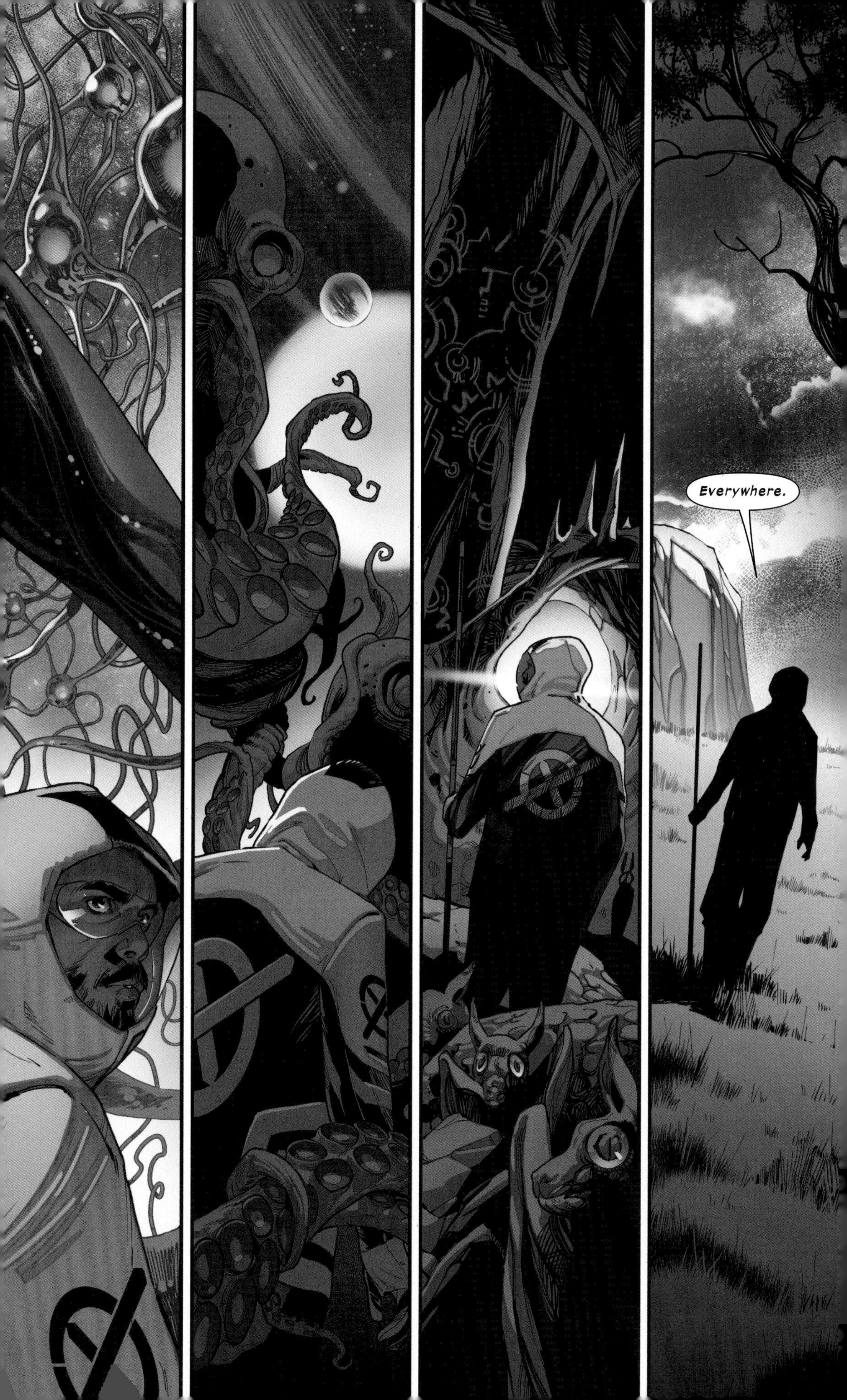
Everywhere.

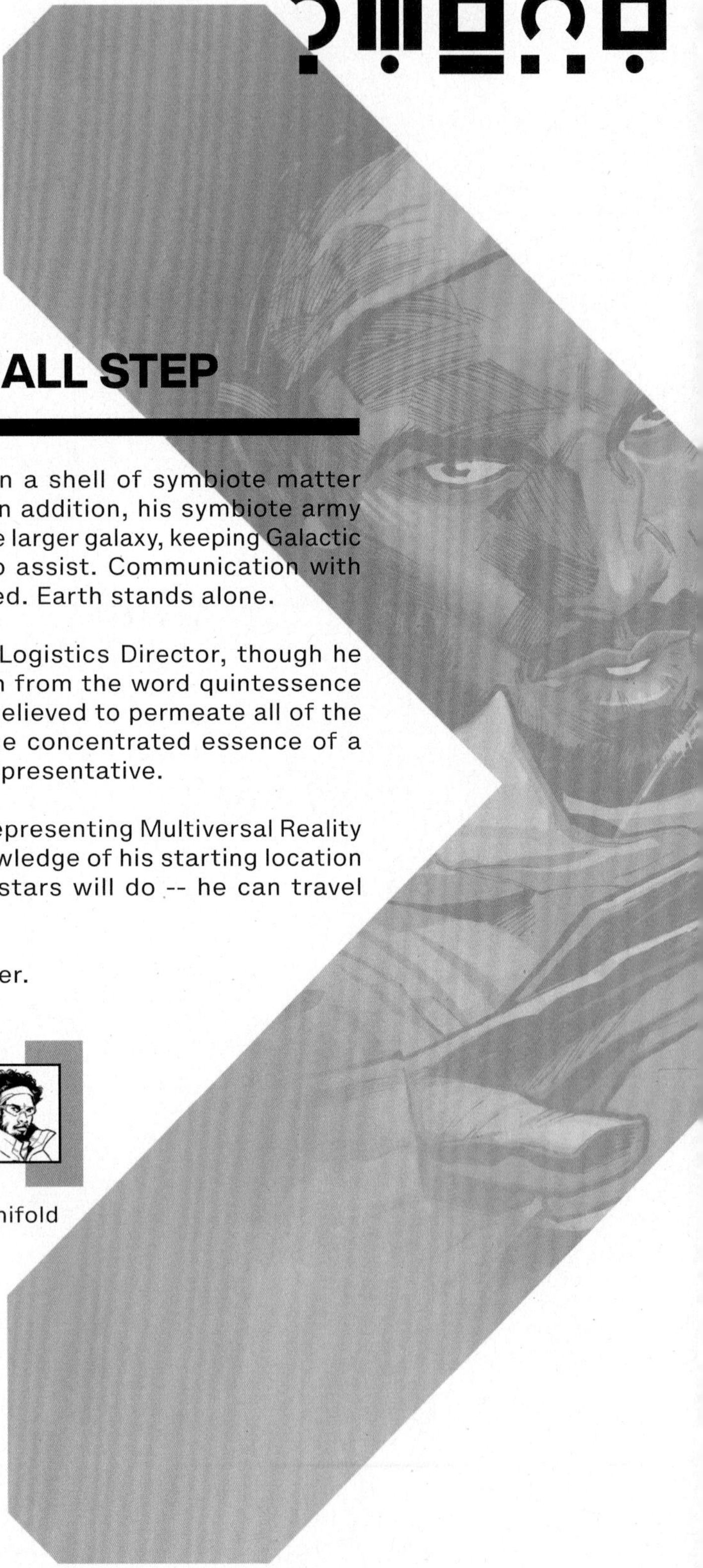

ONE SMALL STEP

Earth has been encased in a shell of symbiote matter by Knull, god of the void. In addition, his symbiote army continues to lay waste to the larger galaxy, keeping Galactic Council forces too busy to assist. Communication with the planet has been severed. Earth stands alone.

Eden Fesi is S.W.O.R.D.'s Logistics Director, though he prefers "Quintician," taken from the word quintessence -- the fifth element once believed to permeate all of the universe. It also means the concentrated essence of a thing or its most typical representative.

Eden Fesi is the Manifold representing Multiversal Reality 616. As long as he has knowledge of his starting location -- even a glimpse of the stars will do -- he can travel anywhere in our universe.

Eden Fesi is not a teleporter.

Manifold

S.W.O.R.D.
[X_03]

[ISSUE THREE]...............................
...........................EVERYWHERE MAN

AL EWING.....................................[WRITER]
VALERIO SCHITI, RAY-ANTHONY HEIGHT, BERNARD CHANG..........
& NICO LEON.....................................[ARTISTS]
MARTE GRACIA...............................[COLOR ARTIST]
VC's ARIANA MAHER..............................[LETTERER]
TOM MULLER.......................................[DESIGN]

VALERIO SCHITI & MARTE GRACIA...............[COVER ARTISTS]
TAKESHI MIYAZAWA & IAN HERRING......[VARIANT COVER ARTISTS]

JONATHAN HICKMAN..............................[HEAD OF X]
NICK RUSSELL..................................[PRODUCTION]
ANNALISE BISSA..........................[ASSOCIATE EDITOR]
JORDAN D. WHITE..................................[EDITOR]
C.B. CEBULSKI..........................[EDITOR IN CHIEF]

[00__king]
[00_black]

[00_00....0]
[00_00...03]

[00_knull_]
[00_____]

[00_____]

[00_____X]

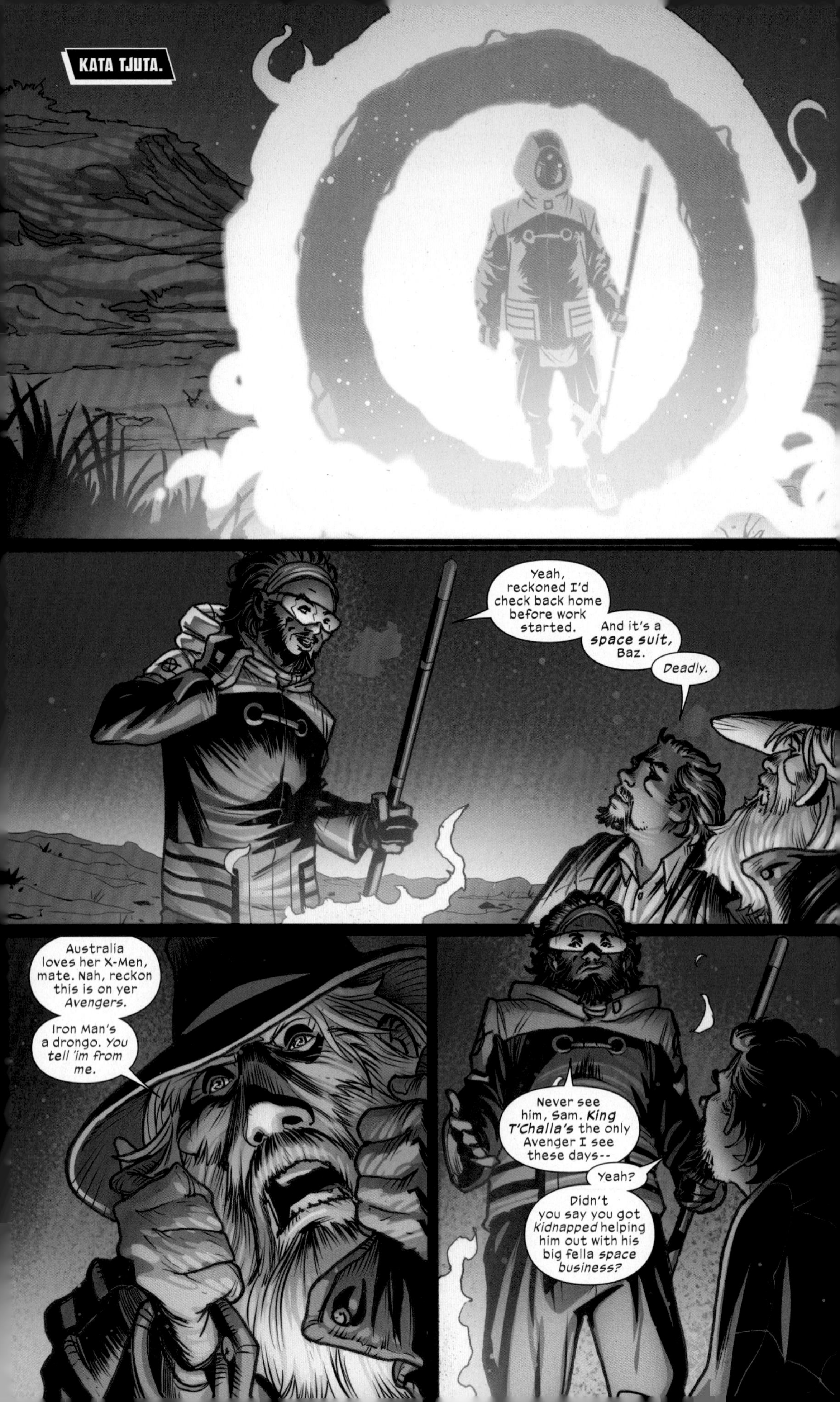
KATA TJUTA.
Yeah, reckoned I'd check back home before work started.
And it's a *space suit*, Baz.
Deadly.
Australia loves her X-Men, mate. Nah, reckon this is on yer *Avengers*.
Iron Man's a drongo. *You tell 'im from me.*
Never see him, Sam. *King T'Challa's* the only Avenger I see these days--
Yeah?
Didn't you say you got *kidnapped* helping him out with his big fella *space business?*

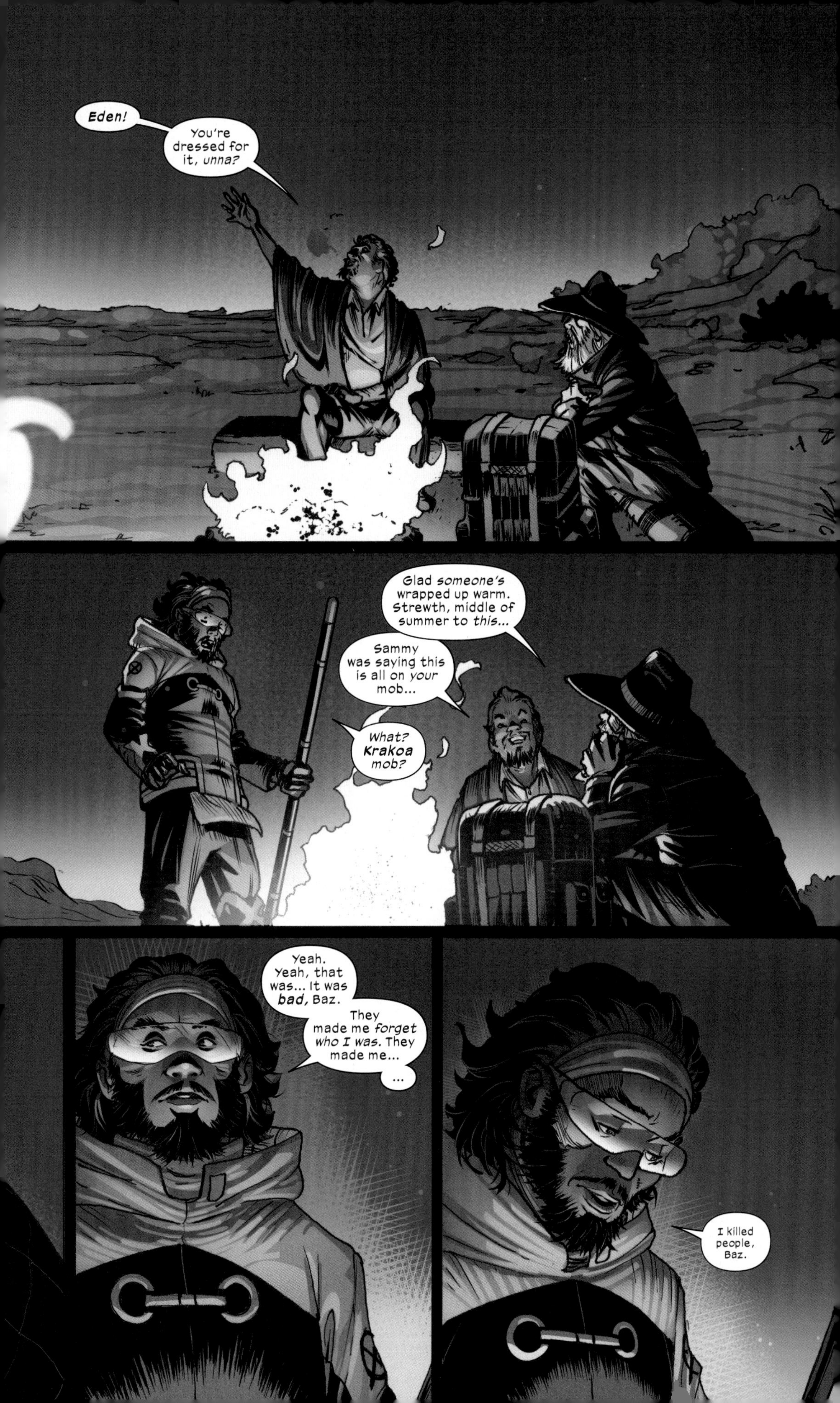
Eden!
You're dressed for it, unna?
Glad someone's wrapped up warm. Strewth, middle of summer to this...
Sammy was saying this is all on your mob...
What? Krakoa mob?
Yeah. Yeah, that was... It was bad, Baz.
They made me forget who I was. They made me...
...
I killed people, Baz.

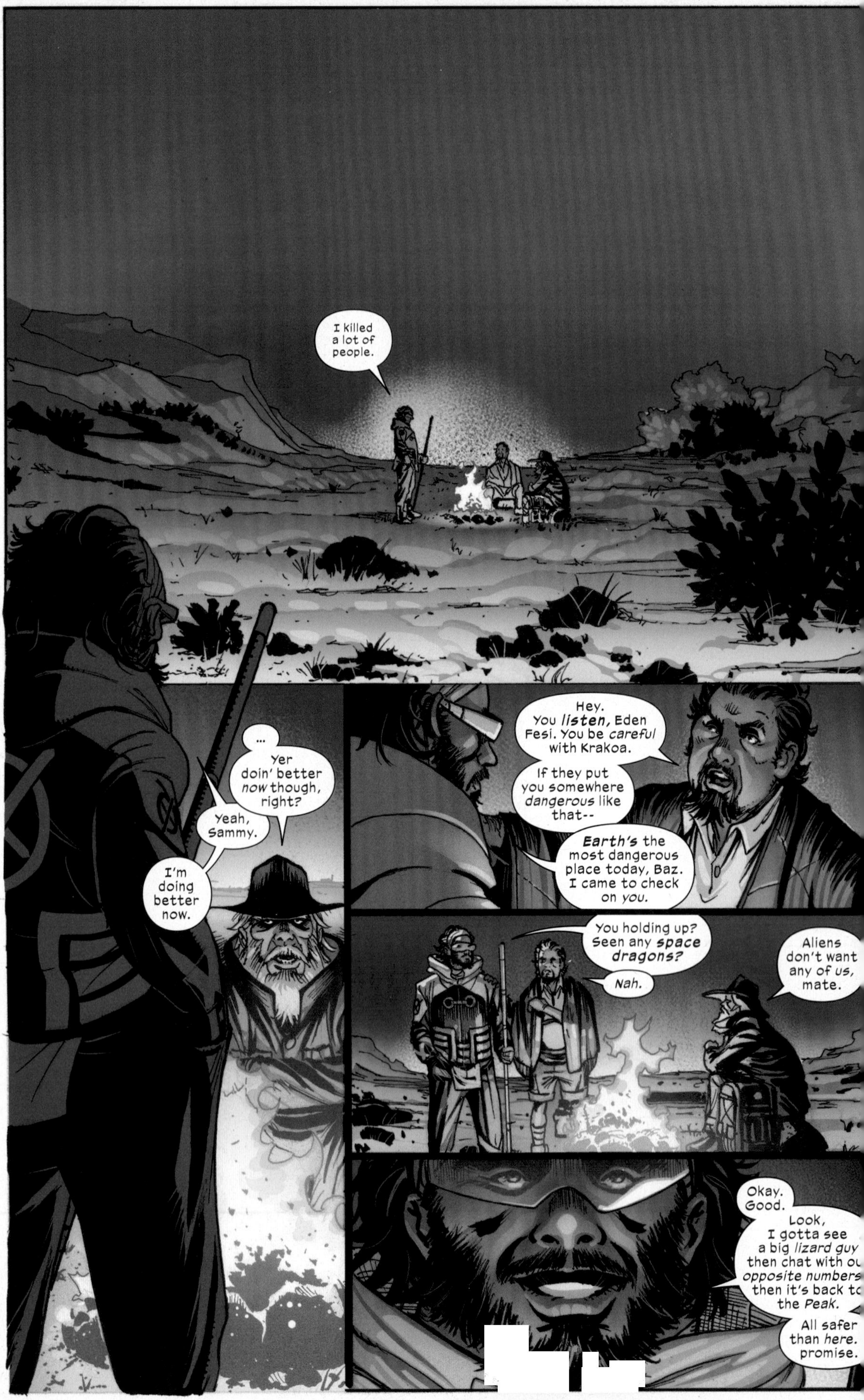

I killed a lot of people.
...
Yer doin' better *now* though, right?
Yeah, Sammy.
I'm doing better now.
Hey. You *listen,* Eden Fesi. You be *careful* with Krakoa.
If they put you somewhere *dangerous* like that--
Earth's the most dangerous place today, Baz. I came to check on *you.*
You holding up? Seen any *space dragons?*
Nah.
Aliens don't want any of *us,* mate.
Okay. Good.
Look, I gotta see a big *lizard guy* then chat with ou *opposite numbers* then it's back t the *Peak.*
All safer than *here.* promise.

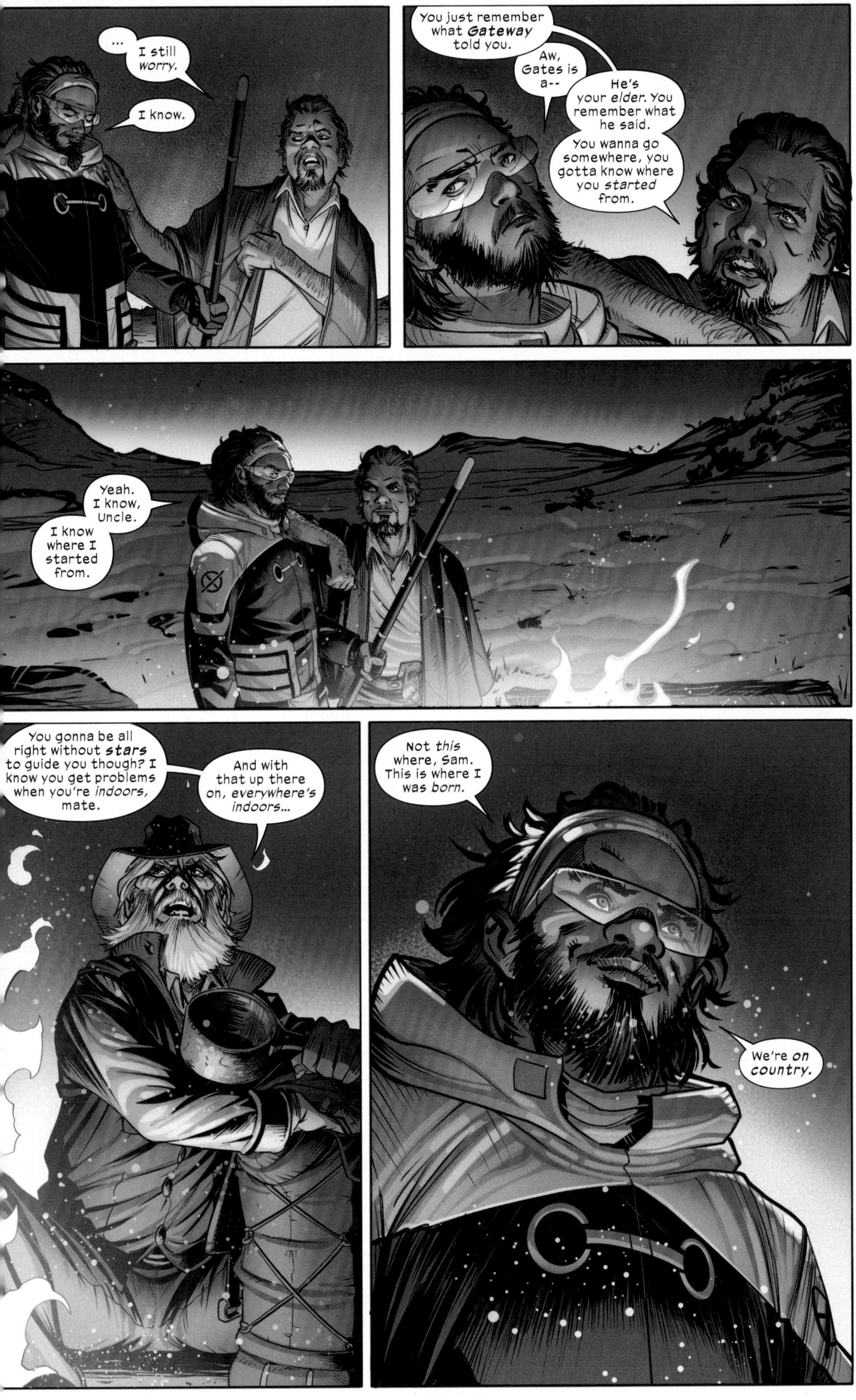
...
I still worry.
I know.
You just remember what Gateway told you.
Aw, Gates is a--
He's your elder. You remember what he said.
You wanna go somewhere, you gotta know where you started from.
Yeah. I know, Uncle.
I know where I started from.
You gonna be all right without stars to guide you though? I know you get problems when you're indoors, mate.
And with that up there on, everywhere's indoors...
Not this where, Sam. This is where I was born.
We're on country.

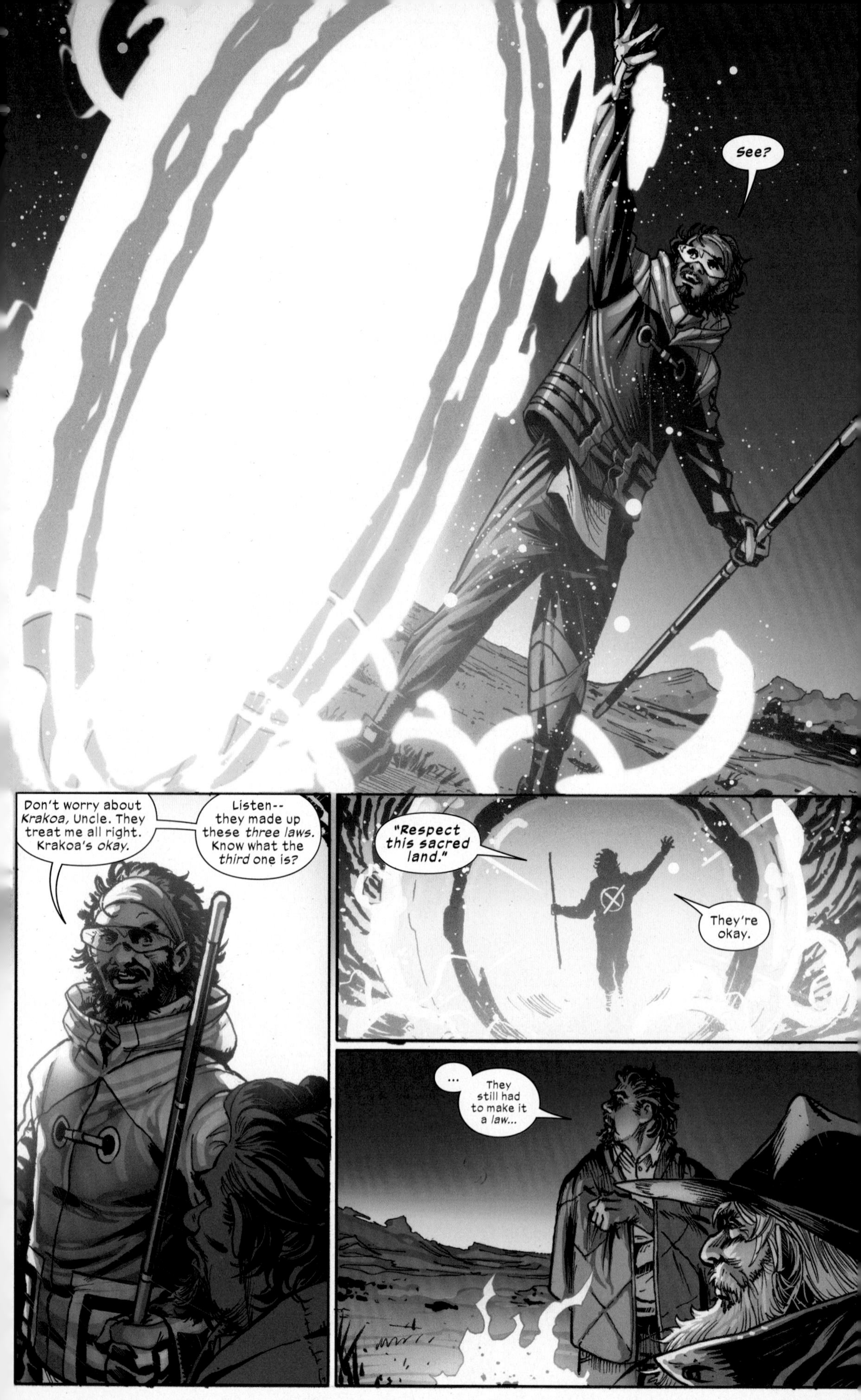
See?
Don't worry about *Krakoa,* Uncle. They treat me all right. Krakoa's *okay.*
Listen-- they made up these *three laws.* Know what the *third* one is?
"Respect this sacred land."
They're okay.
...
They still had to make it a *law...*

SNARKWAR

Snarkwar is the colloquial term for a **Zn'rx War of Succession**.

Xenobiology has yet to tell us exactly how the children of a **Zn'rx regent** know instantly that the regent has died. However, the immediate reaction is always a violent urge on the part of the fallen regent's heirs to claim the vacant alpha position by any means necessary, heedless of any collateral damage caused. Though the urge can be resisted or satisfied through single combat, recent attempts at modernizing the succession process were derailed by the **Hyinar Usurpation** and the resultant rise to power of the traditionalist **Stote**, who undid many of the Bhadsha era's reforms during his brief time on the throne.

HEIRS OF EMPEROR STOTE *[ranked by odds of succession]*

Kuga of Bhoa Clan	*[25/1]*	Eldest of the current heirs. Radical modernist. Currently in retreat after a catastrophic defeat in the Ortuua System.
Wezel of Chita Clan	*[14/1]*	Traditionalist. Currently besieged at the edge of Utopian Kree space. Attempting negotiation with the Supremor for safe passage.
Khondor of Gylar Clan	*[4/1]*	Youngest of the current heirs. Moderate reformists. Currently in an agreed alliance until only they remain, whereupon the war will shift to a process of single combat.
Lyga of Gylar Clan	*[4/1]*	
Djagyar of Bhoa Clan	*[3/2]*	Radical traditionalist. Eschews a fixed power base in favor of a guerrilla fleet. Current favorite to succeed Stote on the Zn'rx throne.

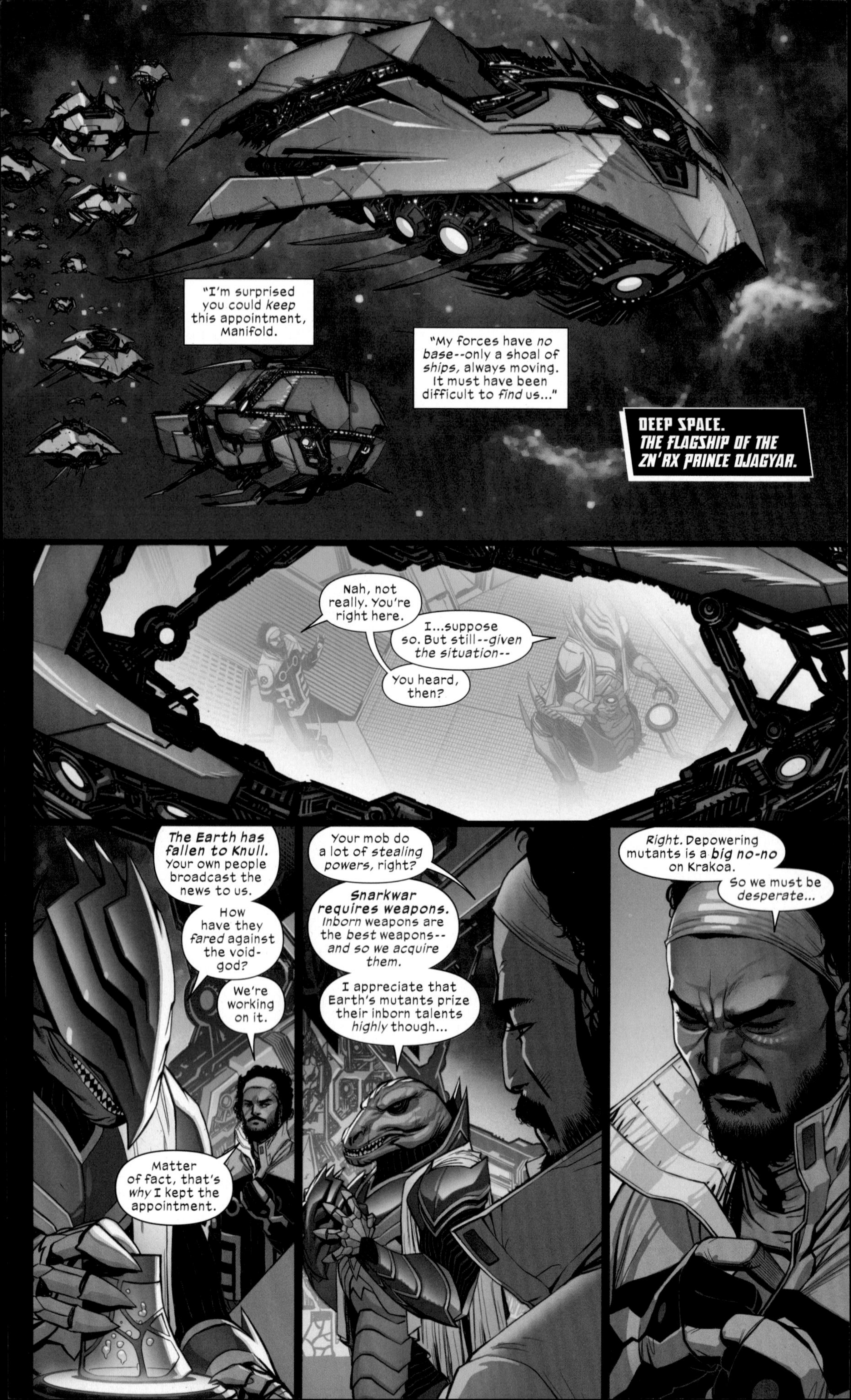
"I'm surprised you could keep this appointment, Manifold.
"My forces have no base--only a shoal of ships, always moving. It must have been difficult to find us..."
DEEP SPACE. THE FLAGSHIP OF THE ZN'RX PRINCE DJAGYAR.
Nah, not really. You're right here.
I...suppose so. But still--given the situation--
You heard, then?
The Earth has fallen to Knull. Your own people broadcast the news to us.
How have they fared against the void-god?
We're working on it.
Matter of fact, that's why I kept the appointment.
Your mob do a lot of stealing powers, right?
Snarkwar requires weapons. Inborn weapons are the best weapons--and so we acquire them.
I appreciate that Earth's mutants prize their inborn talents highly though...
Right. Depowering mutants is a big no-no on Krakoa.
So we must be desperate...

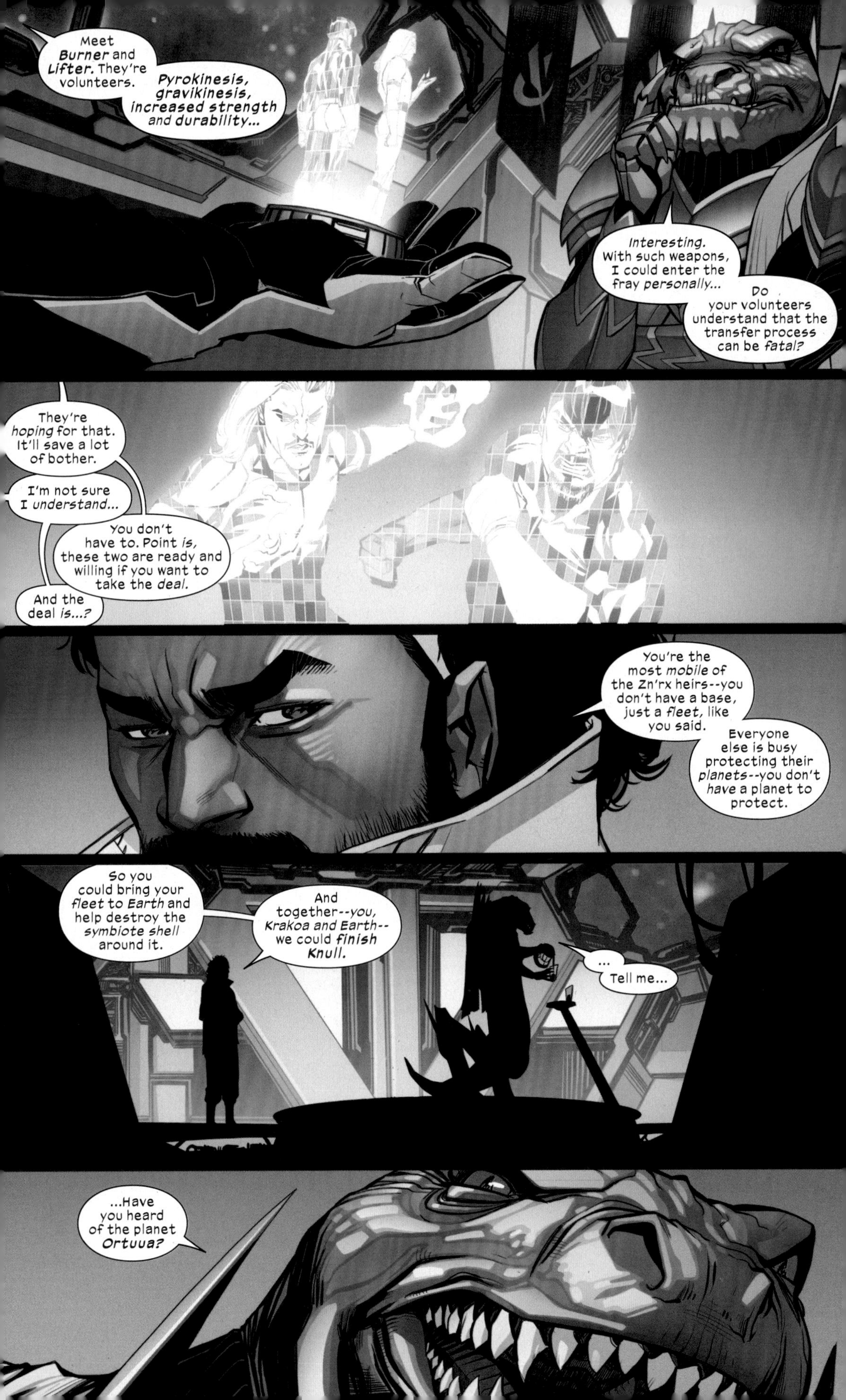
Meet Burner and Lifter. They're volunteers.
Pyrokinesis, gravikinesis, increased strength and durability...
Interesting. With such weapons, I could enter the fray personally...
Do your volunteers understand that the transfer process can be fatal?
They're hoping for that. It'll save a lot of bother.
I'm not sure I understand...
You don't have to. Point is, these two are ready and willing if you want to take the deal.
And the deal is...?
You're the most mobile of the Zn'rx heirs--you don't have a base, just a fleet, like you said.
Everyone else is busy protecting their planets--you don't have a planet to protect.
So you could bring your fleet to Earth and help destroy the symbiote shell around it.
And together--you, Krakoa and Earth--we could finish Knull.
...
Tell me...
...Have you heard of the planet Ortuua?

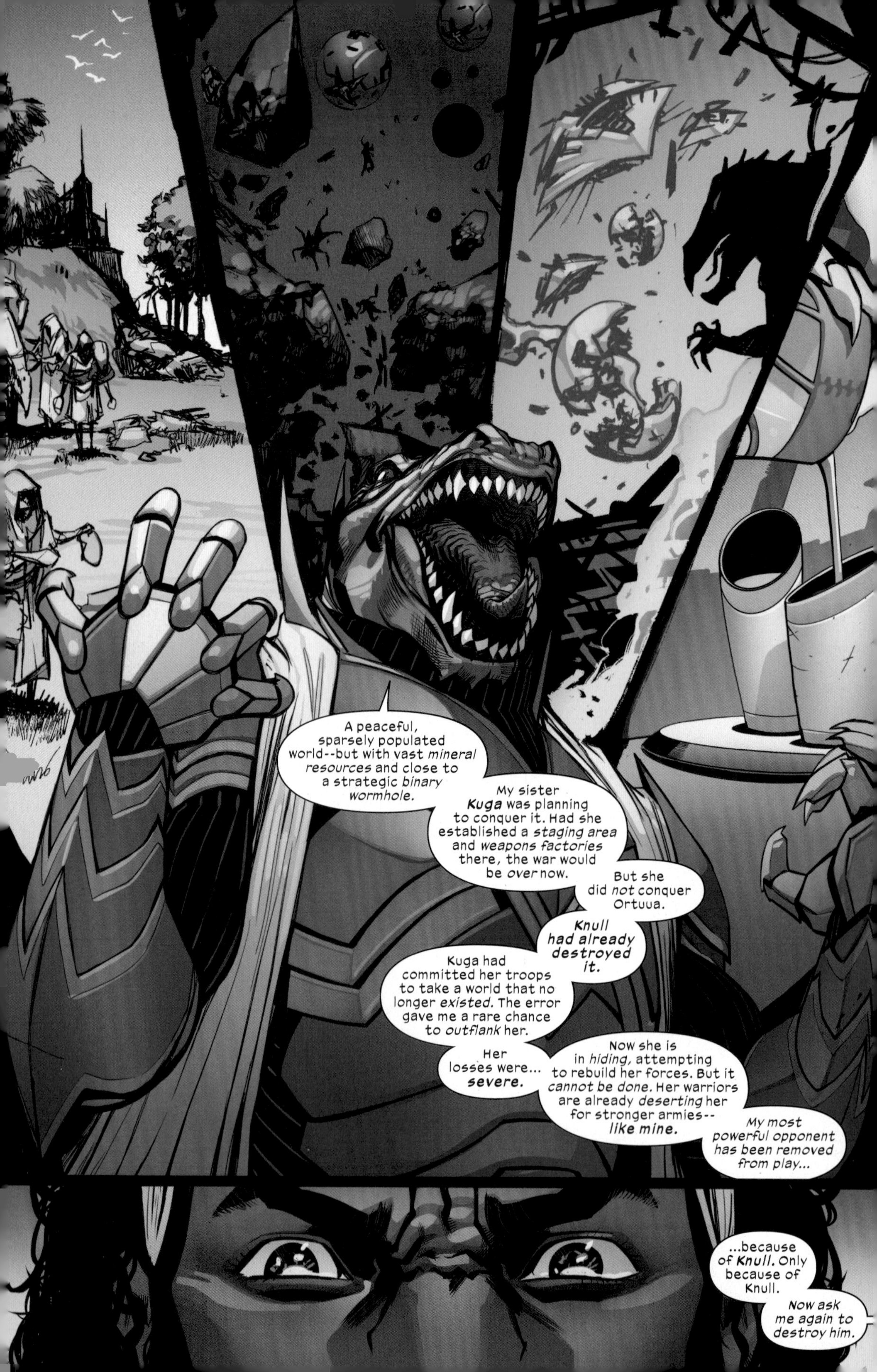

A peaceful, sparsely populated world--but with vast *mineral resources* and close to a strategic *binary wormhole.*
My sister ***Kuga*** was planning to conquer it. Had she established a *staging area* and *weapons factories* there, the war would be *over* now.
But she did *not* conquer Ortuua.
Knull had already destroyed it.
Kuga had committed her troops to take a world that no longer *existed.* The error gave me a rare chance to *outflank* her.
Her losses were... ***severe.***
Now she is in *hiding,* attempting to rebuild her forces. But it *cannot be done.* Her warriors are already *deserting* her for stronger armies-- ***like mine.***
My most powerful opponent has been removed from play...
...because of ***Knull.*** Only because of Knull.
Now ask me again to destroy him.

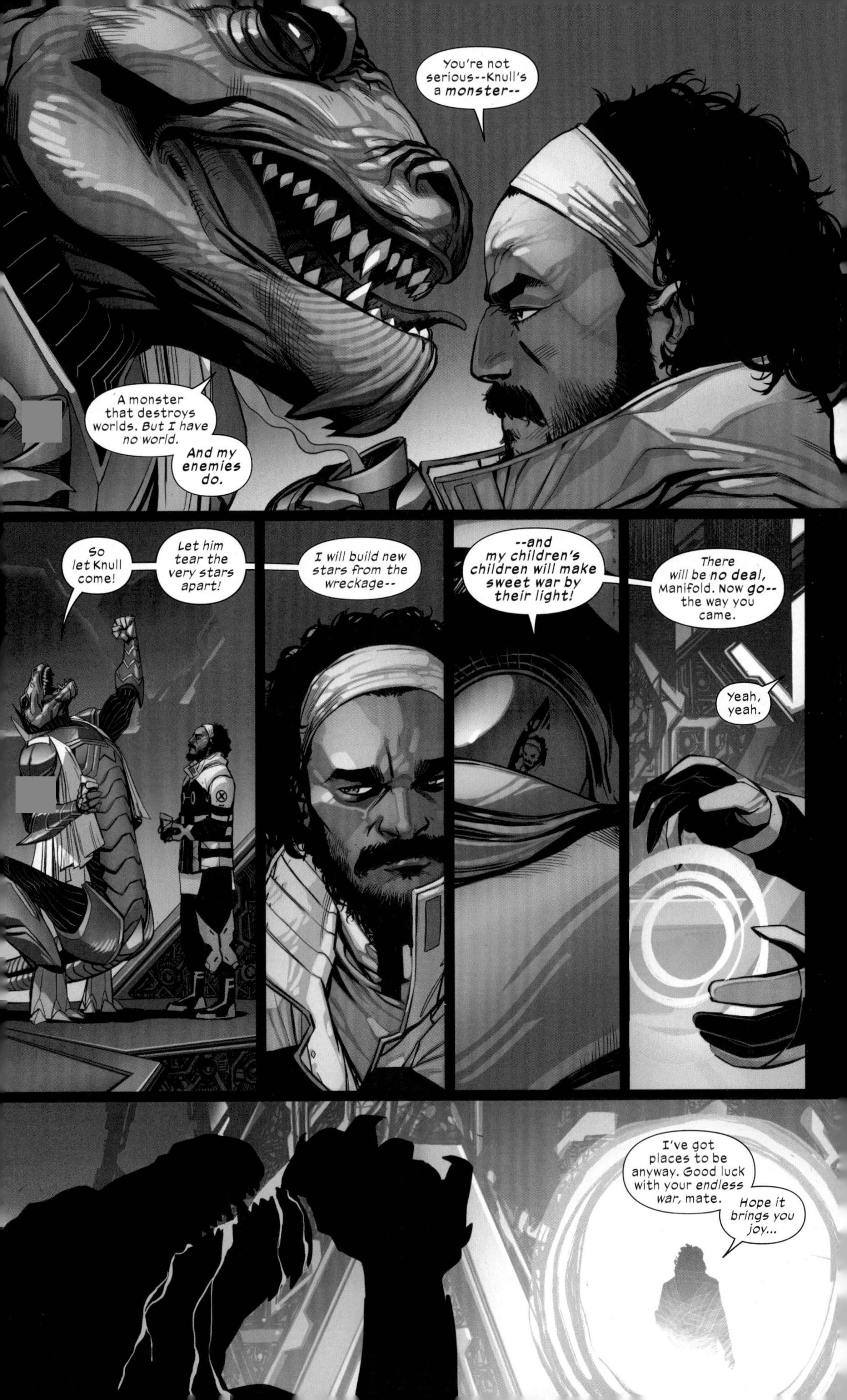
You're not serious--Knull's a monster--
A monster that destroys worlds. But I have no world.
And my enemies do.
So let Knull come!
Let him tear the very stars apart!
I will build new stars from the wreckage--
--and my children's children will make sweet war by their light!
There will be no deal, Manifold. Now go--the way you came.
Yeah, yeah.
I've got places to be anyway. Good luck with your endless war, mate.
Hope it brings you joy...

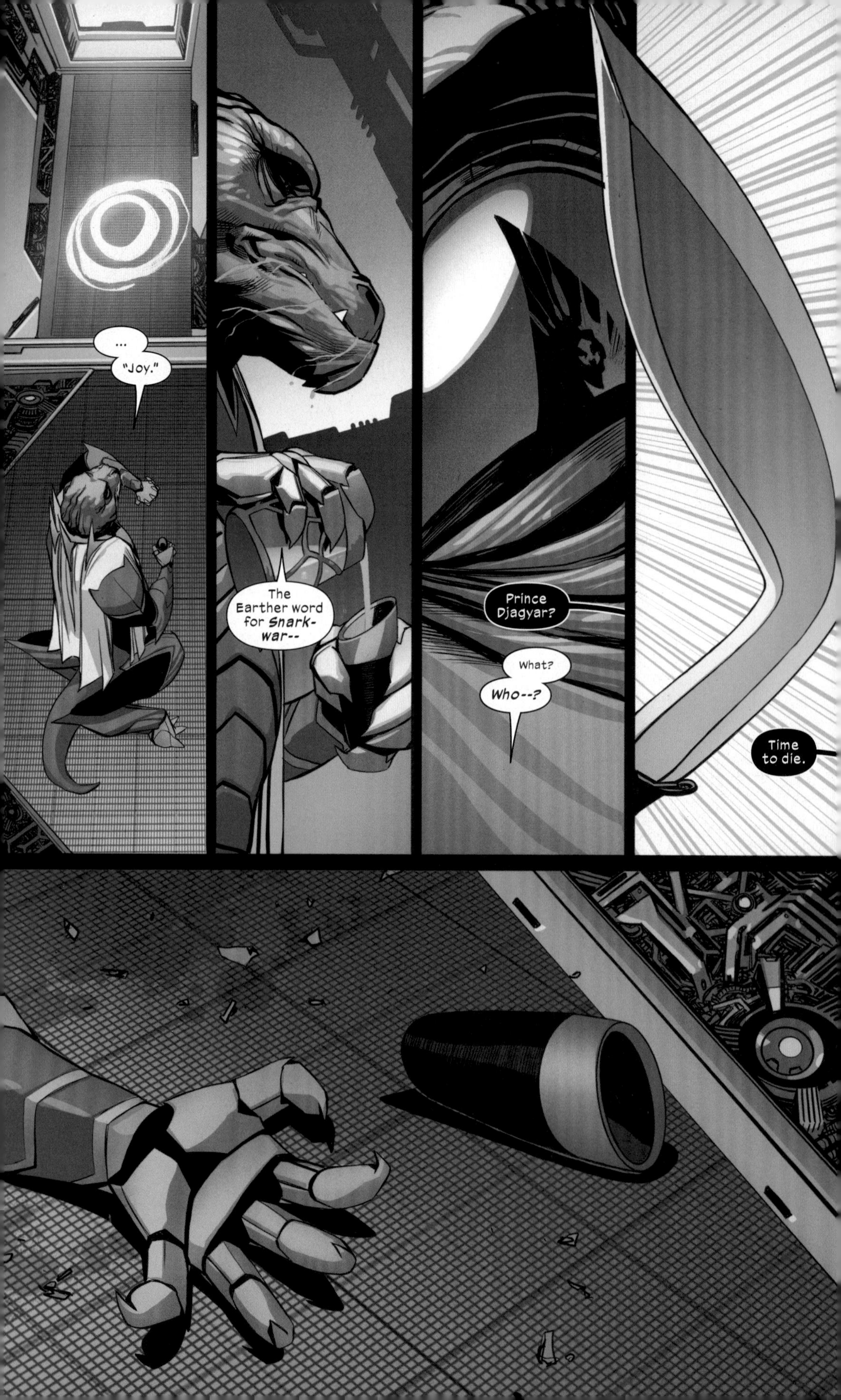
...
"Joy."
The Earther word for Snark-war--
Prince Djagyar?
What?
Who--?
Time to die.

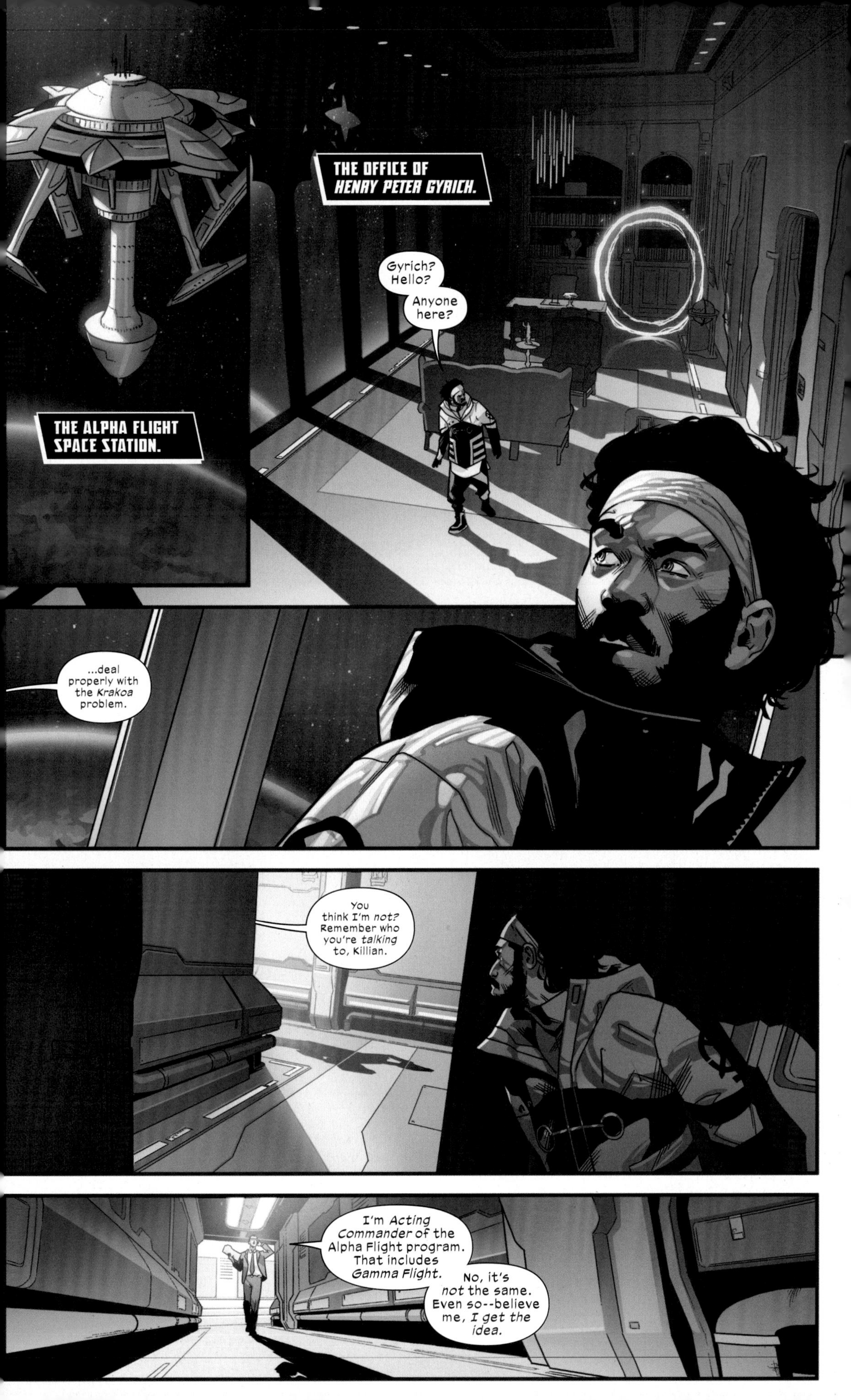
THE ALPHA FLIGHT SPACE STATION.
THE OFFICE OF HENRY PETER GYRICH.
Gyrich? Hello?
Anyone here?
...deal properly with the Krakoa problem.
You think I'm not? Remember who you're talking to, Killian.
I'm Acting Commander of the Alpha Flight program. That includes Gamma Flight.
No, it's not the same. Even so--believe me, I get the idea.

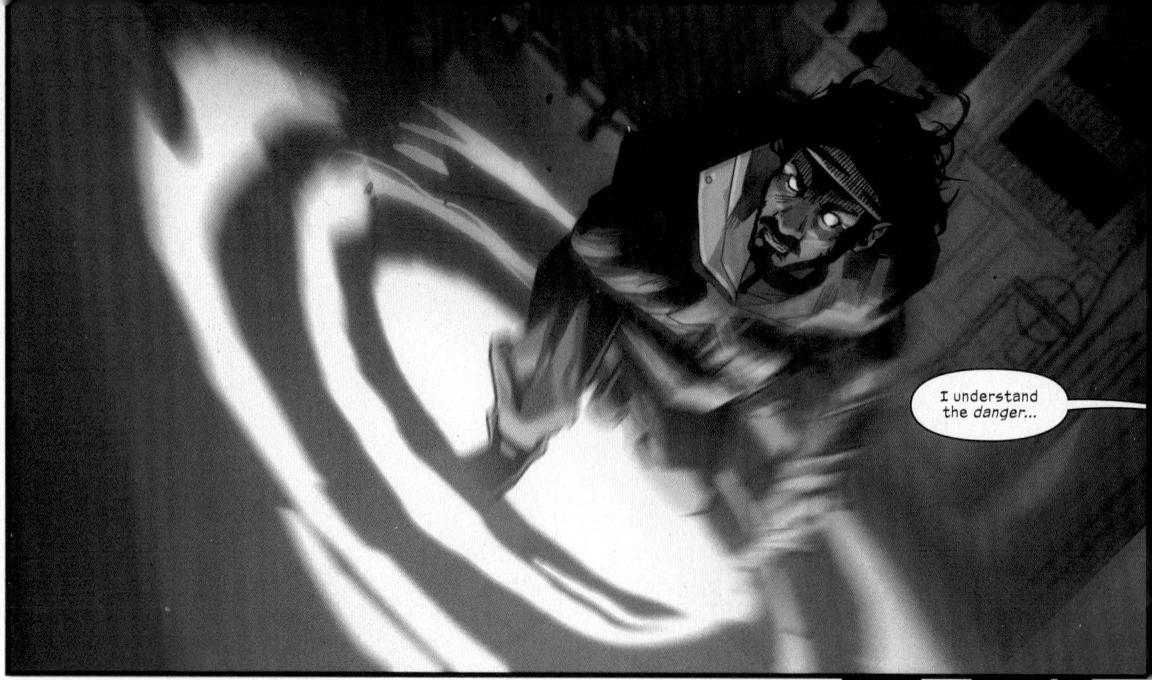
I understand the *danger*...

PERSONNEL NOTES :: EDEN FESI/*MANIFOLD*

ABIGAIL BRAND :: E-7-12 11/05 :: GSTC 0833

Eden Fesi is not a teleporter. People treat him like one, but that's not what he is at all.

Eden Fesi talks to space.

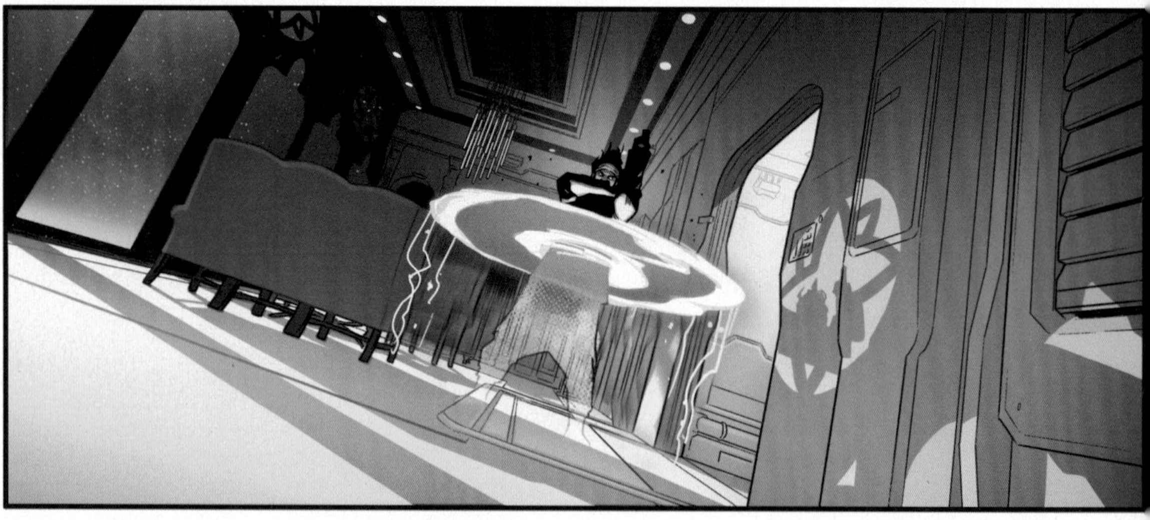

If he tells the universe to fold itself until he can walk across it in a single step -- it does. If he tells space to warp so light passes all the way around it without ever hitting him -- to form a little bubble of invisibility just for him -- it will.

He says it's not "telling." It's "asking." It still terrifies me if I think about it for too long.

That aside, he's a really nice guy.

—

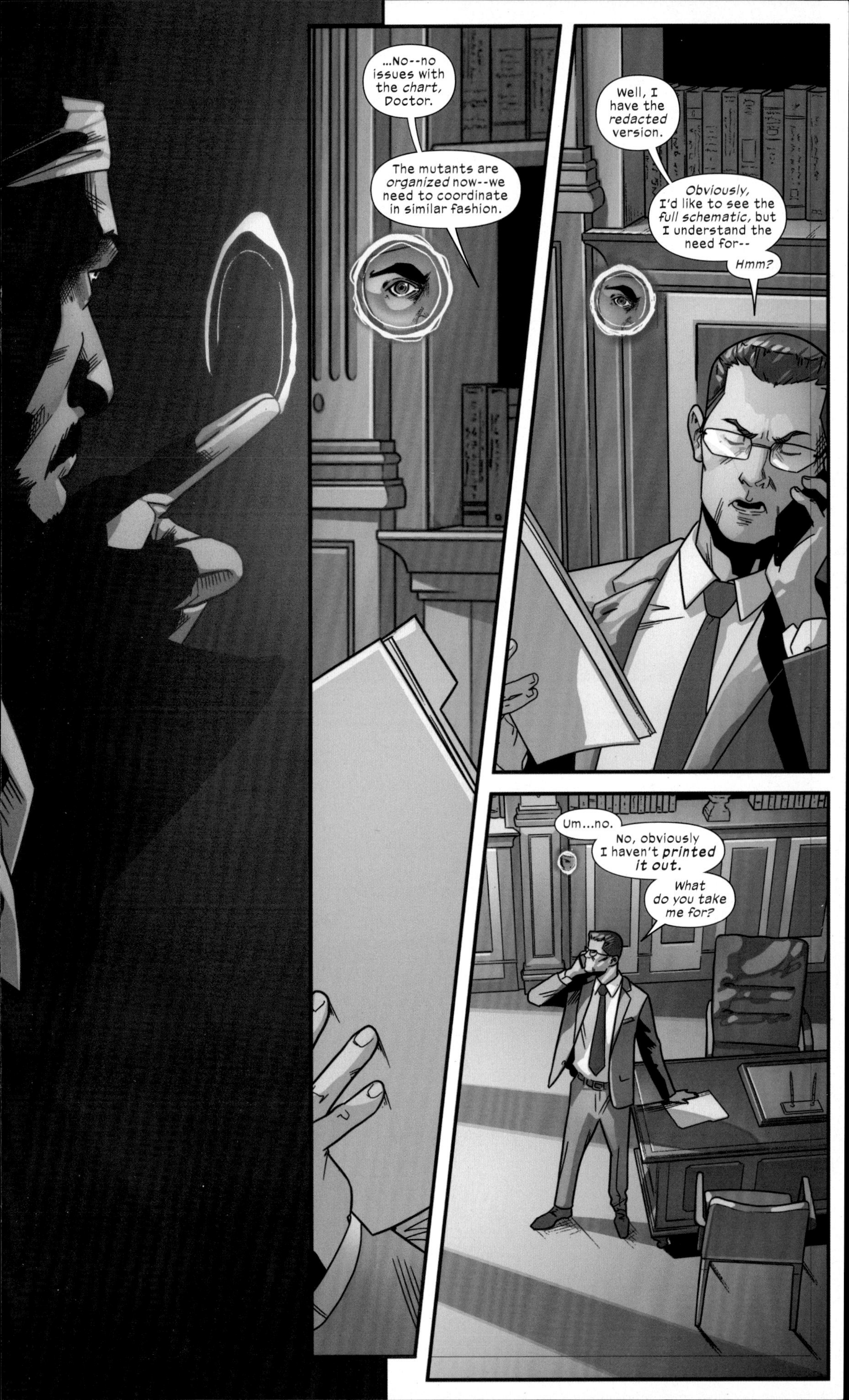

...No--no issues with the *chart,* Doctor.
The mutants are *organized* now--we need to coordinate in similar fashion.
Well, I have the *redacted* version.
Obviously, I'd like to see the *full schematic,* but I understand the need for--
Hmm?
Um...no.
No, obviously I haven't **printed it out.**
What do you take me for?

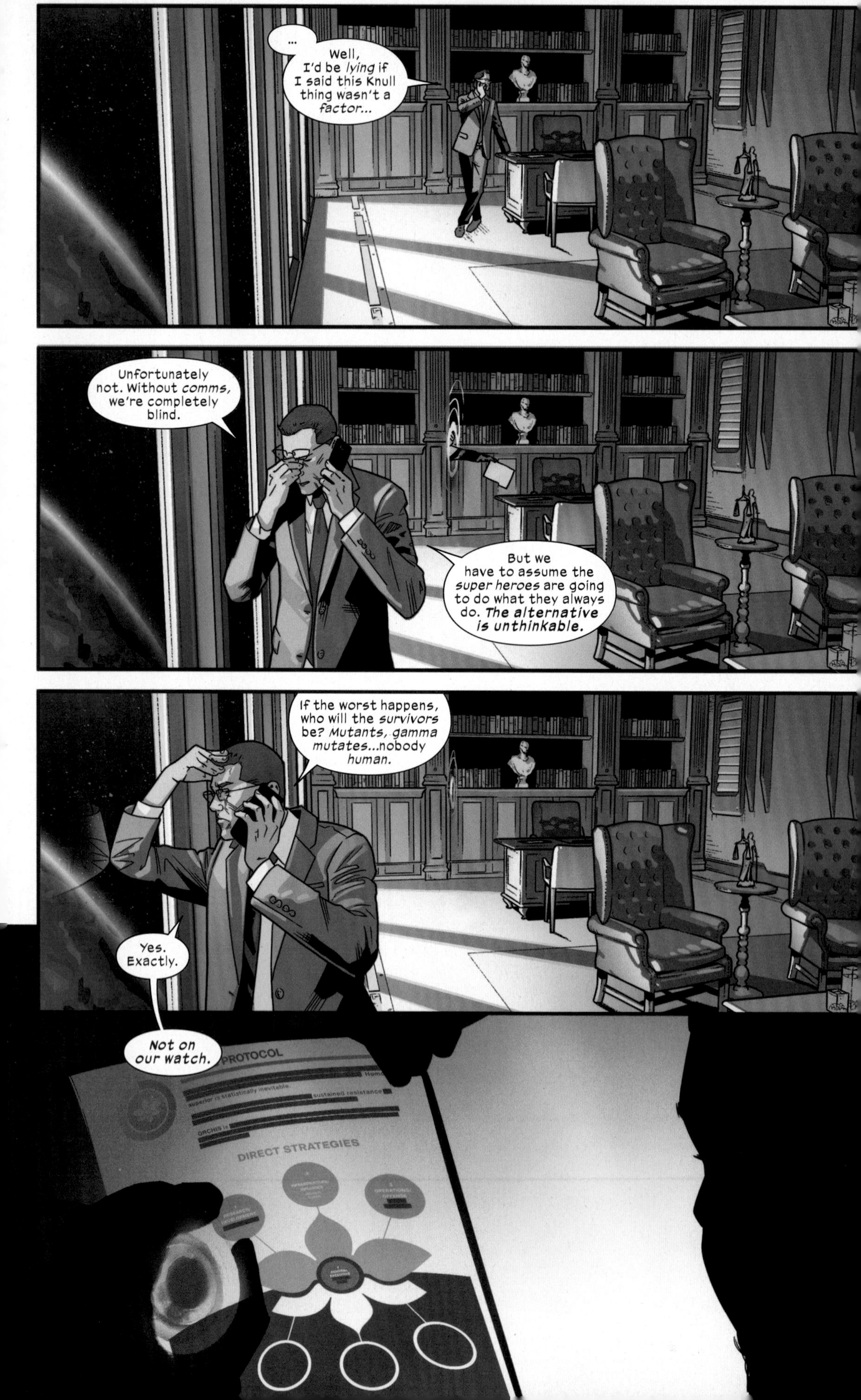
...
Well, I'd be *lying* if I said this Knull thing wasn't a *factor*...
Unfortunately not. Without *comms*, we're completely blind.
But we have to assume the *super heroes* are going to do what they always do. ***The alternative is unthinkable.***
If the worst happens, who will the *survivors* be? *Mutants, gamma mutates*...nobody *human.*
Yes. Exactly.
Not on our watch.
PROTOCOL
DIRECT STRATEGIES

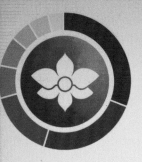

ORCHIS PROTOCOL

[redacted] ***Homo superior*** is statistically inevitable.

[redacted] sustained resistance [redacted]

ORCHIS is [redacted]

DIRECT STRATEGIES

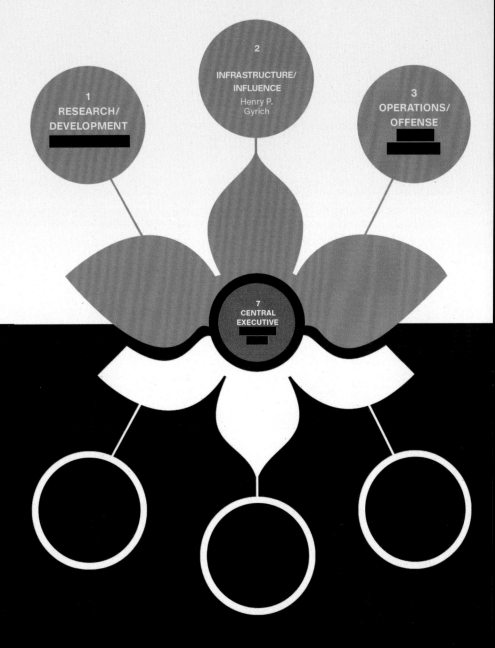

1
RESEARCH/
DEVELOPMENT
[redacted]
2
INFRASTRUCTURE/
INFLUENCE
Henry P.
Gyrich
3
OPERATIONS/
OFFENSE
[redacted]
7
CENTRAL
EXECUTIVE
[redacted]

[CLASSIFIED]

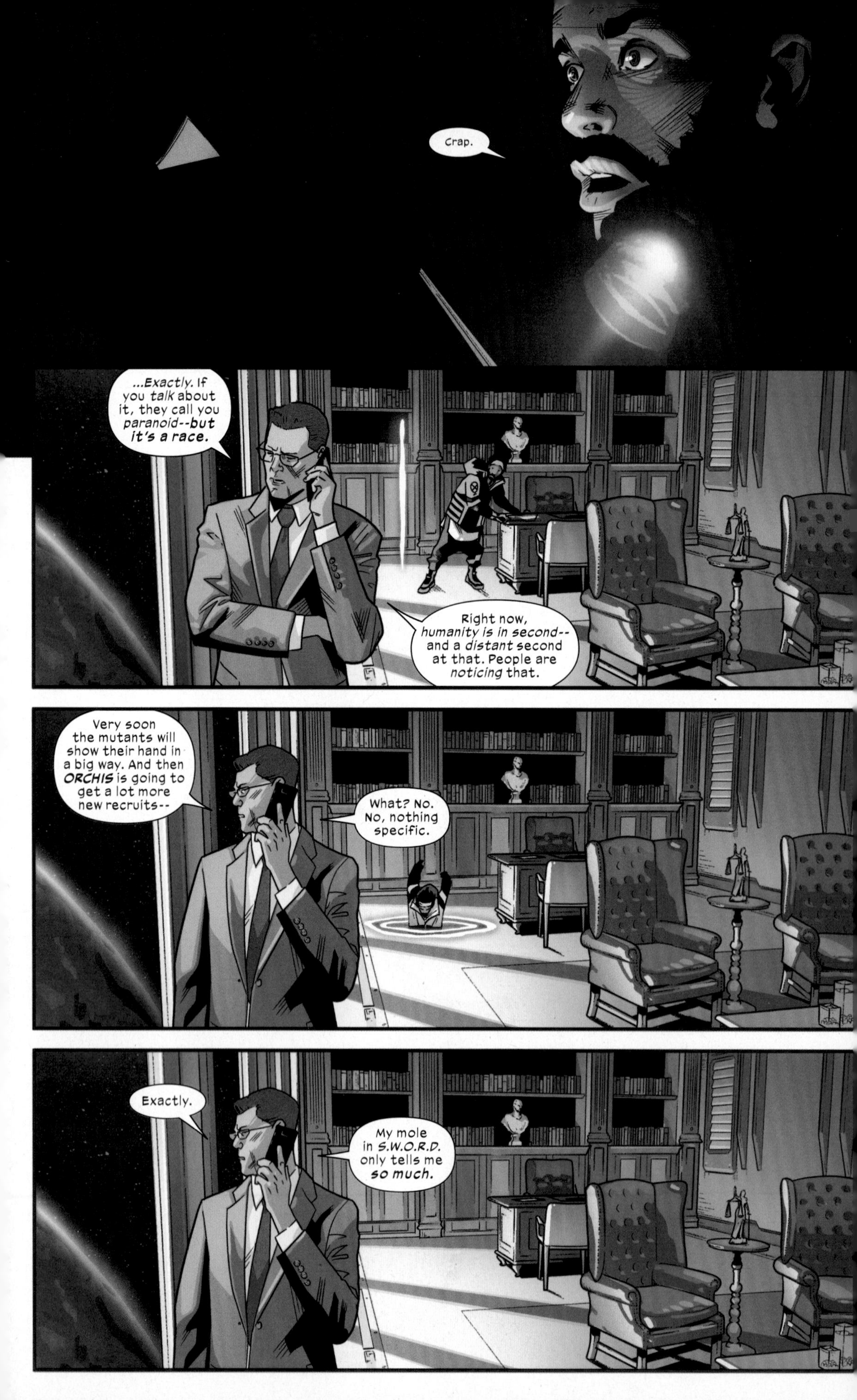
Crap.
...Exactly. If you talk about it, they call you paranoid--but it's a race.
Right now, humanity is in second--and a distant second at that. People are noticing that.
Very soon the mutants will show their hand in a big way. And then ORCHIS is going to get a lot more new recruits--
What? No. No, nothing specific.
Exactly.
My mole in S.W.O.R.D. only tells me so much.

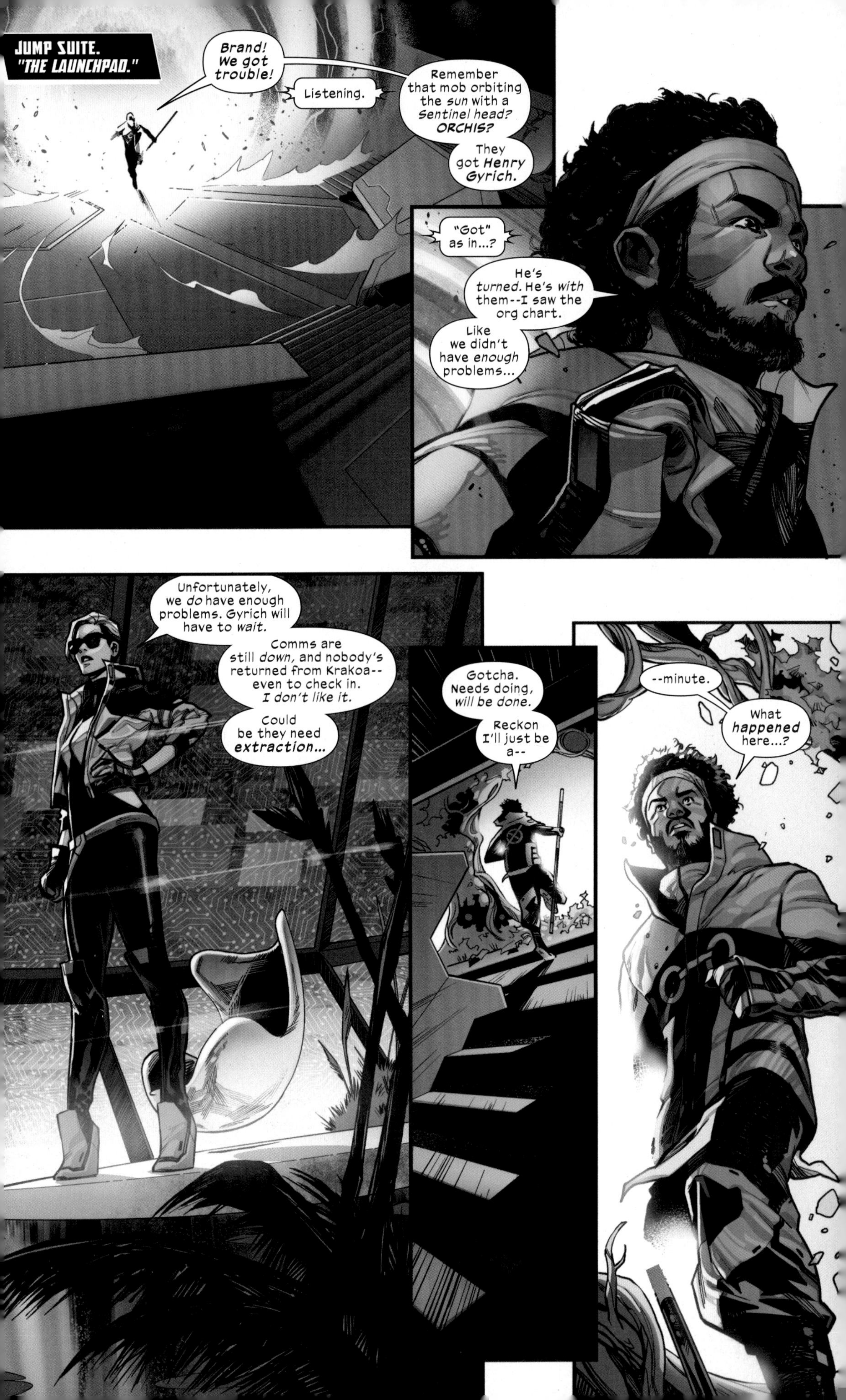
JUMP SUITE. "THE LAUNCHPAD."
Brand! We got trouble!
Listening.
Remember that mob orbiting the sun with a Sentinel head? ORCHIS?
They got Henry Gyrich.
"Got" as in...?
He's turned. He's with them--I saw the org chart.
Like we didn't have enough problems...
Unfortunately, we do have enough problems. Gyrich will have to wait.
Comms are still down, and nobody's returned from Krakoa--even to check in. I don't like it.
Could be they need extraction...
Gotcha. Needs doing, will be done.
Reckon I'll just be a--
--minute.
What happened here...?

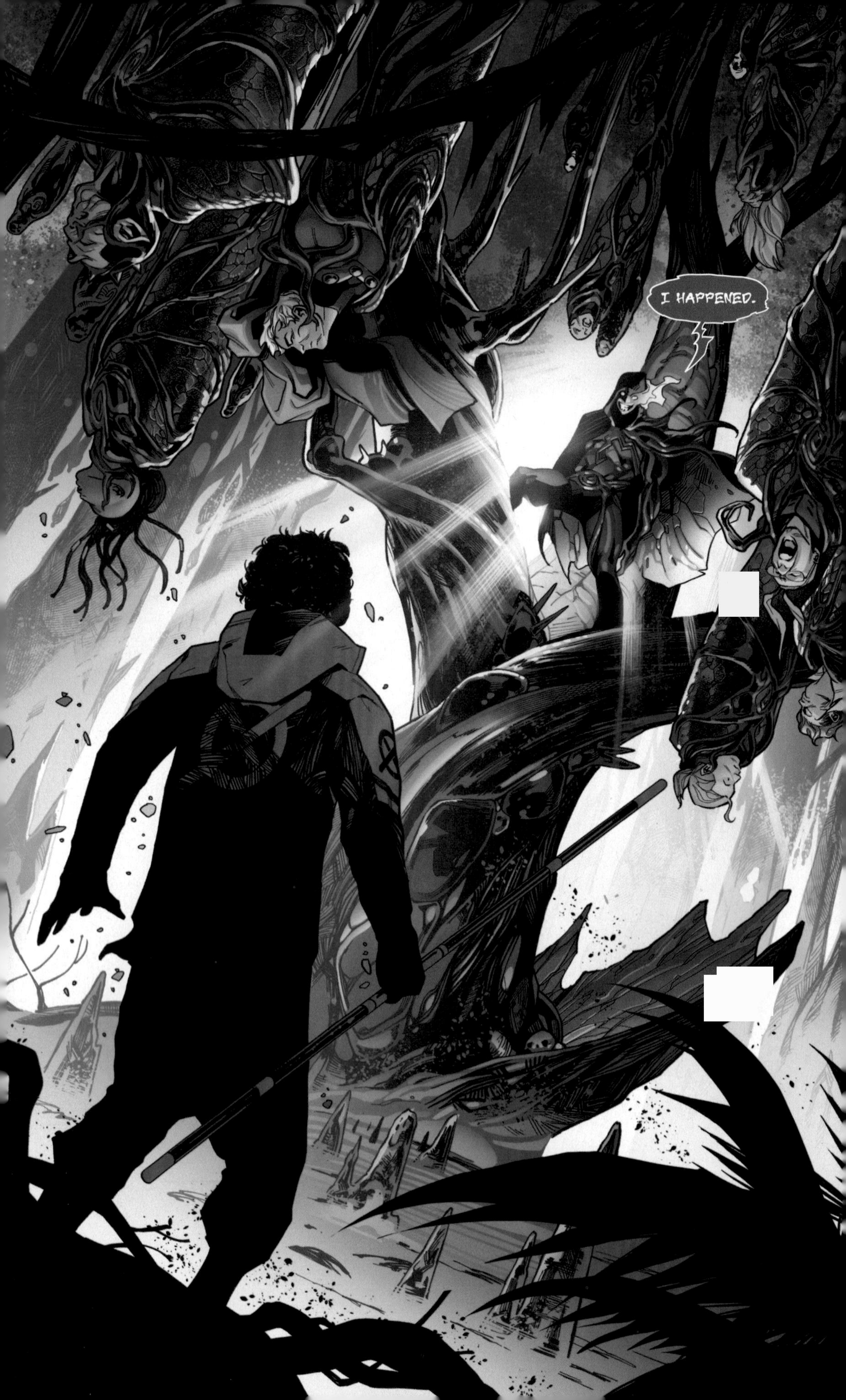
I HAPPENED.

[reign_of_x]

[kra_]
[koa_]

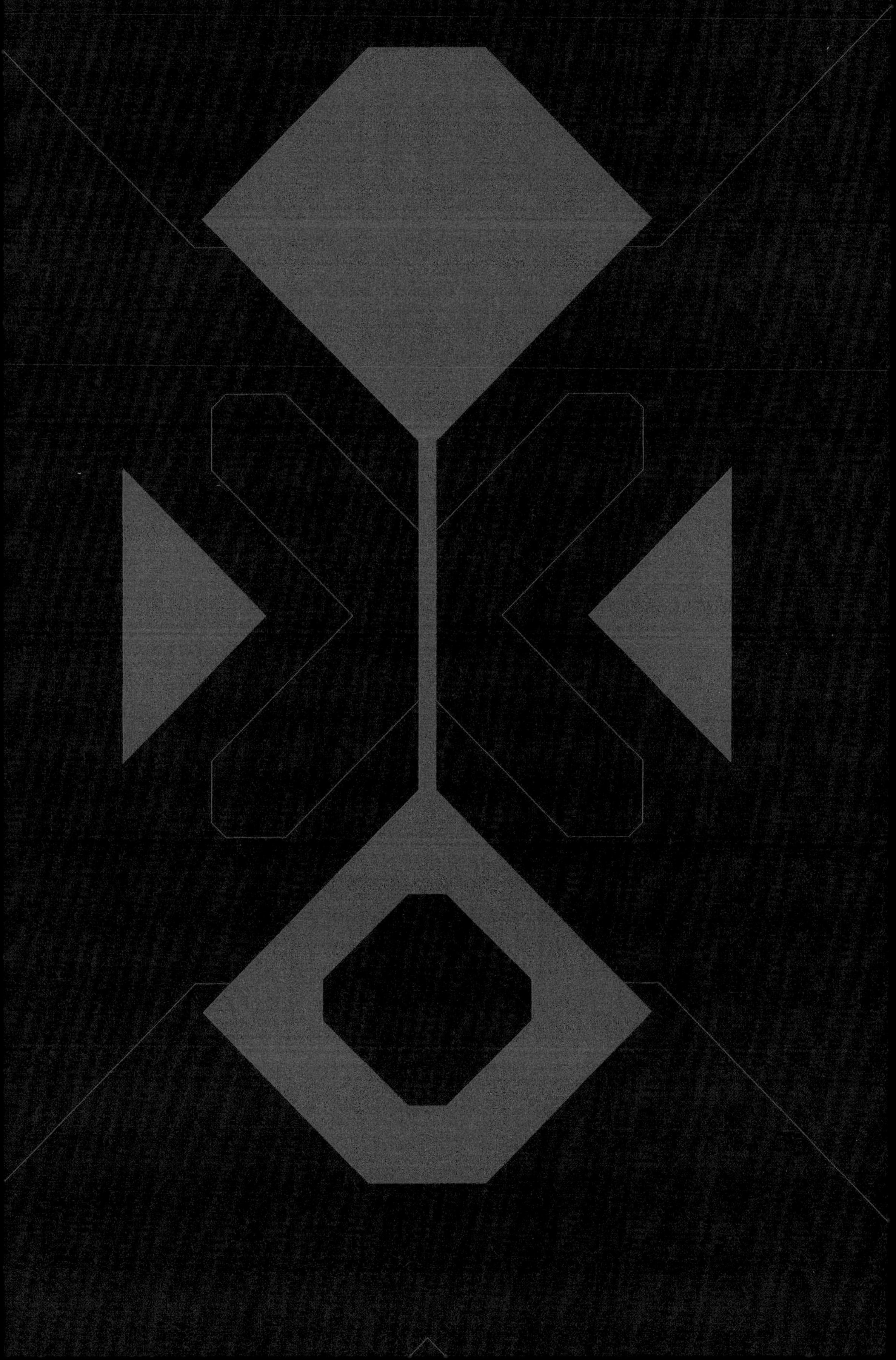

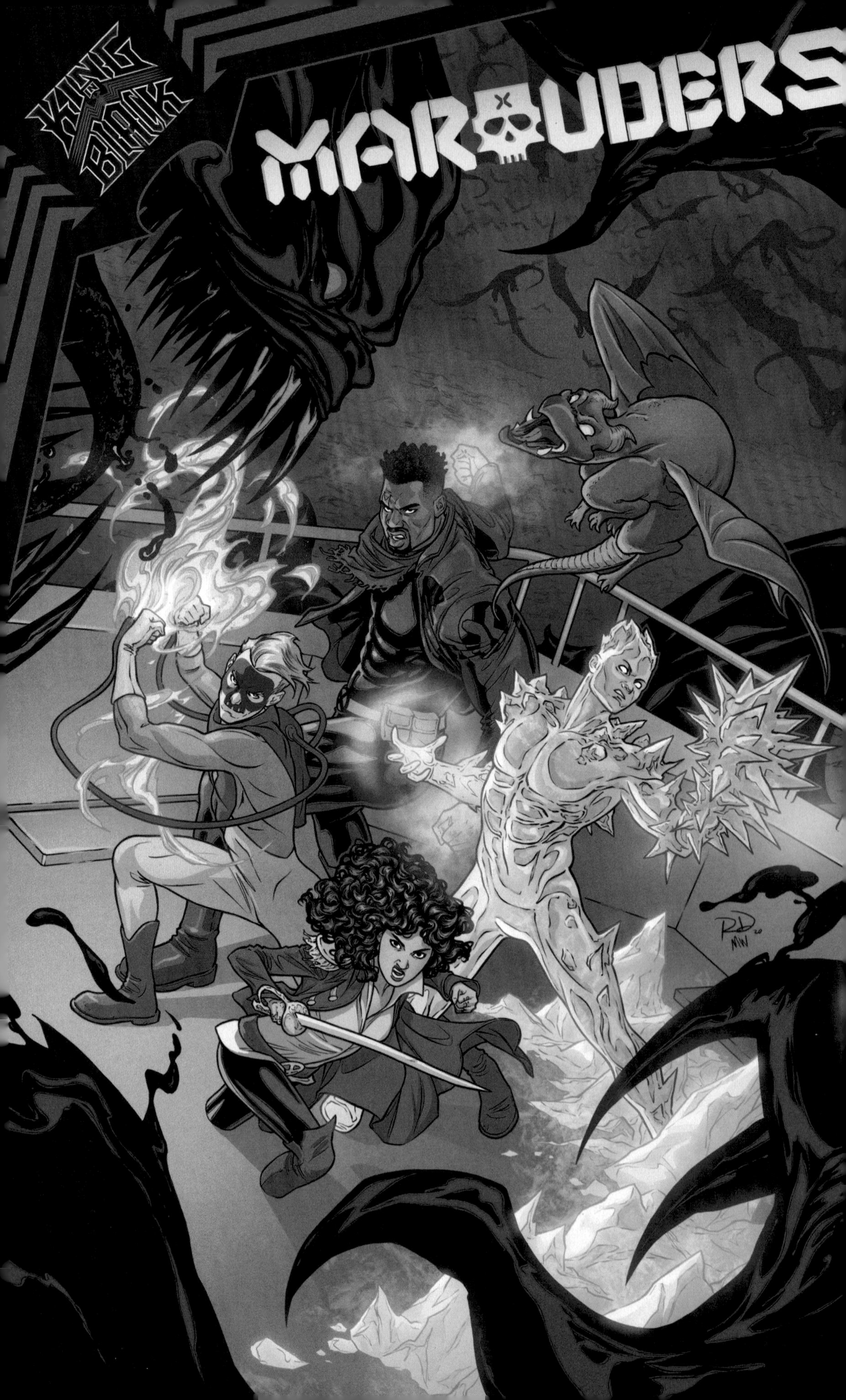
KING IN BLACK
MARAUDERS

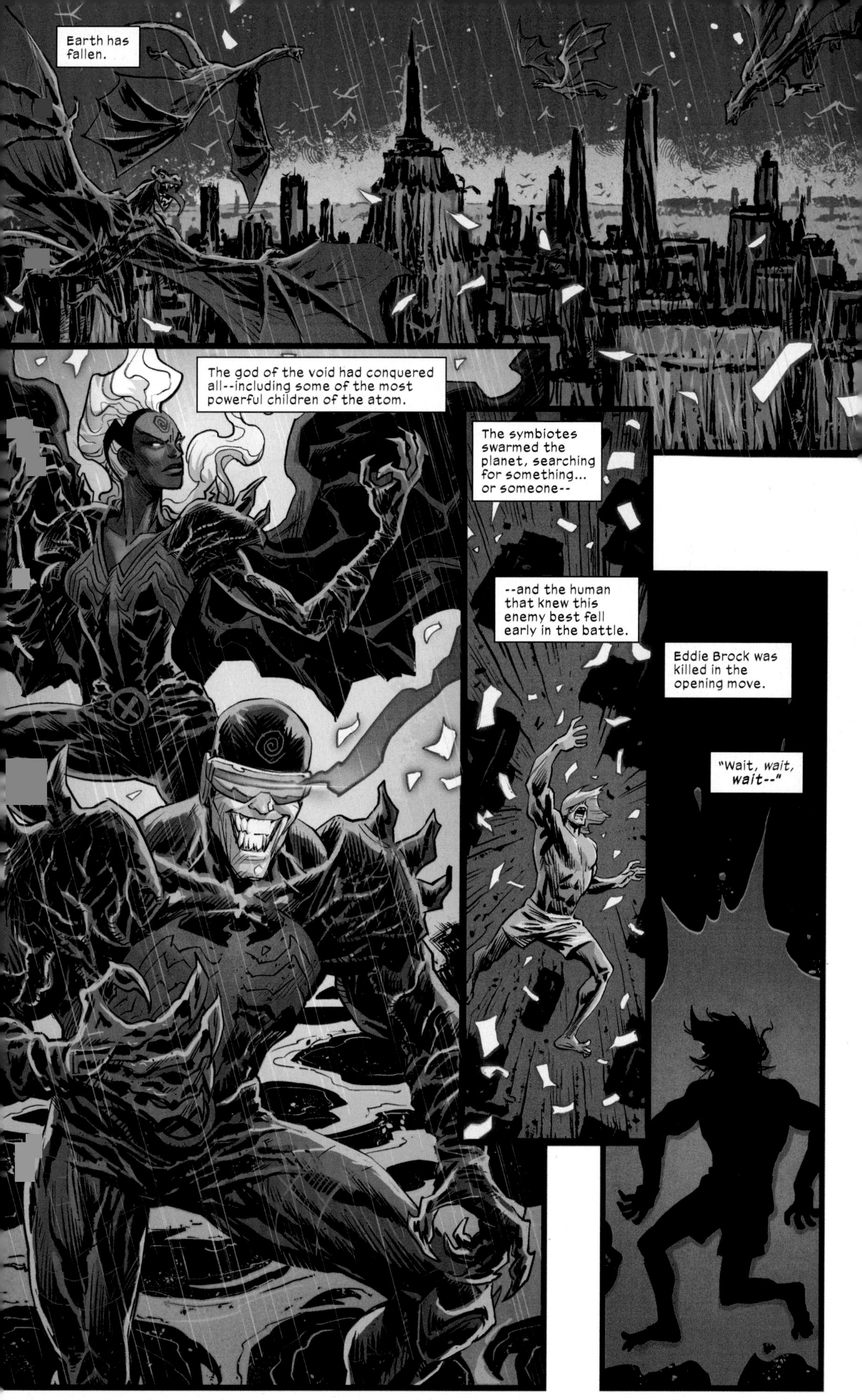
Earth has fallen.
The god of the void had conquered all--including some of the most powerful children of the atom.
The symbiotes swarmed the planet, searching for something... or someone--
--and the human that knew this enemy best fell early in the battle.
Eddie Brock was killed in the opening move.
"Wait, *wait*, ***wait***--"

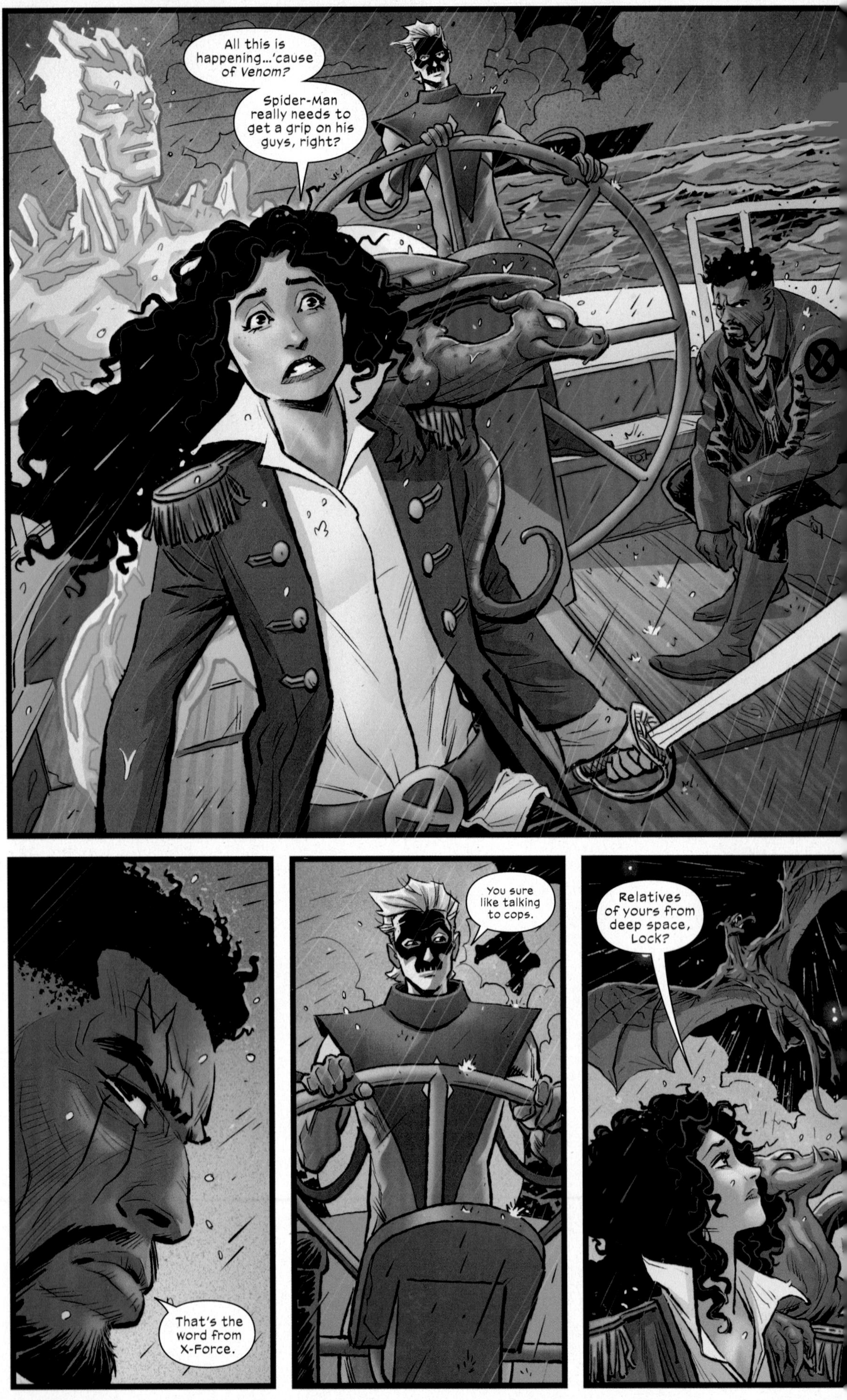
All this is happening...'cause of *Venom?*
Spider-Man really needs to get a grip on his guys, right?
That's the word from X-Force.
You sure like talking to cops.
Relatives of yours from deep space, Lock?

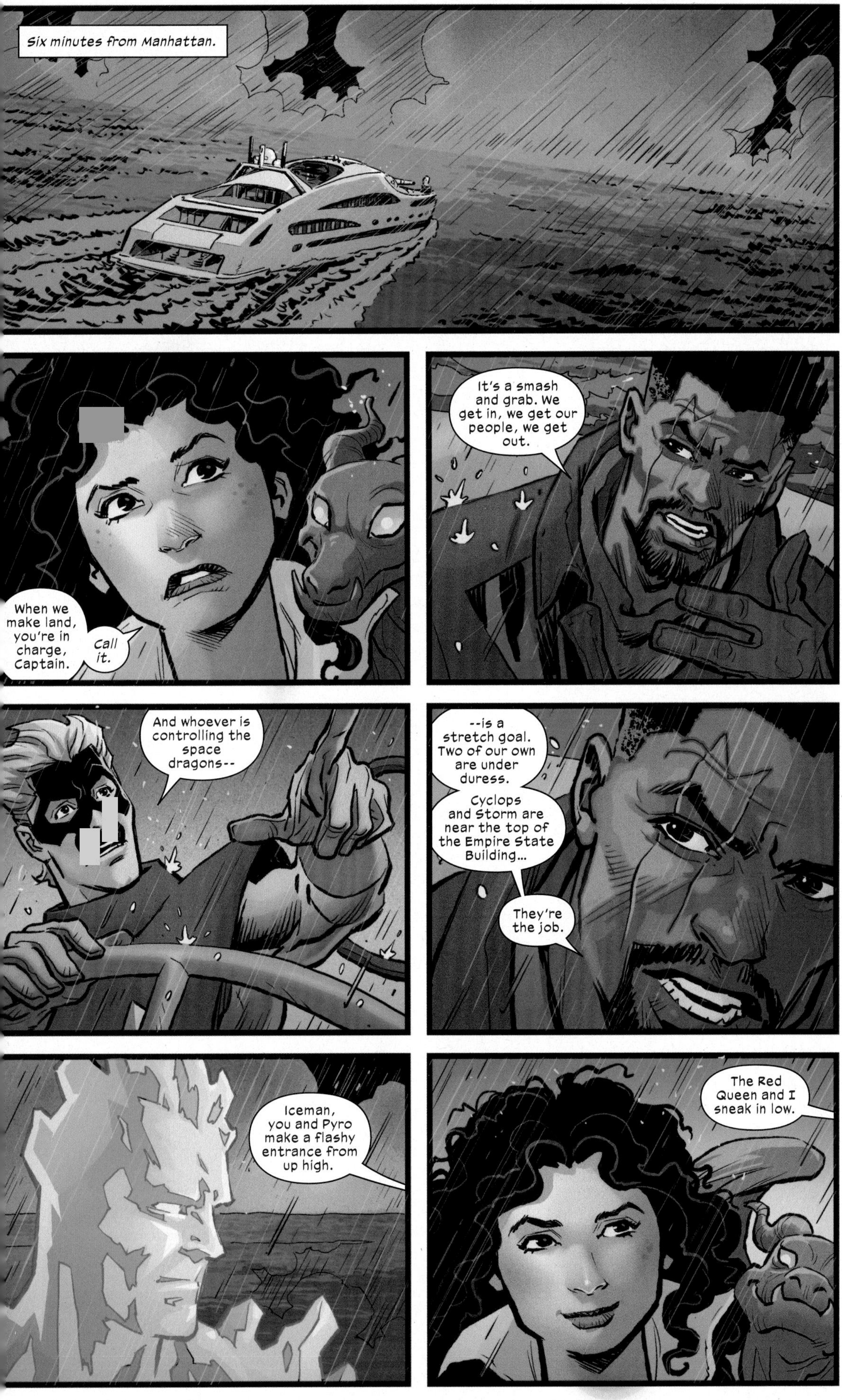
Six minutes from Manhattan.
When we make land, you're in charge, Captain.
Call it.
It's a smash and grab. We get in, we get our people, we get out.
And whoever is controlling the space dragons--
--is a stretch goal. Two of our own are under duress.
Cyclops and Storm are near the top of the Empire State Building...
They're the job.
Iceman, you and Pyro make a flashy entrance from up high.
The Red Queen and I sneak in low.

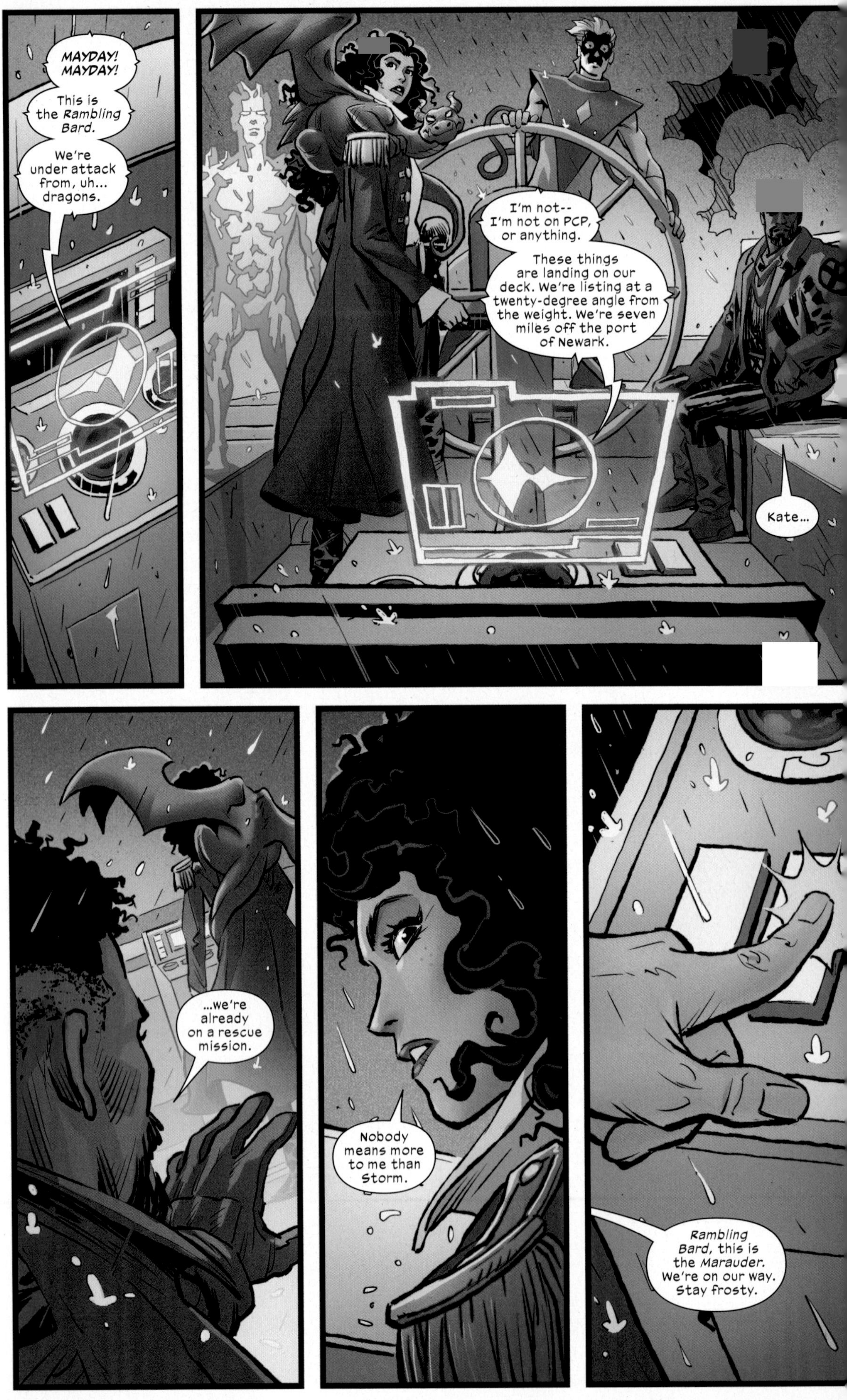

MAYDAY! MAYDAY!
This is the Rambling Bard.
We're under attack from, uh... dragons.
I'm not-- I'm not on PCP, or anything.
These things are landing on our deck. We're listing at a twenty-degree angle from the weight. We're seven miles off the port of Newark.
Kate...
...we're already on a rescue mission.
Nobody means more to me than Storm.
Rambling Bard, this is the Marauder. We're on our way. Stay frosty.

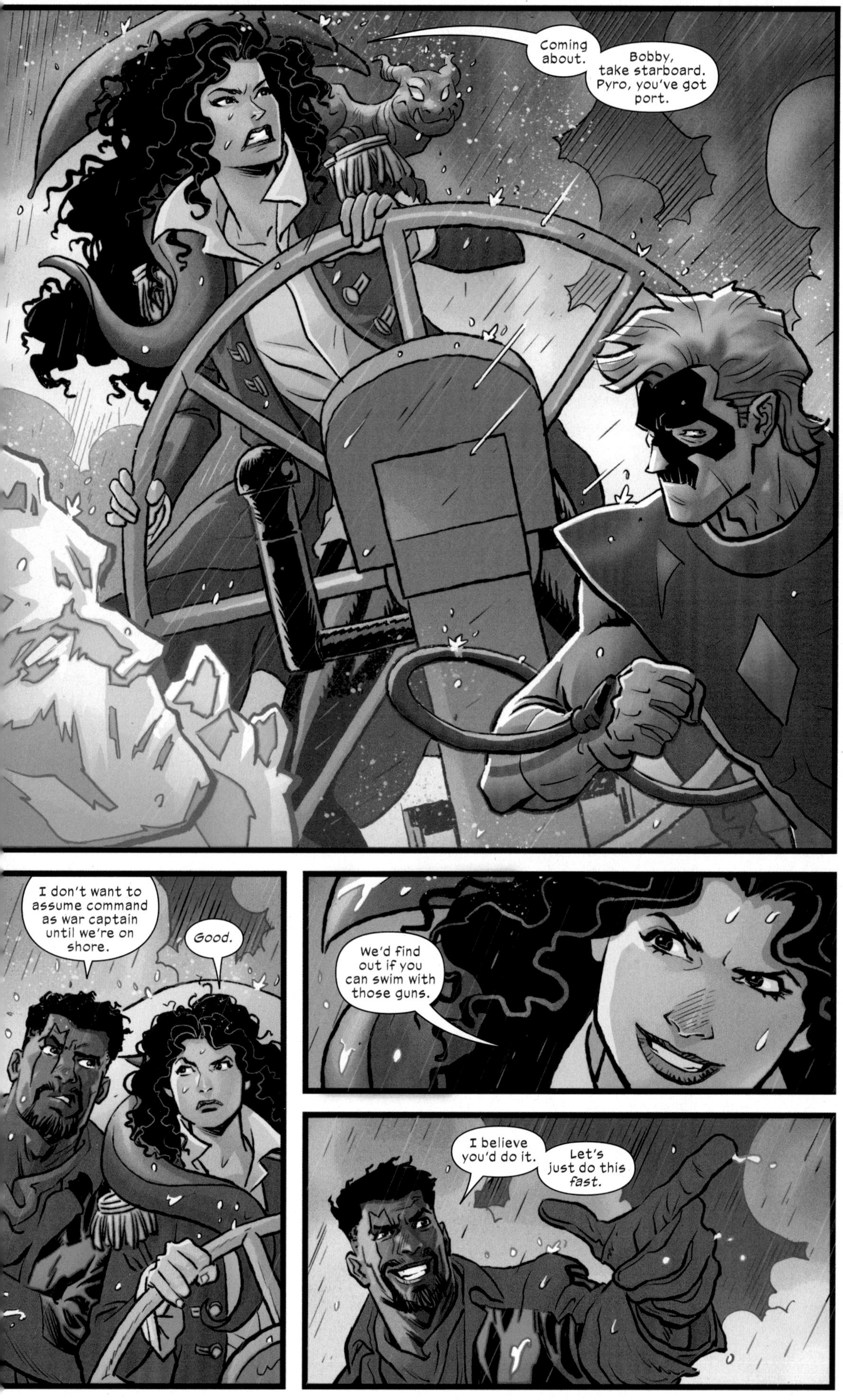
Coming about.
Bobby, take starboard. Pyro, you've got port.
I don't want to assume command as war captain until we're on shore.
Good.
We'd find out if you can swim with those guns.
I believe you'd do it.
Let's just do this *fast.*

KING IN BLACK: MARAUDERS

Knull, symbiote god of the void, has laid waste to the Earth. The entire planet has been enclosed in a symbiote, cutting off interplanetary communication...leaving humanity (and mutantkind) at the mercy of Knull's symbiote dragons.

Fighting dragons on the high seas? Sounds like a job for the MARAUDERS.

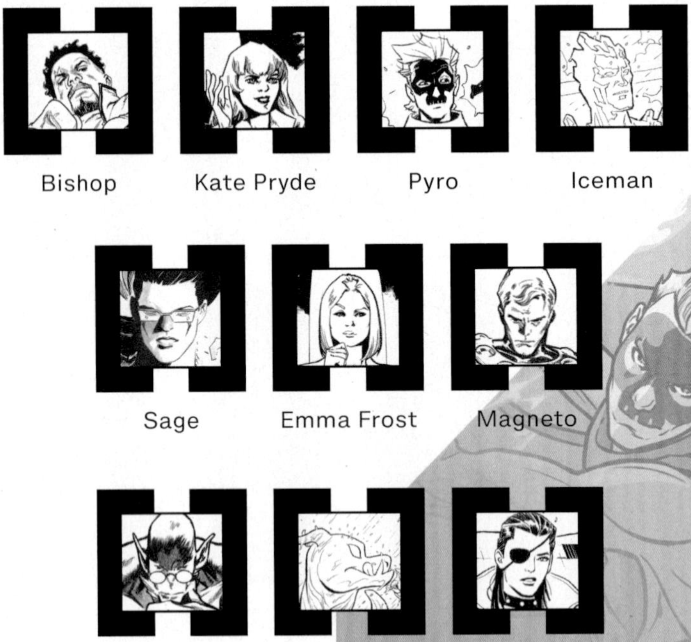

Bishop · Kate Pryde · Pyro · Iceman

Sage · Emma Frost · Magneto

Beast · Lockheed · Callisto

[00_Reign]
[00___ofX]

MARAUDERS [KIB_01]

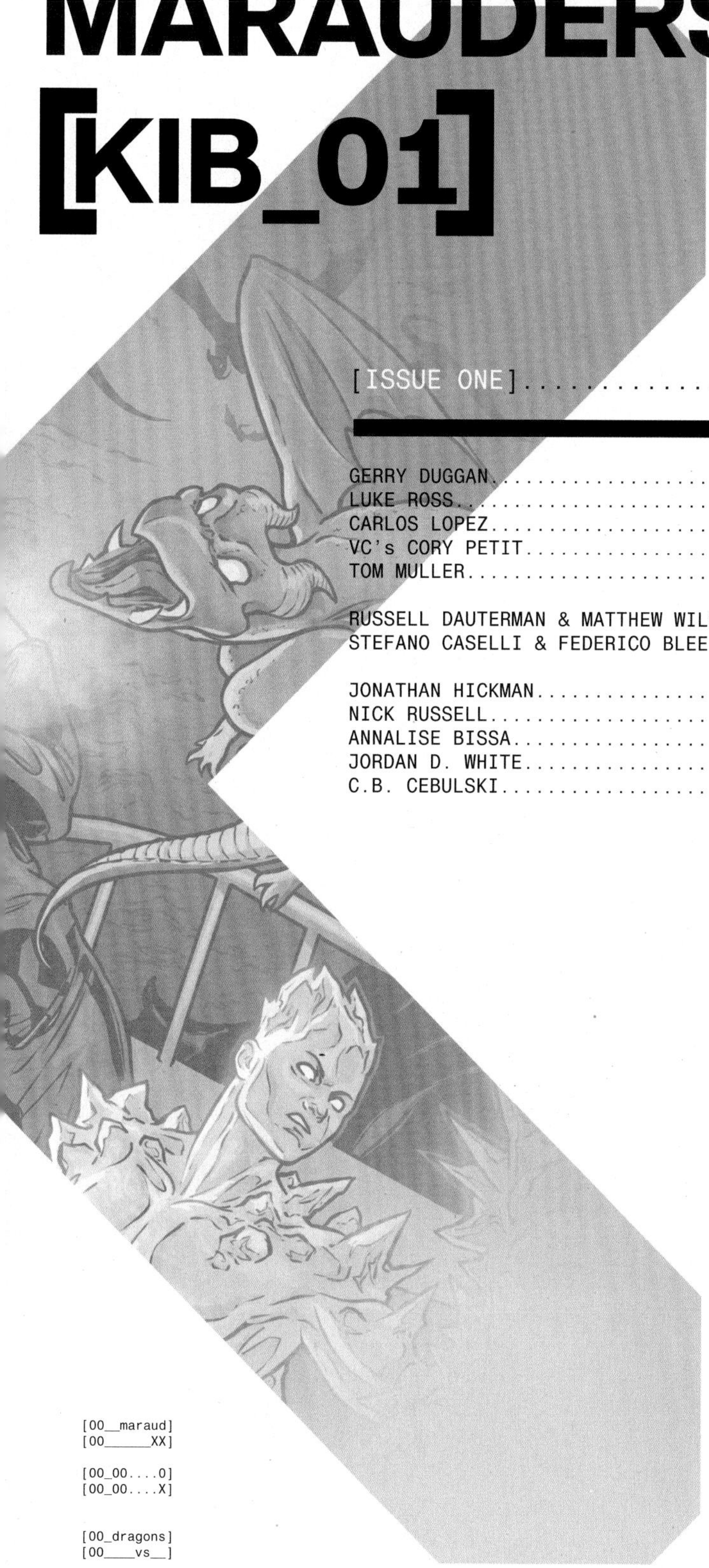

[ISSUE ONE]........................QUEEN IN RED

GERRY DUGGAN..[WRITER]
LUKE ROSS...[ARTIST]
CARLOS LOPEZ...................................[COLOR ARTIST]
VC's CORY PETIT....................................[LETTERER]
TOM MULLER..[DESIGN]

RUSSELL DAUTERMAN & MATTHEW WILSON..........[COVER ARTISTS]
STEFANO CASELLI & FEDERICO BLEE.....[VARIANT COVER ARTISTS]

JONATHAN HICKMAN.................................[HEAD OF X]
NICK RUSSELL....................................[PRODUCTION]
ANNALISE BISSA.............................[ASSOCIATE EDITOR]
JORDAN D. WHITE.....................................[EDITOR]
C.B. CEBULSKI..............................[EDITOR IN CHIEF]

[00__maraud]
[00______XX]

[00_00....0]
[00_00....X]

[00_dragons]
[00____vs__]

[00_______]

[00_pirates]

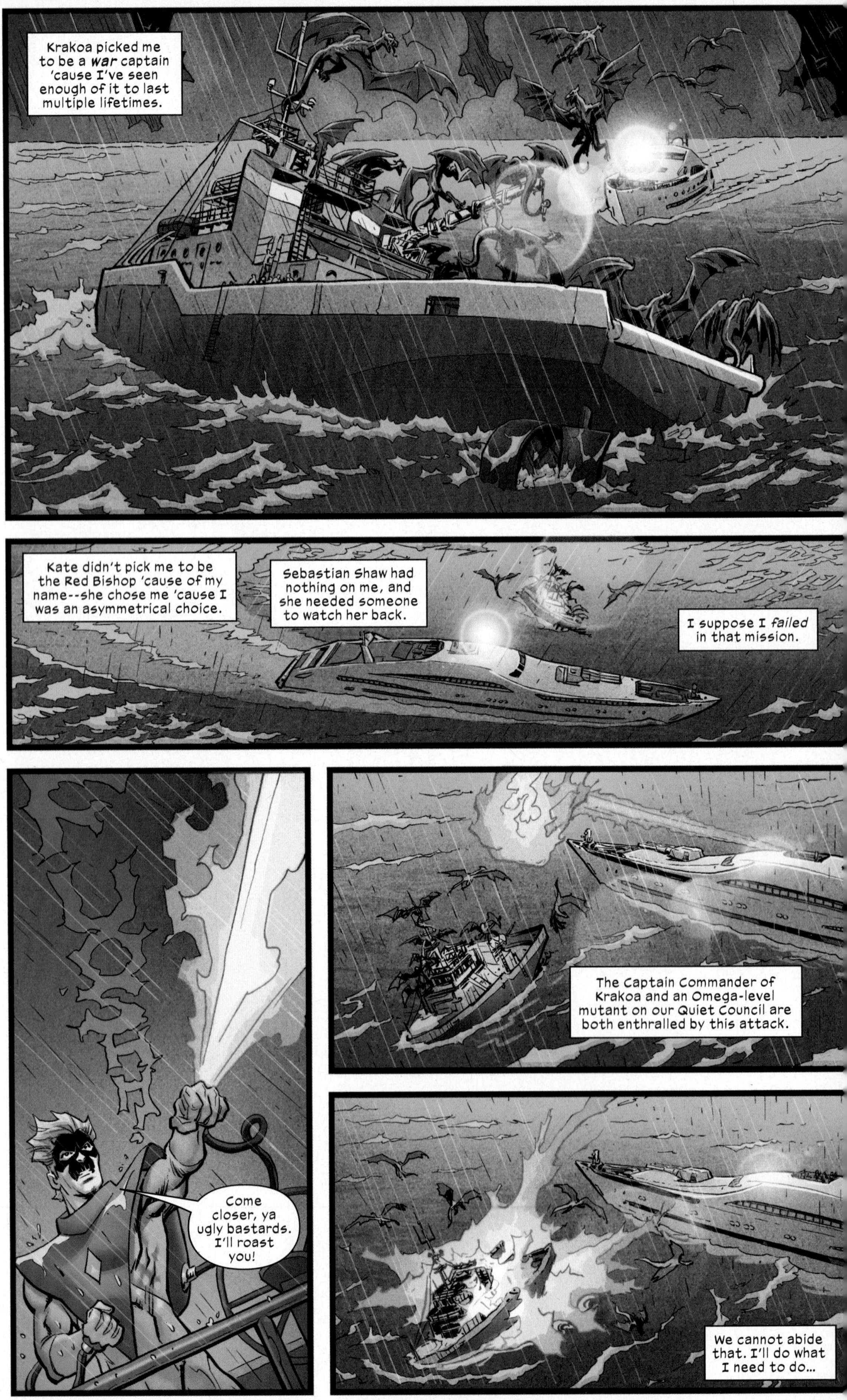

Krakoa picked me to be a *war* captain 'cause I've seen enough of it to last multiple lifetimes.
Kate didn't pick me to be the Red Bishop 'cause of my name--she chose me 'cause I was an asymmetrical choice.
Sebastian Shaw had nothing on me, and she needed someone to watch her back.
I suppose I *failed* in that mission.
Come closer, ya ugly bastards. I'll roast you!
The Captain Commander of Krakoa and an Omega-level mutant on our Quiet Council are both enthralled by this attack.
We cannot abide that. I'll do what I need to do...

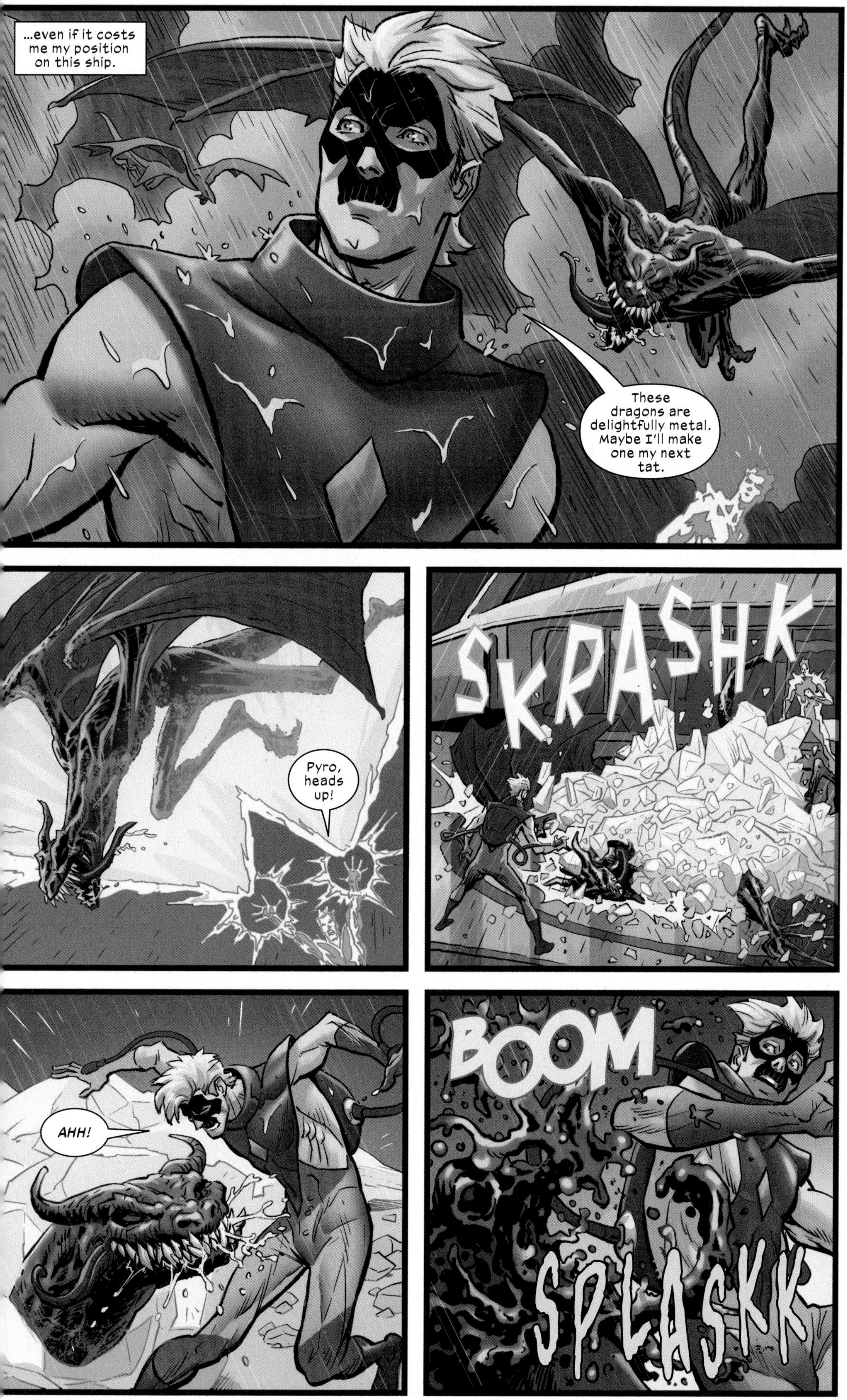

...even if it costs me my position on this ship.
These dragons are delightfully metal. Maybe I'll make one my next tat.
Pyro, heads up!
SKRASHK
AHH!
BOOM
SPLASKK

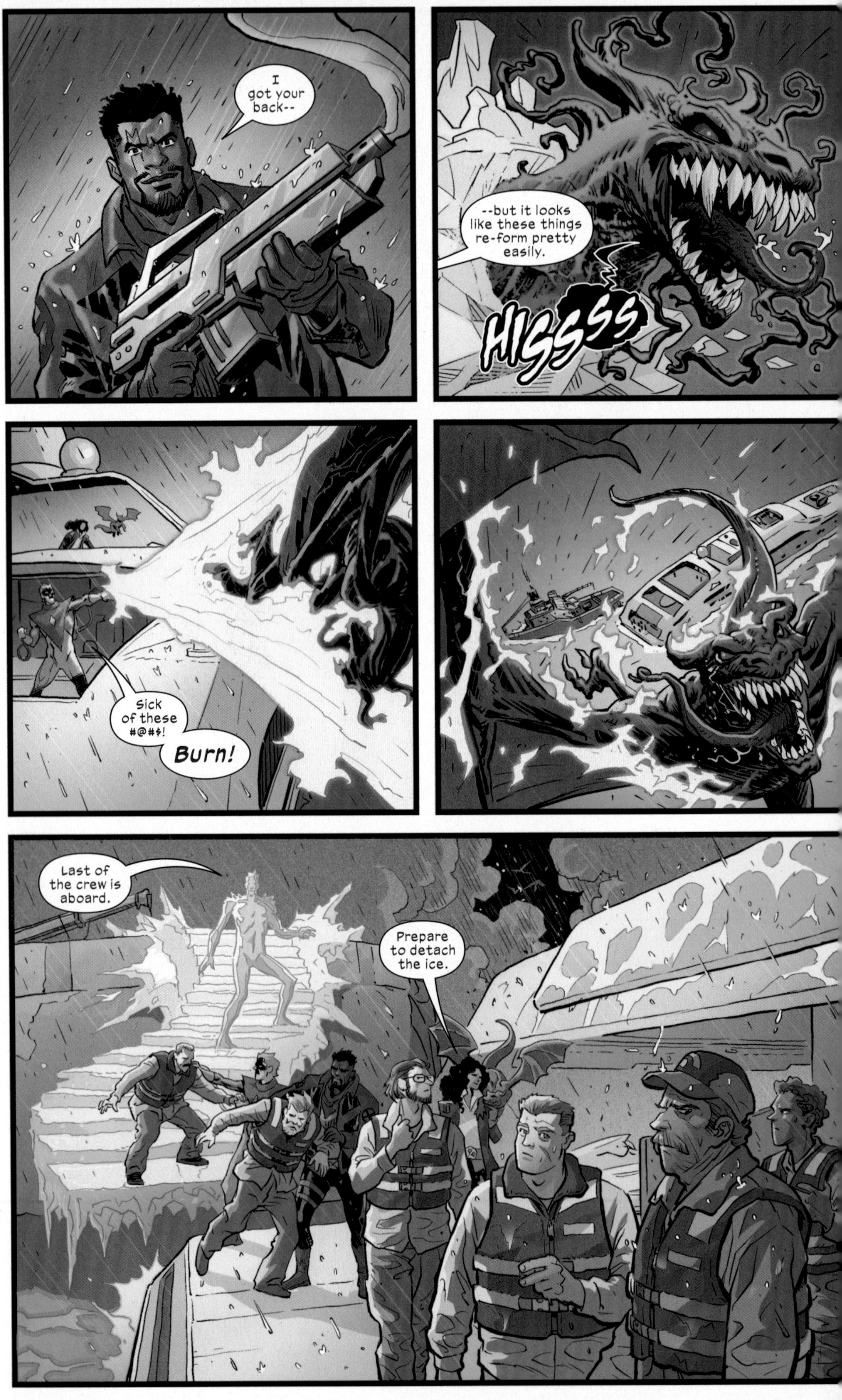
I got your back--
--but it looks like these things re-form pretty easily.
HISSSS
Sick of these #@#$!
Burn!
Last of the crew is aboard.
Prepare to detach the ice.

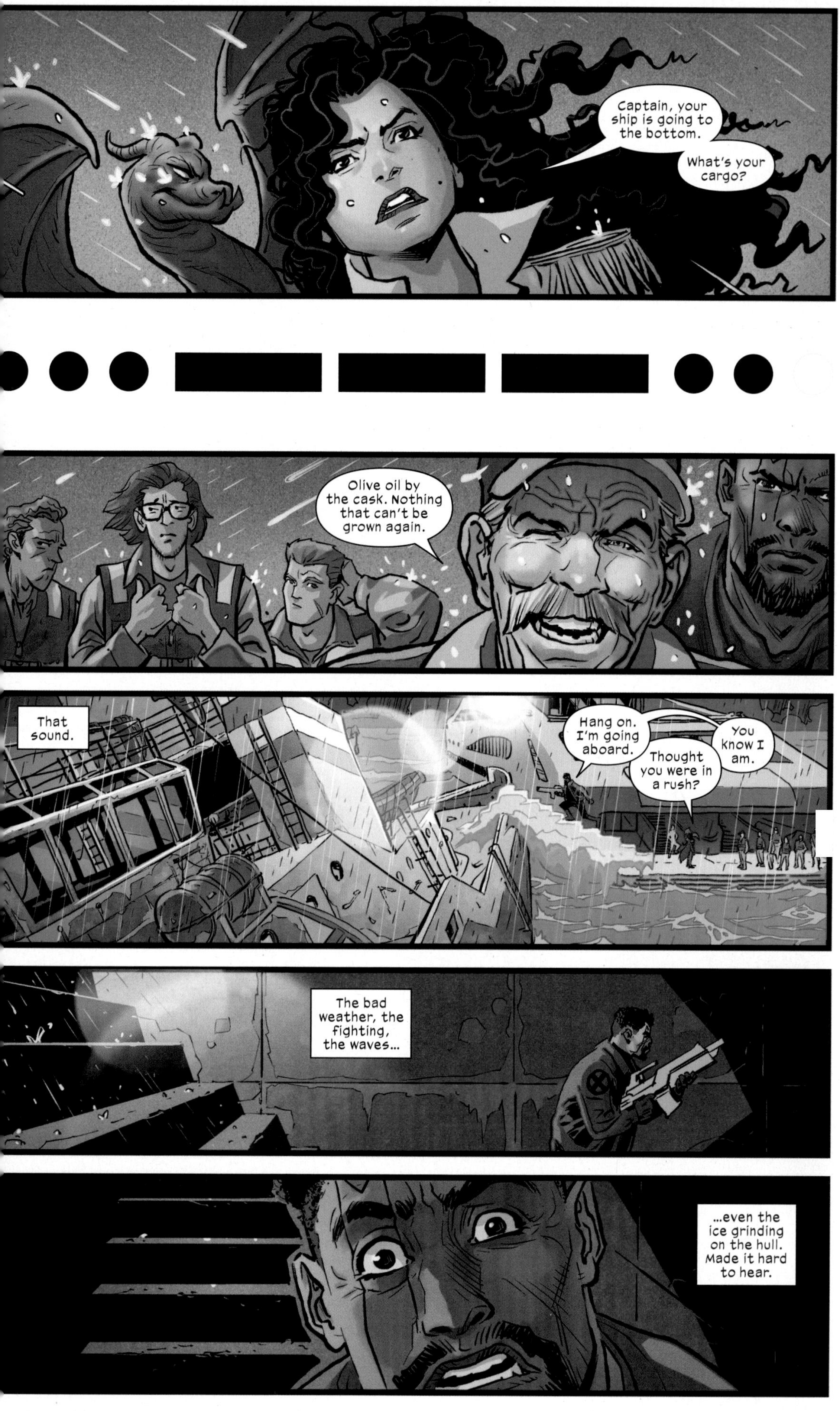
Captain, your ship is going to the bottom.
What's your cargo?
Olive oil by the cask. Nothing that can't be grown again.
That sound.
Hang on. I'm going aboard.
Thought you were in a rush?
You know I am.
The bad weather, the fighting, the waves...
...even the ice grinding on the hull. Made it hard to hear.

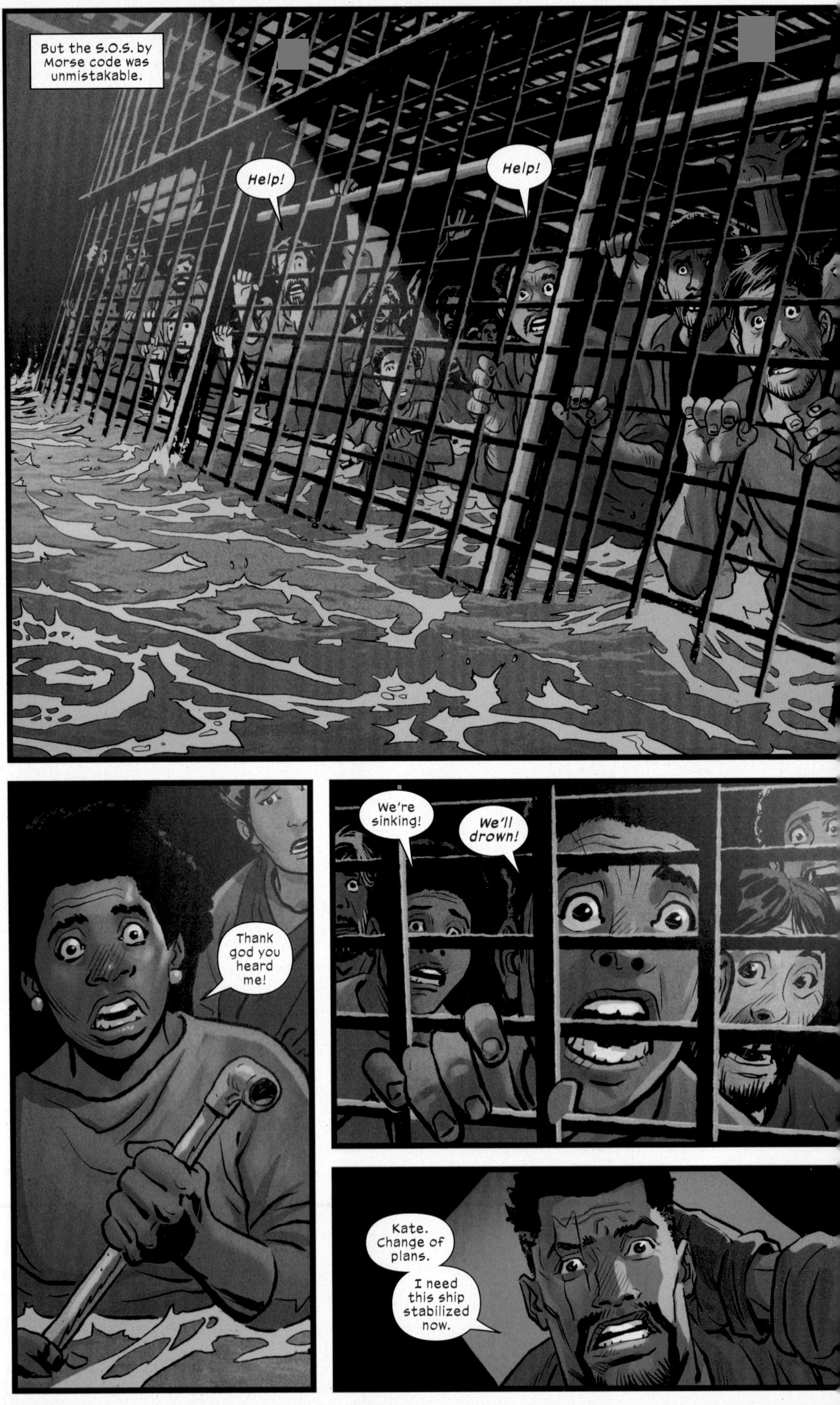
But the S.O.S. by Morse code was unmistakable.
Help!
Help!
Thank god you heard me!
We're sinking!
We'll drown!
Kate. Change of plans.
I need this ship stabilized now.

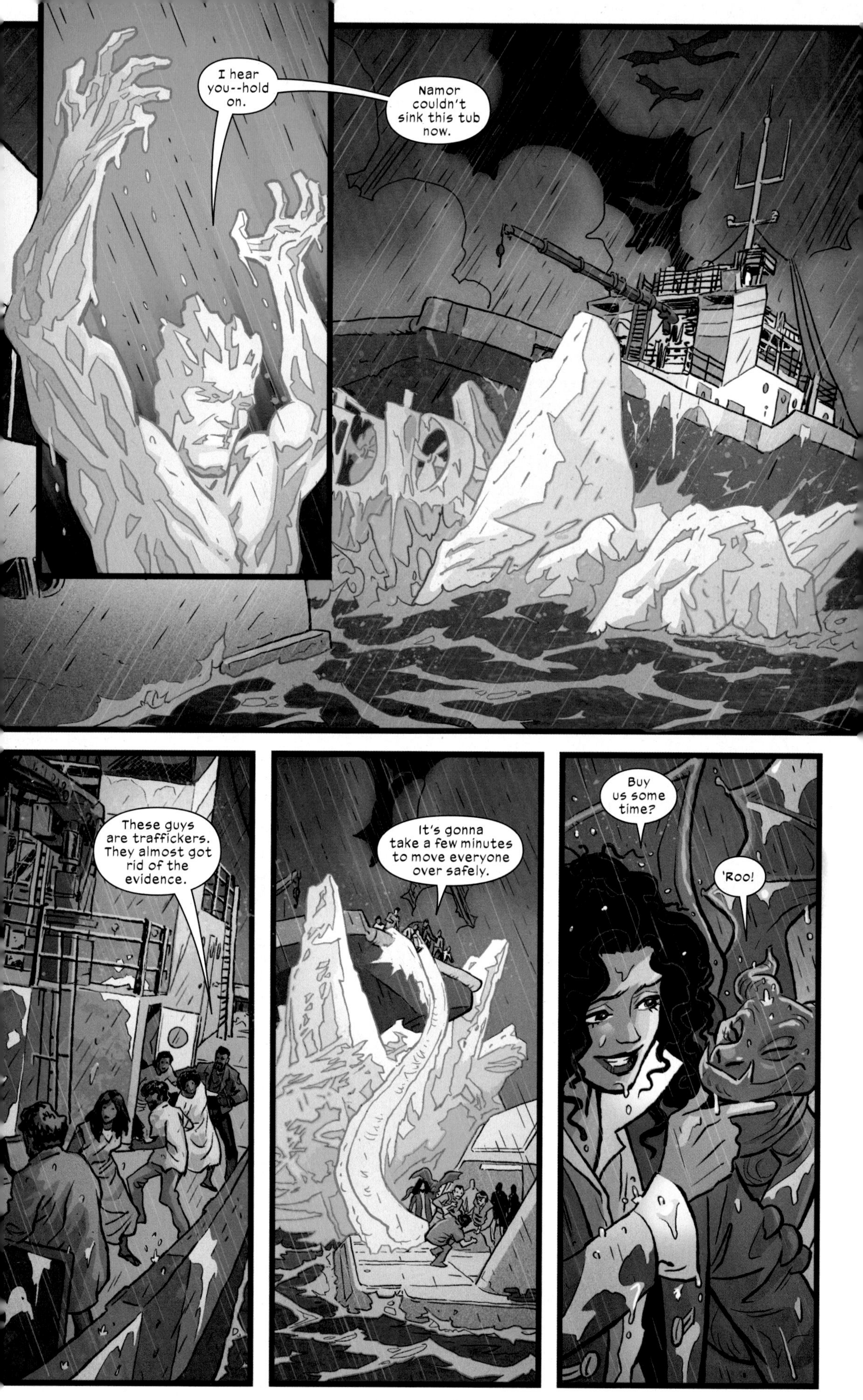
I hear you--hold on.
Namor couldn't sink this tub now.
These guys are traffickers. They almost got rid of the evidence.
It's gonna take a few minutes to move everyone over safely.
Buy us some time?
'Roo!

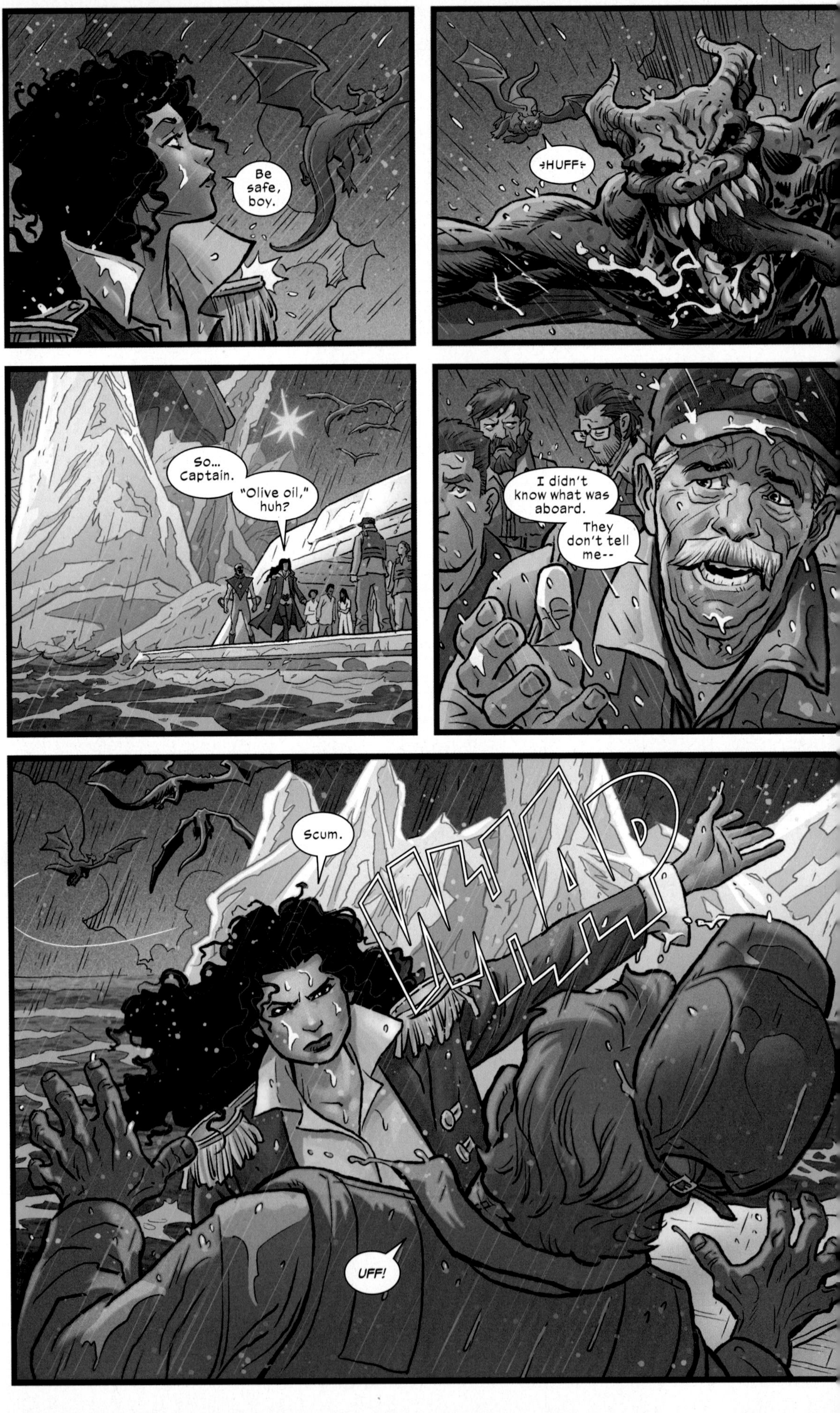
Be safe, boy.
HUFF
So... Captain.
"Olive oil," huh?
I didn't know what was aboard.
They don't tell me--
Scum.
UFF!

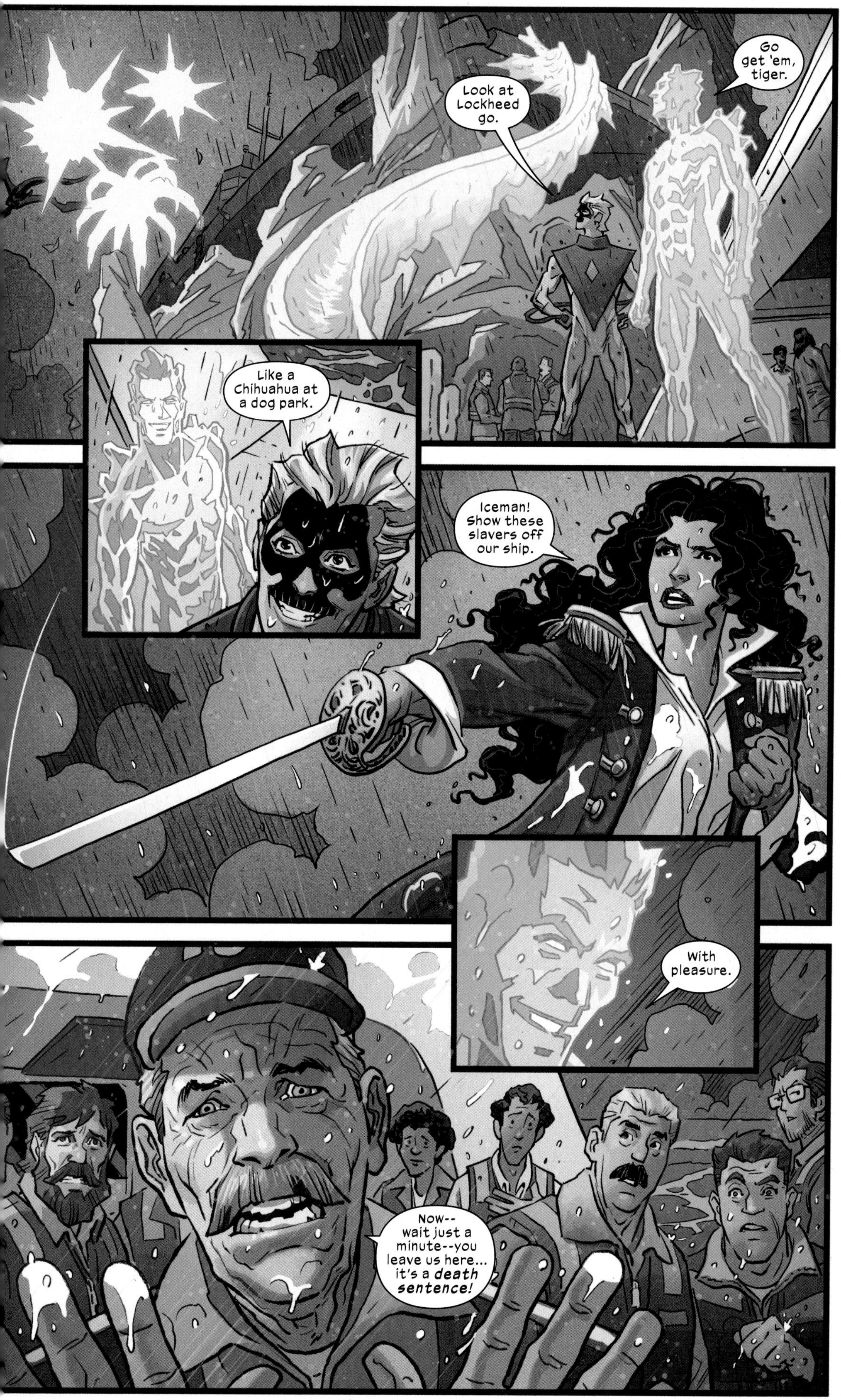
Look at Lockheed go.
Go get 'em, tiger.
Like a Chihuahua at a dog park.
Iceman! Show these slavers off our ship.
With pleasure.
Now-- wait just a minute--you leave us here... it's a *death sentence!*

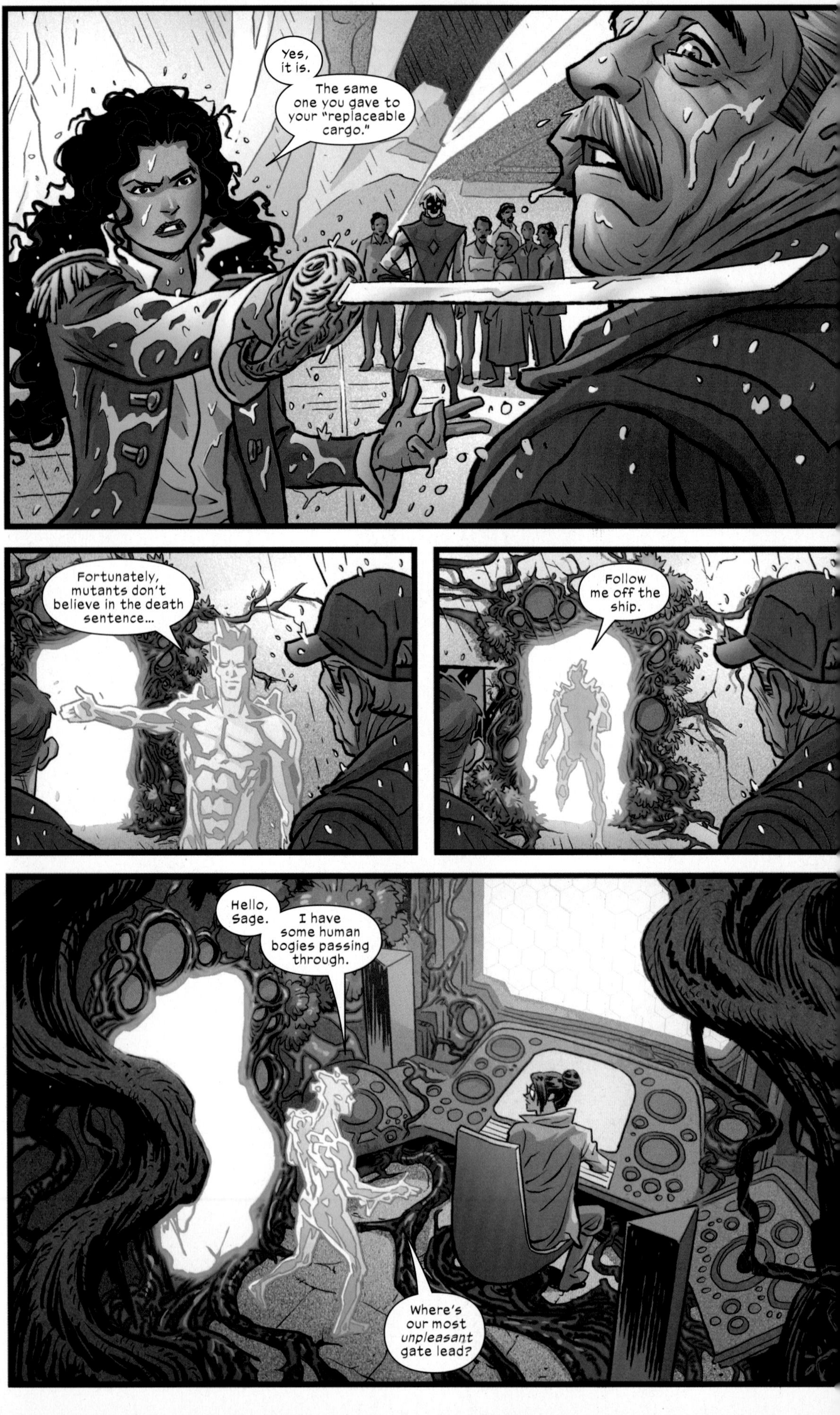

Yes, it is.
The same one you gave to your "replaceable cargo."
Fortunately, mutants don't believe in the death sentence...
Follow me off the ship.
Hello, Sage.
I have some human bogies passing through.
Where's our most *unpleasant* gate lead?

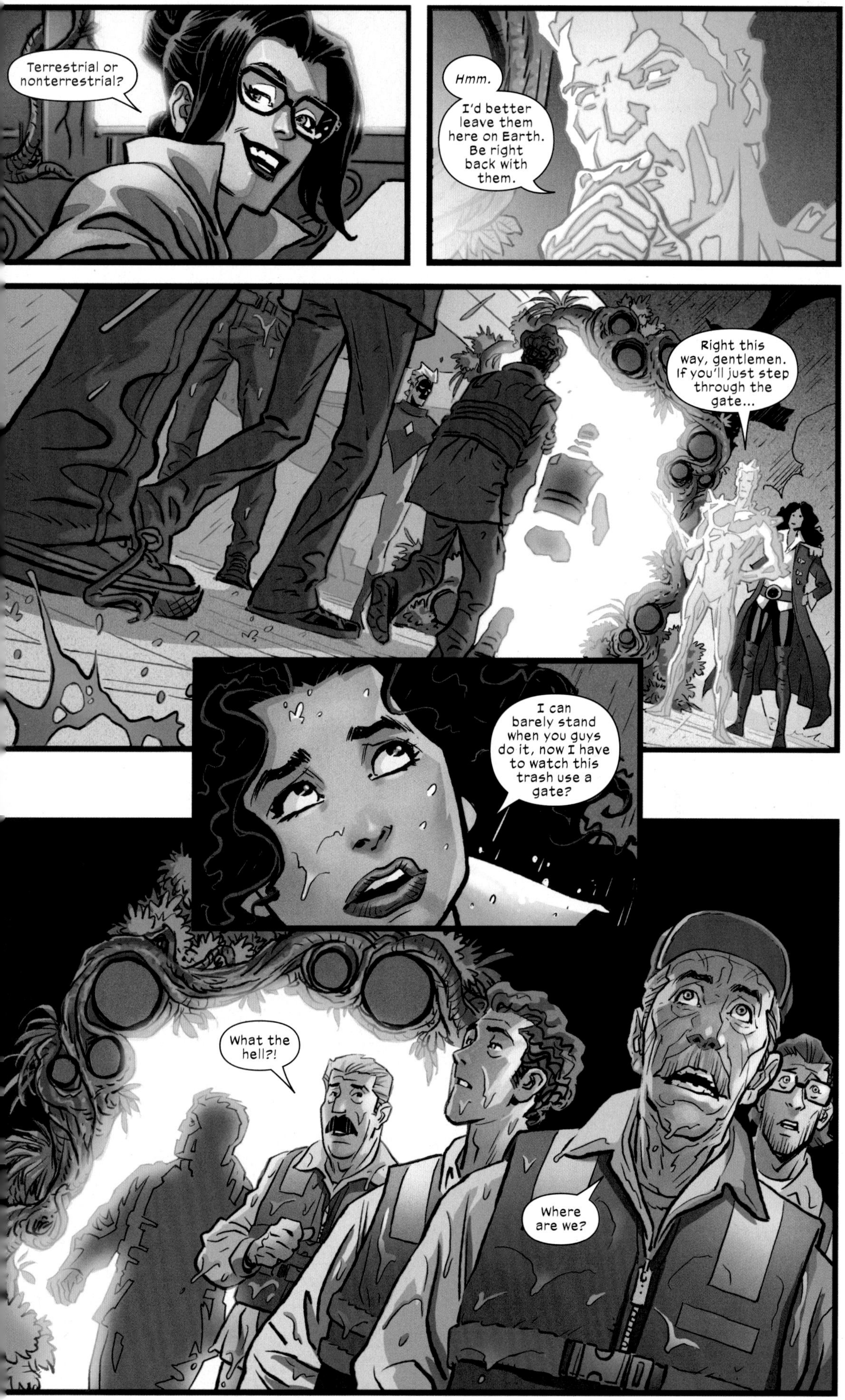
Terrestrial or nonterrestrial?
Hmm.
I'd better leave them here on Earth. Be right back with them.
Right this way, gentlemen. If you'll just step through the gate...
I can barely stand when you guys do it, now I have to watch this trash use a gate?
What the hell?!
Where are we?

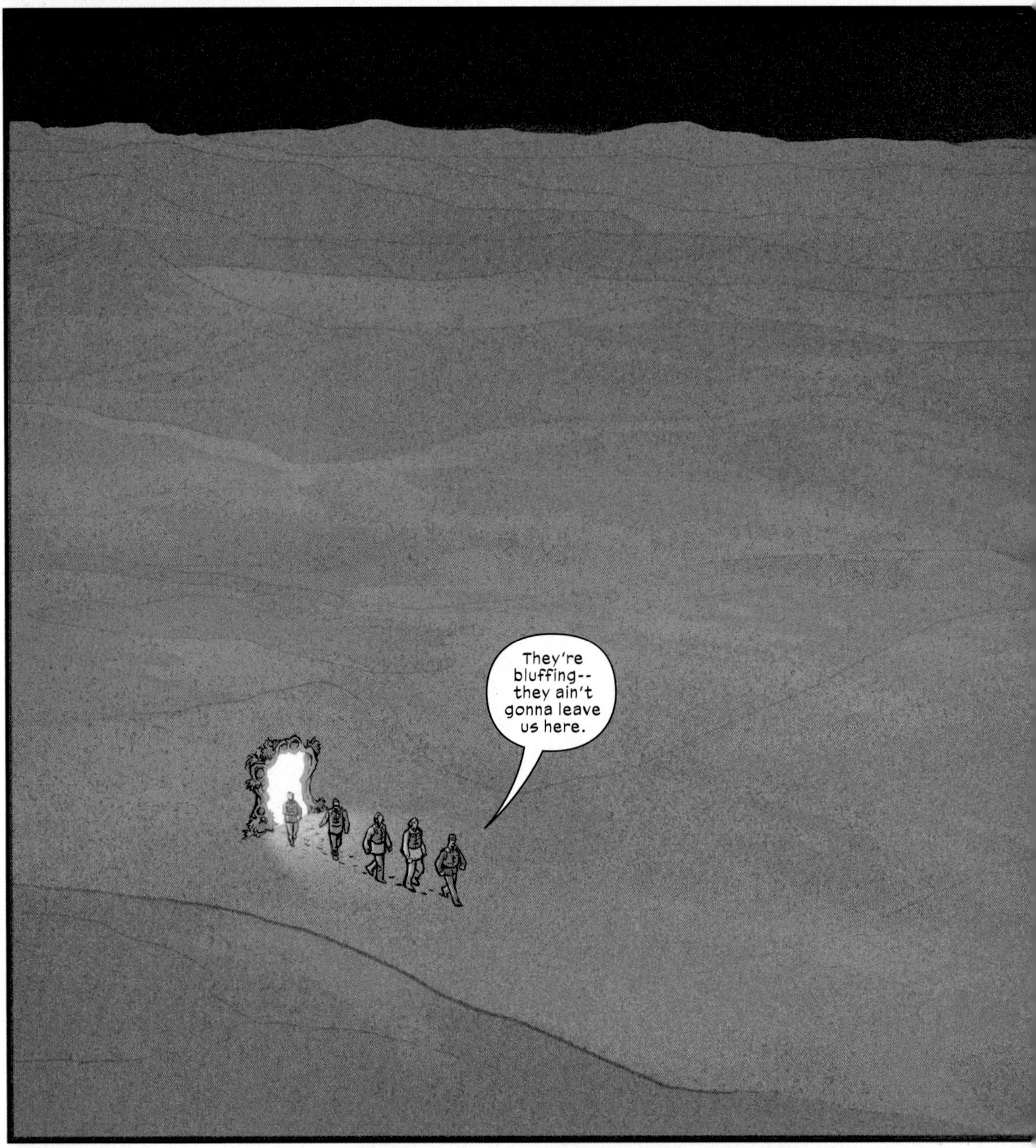
They're bluffing-- they ain't gonna leave us here.

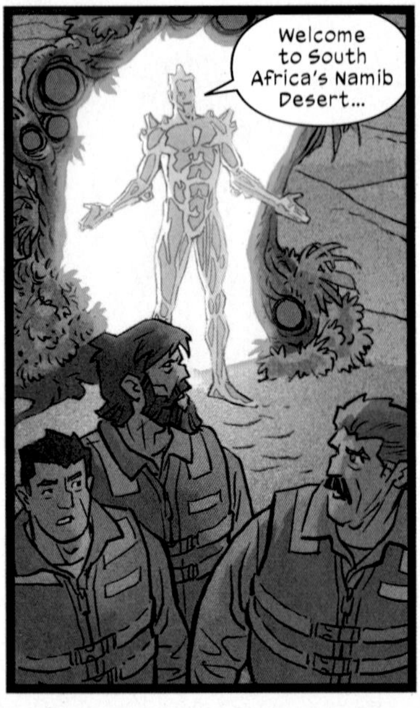
Welcome to South Africa's Namib Desert...

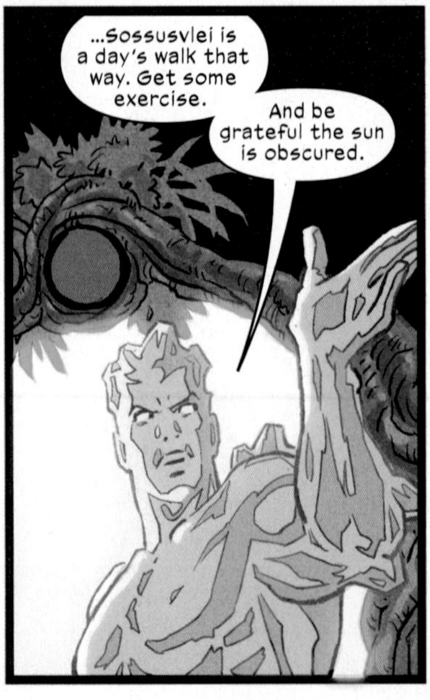
...Sossusvlei is a day's walk that way. Get some exercise.
And be grateful the sun is obscured.

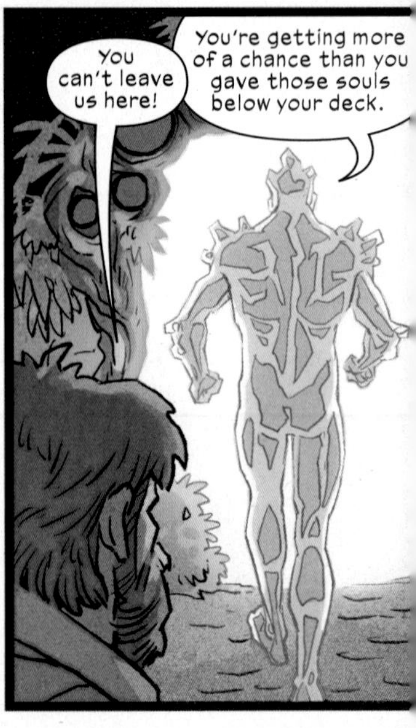
You can't leave us here!
You're getting more of a chance than you gave those souls below your deck.

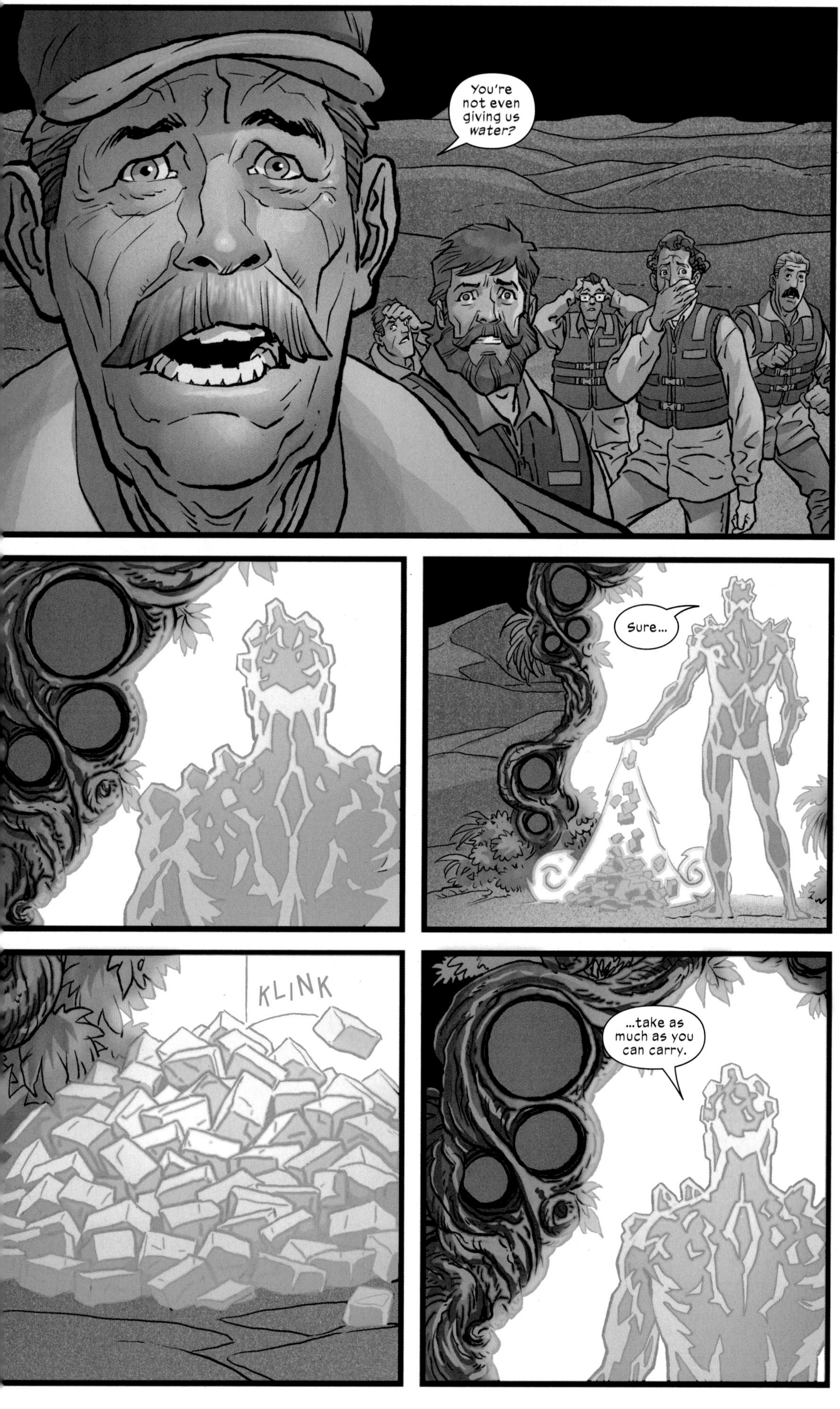
You're not even giving us water?
Sure...
KLINK
...take as much as you can carry.

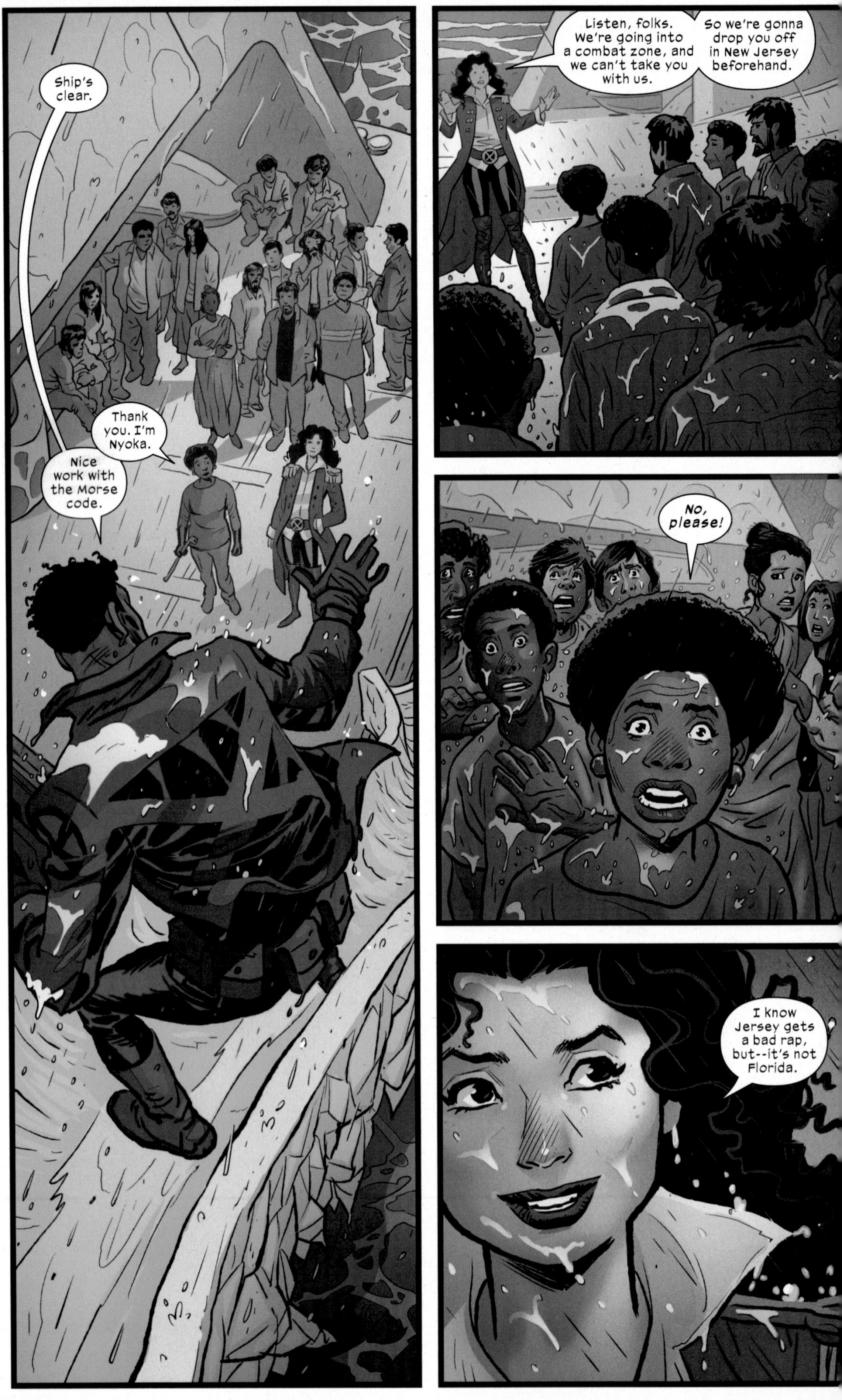
Ship's clear.
Nice work with the Morse code.
Thank you. I'm Nyoka.
Listen, folks. We're going into a combat zone, and we can't take you with us.
So we're gonna drop you off in New Jersey beforehand.
No, please!
I know Jersey gets a bad rap, but--it's not Florida.

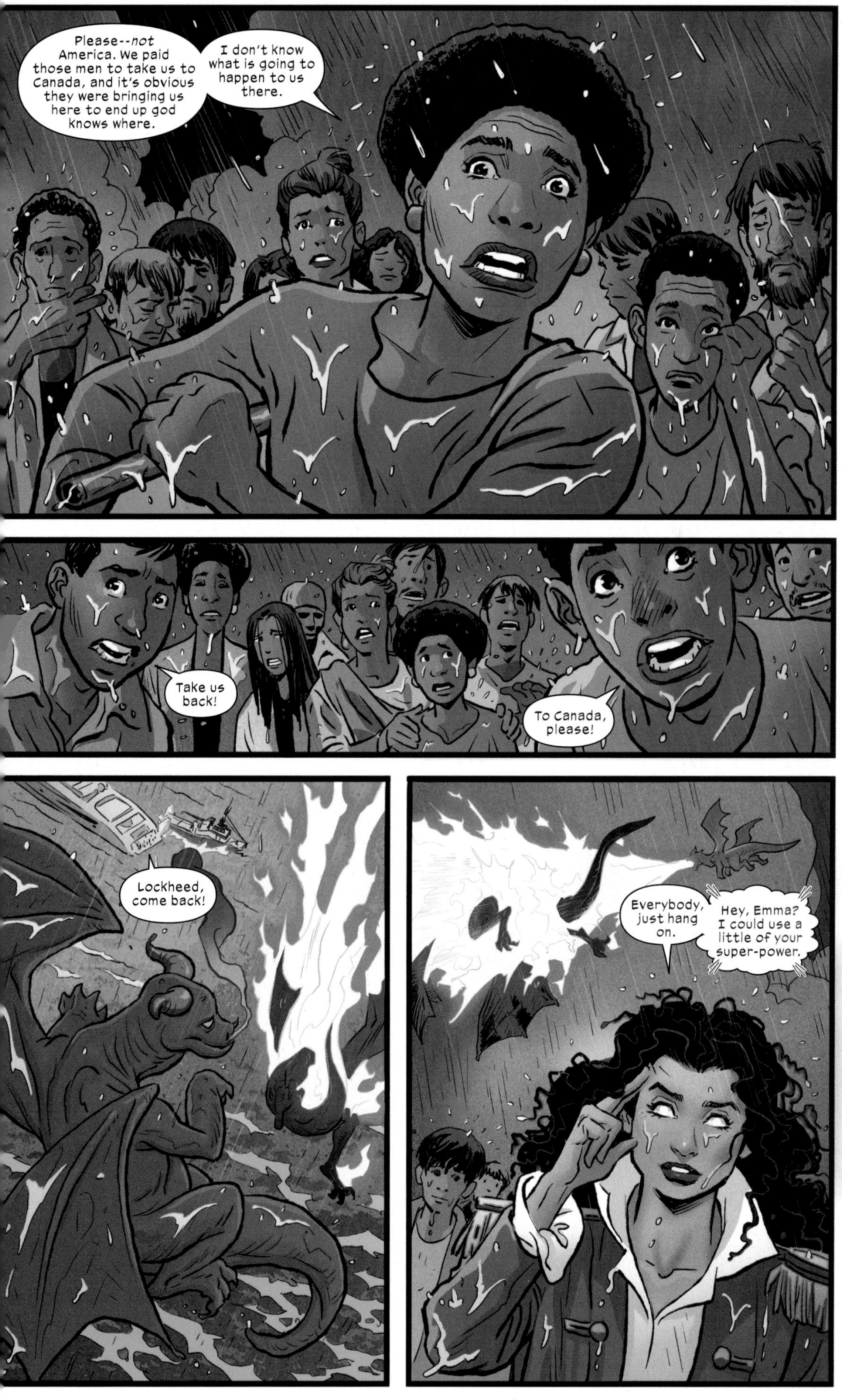
Please--*not* America. We paid those men to take us to Canada, and it's obvious they were bringing us here to end up god knows where.
I don't know what is going to happen to us there.
Take us back!
To Canada, please!
Lockheed, come back!
Everybody, just hang on.
Hey, Emma? I could use a little of your super-power.

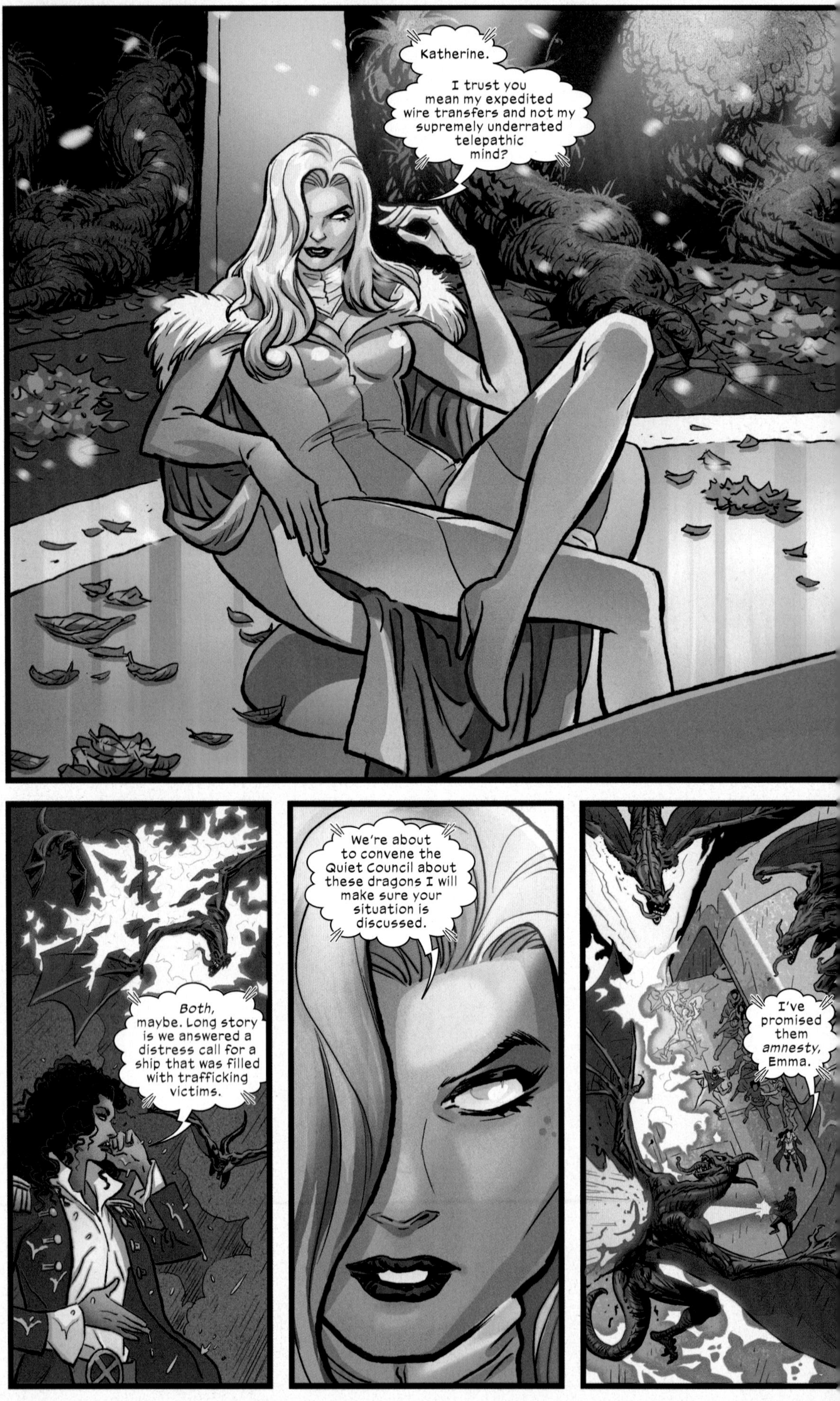
Katherine.
I trust you mean my expedited wire transfers and not my supremely underrated telepathic mind?
Both, maybe. Long story is we answered a distress call for a ship that was filled with trafficking victims.
We're about to convene the Quiet Council about these dragons I will make sure your situation is discussed.
I've promised them amnesty, Emma.

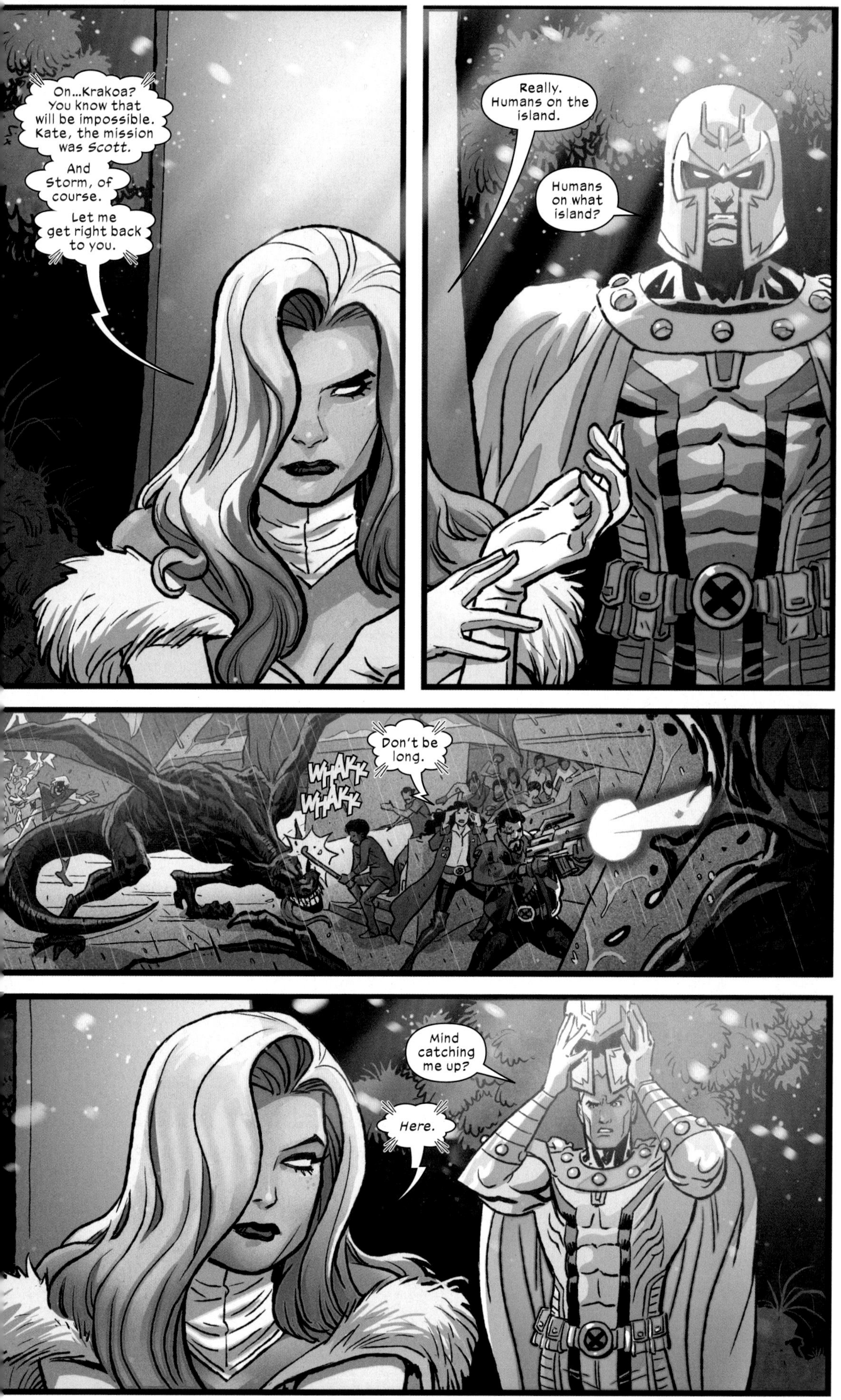
On...Krakoa? You know that will be impossible. Kate, the mission was Scott.
And Storm, of course.
Let me get right back to you.
Really. Humans on the island.
Humans on what island?
WHAKK WHAKK
Don't be long.
Mind catching me up?
Here.

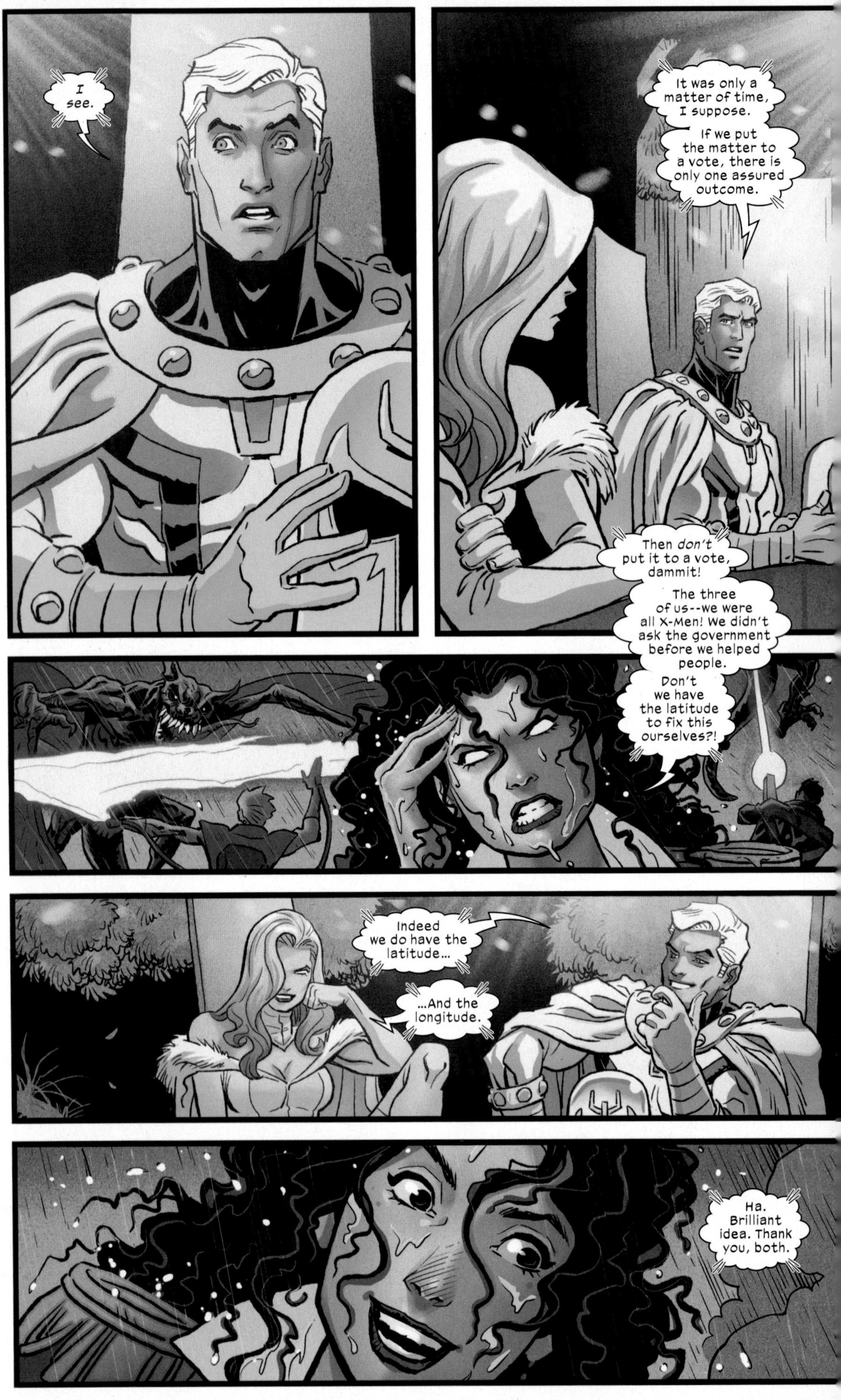
I see.
It was only a matter of time, I suppose.
If we put the matter to a vote, there is only one assured outcome.
Then *don't* put it to a vote, dammit!
The three of us--we were all X-Men! We didn't ask the government before we helped people.
Don't we have the latitude to fix this ourselves?!
Indeed we do have the latitude...
...And the longitude.
Ha. Brilliant idea. Thank you, both.

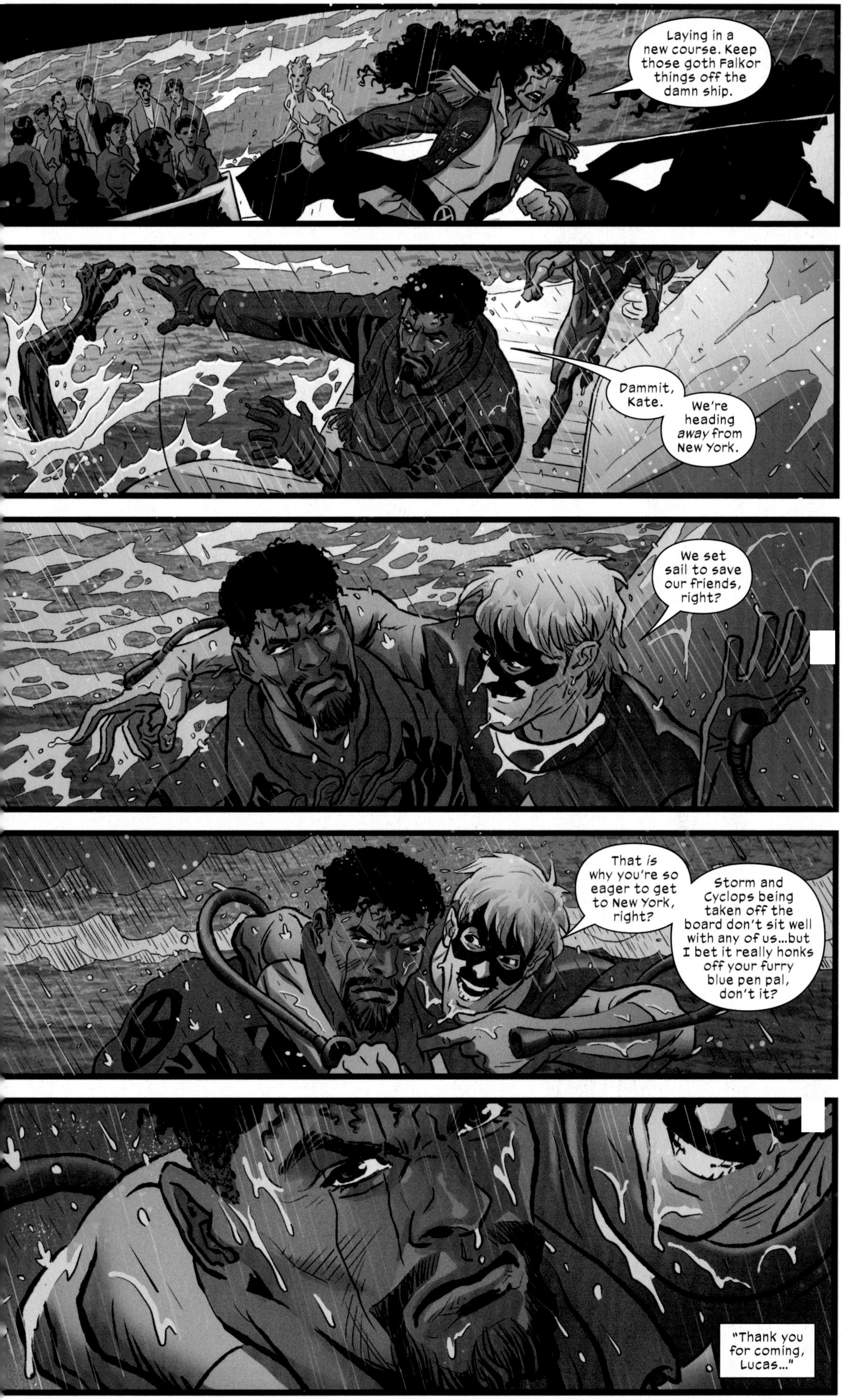
Laying in a new course. Keep those goth Falkor things off the damn ship.
Dammit, Kate.
We're heading *away* from New York.
We set sail to save our friends, right?
That *is* why you're so eager to get to New York, right?
Storm and Cyclops being taken off the board don't sit well with any of us...but I bet it really honks off your furry blue pen pal, don't it?
"Thank you for coming, Lucas..."

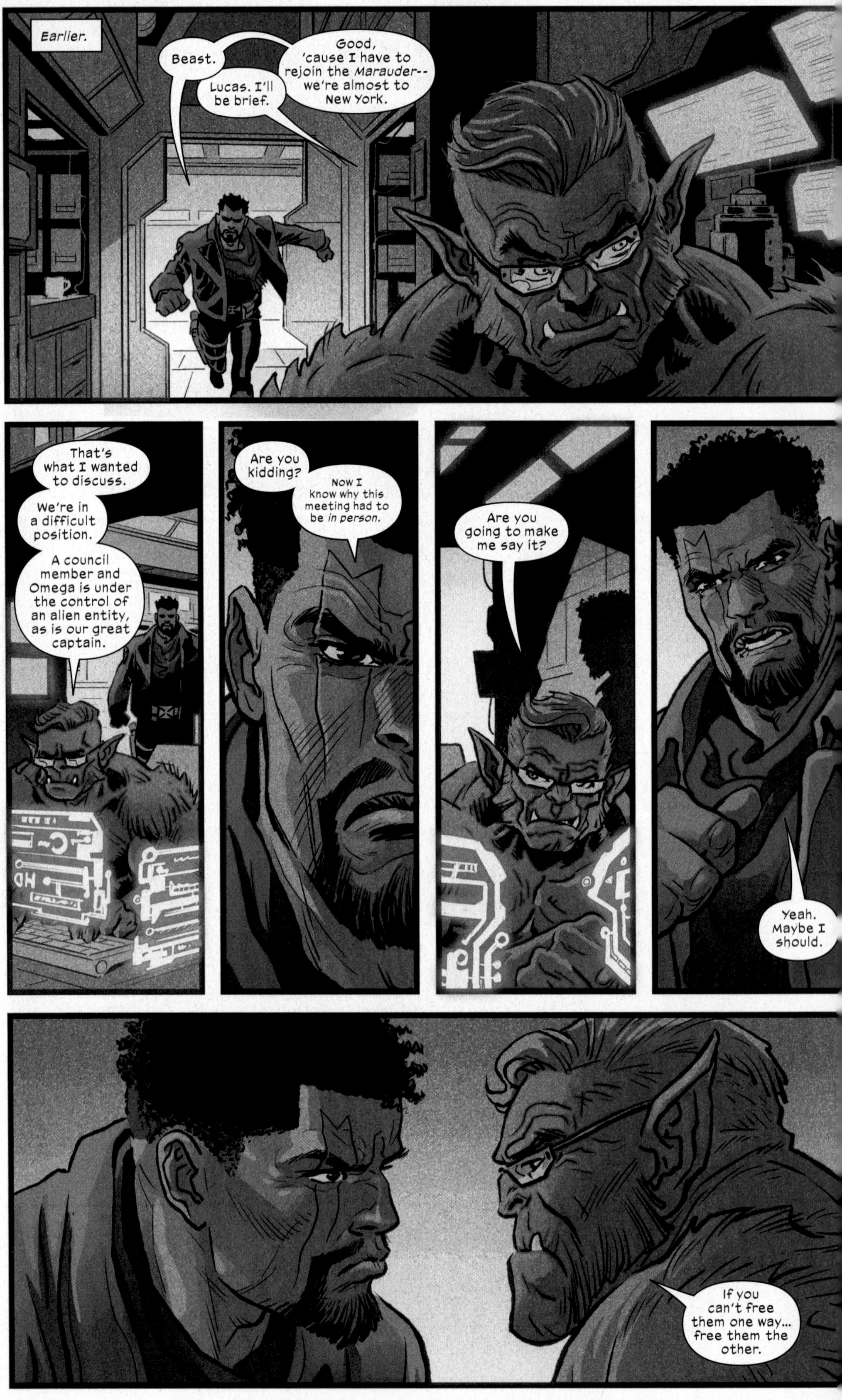
Earlier.
Beast.
Lucas. I'll be brief.
Good, 'cause I have to rejoin the *Marauder*-- we're almost to New York.
That's what I wanted to discuss.
We're in a difficult position.
A council member and Omega is under the control of an alien entity, as is our great captain.
Are you kidding?
Now I know why this meeting had to be *in person*.
Are you going to make me say it?
Yeah. Maybe I should.
If you can't free them one way... free them the other.

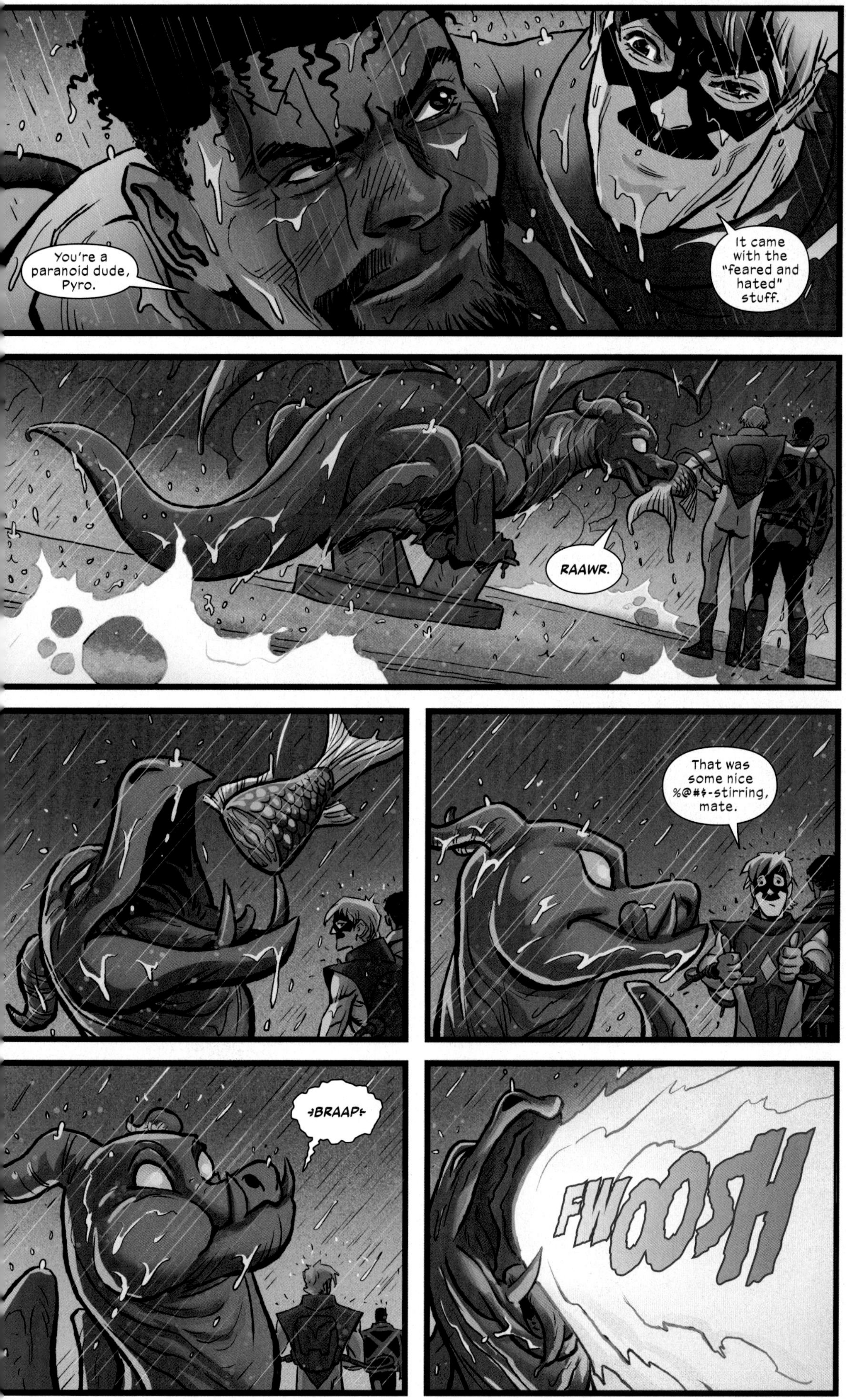

You're a paranoid dude, Pyro.
It came with the "feared and hated" stuff.
RAAWR.
That was some nice %@#$-stirring, mate.
BRAAP
FWOOSH

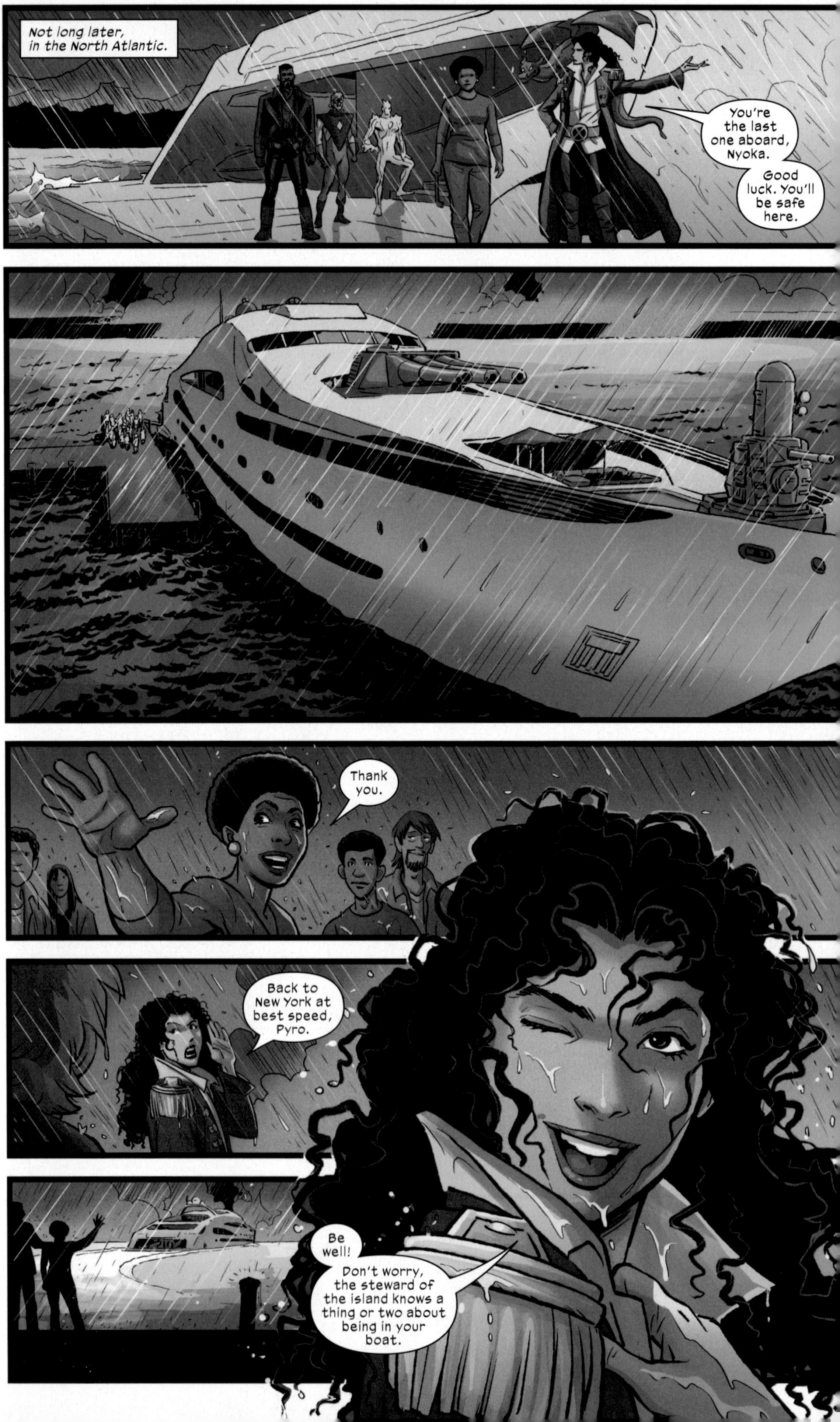
Not long later, in the North Atlantic.
You're the last one aboard, Nyoka.
Good luck. You'll be safe here.
Thank you.
Back to New York at best speed, Pyro.
Be well!
Don't worry, the steward of the island knows a thing or two about being in your boat.

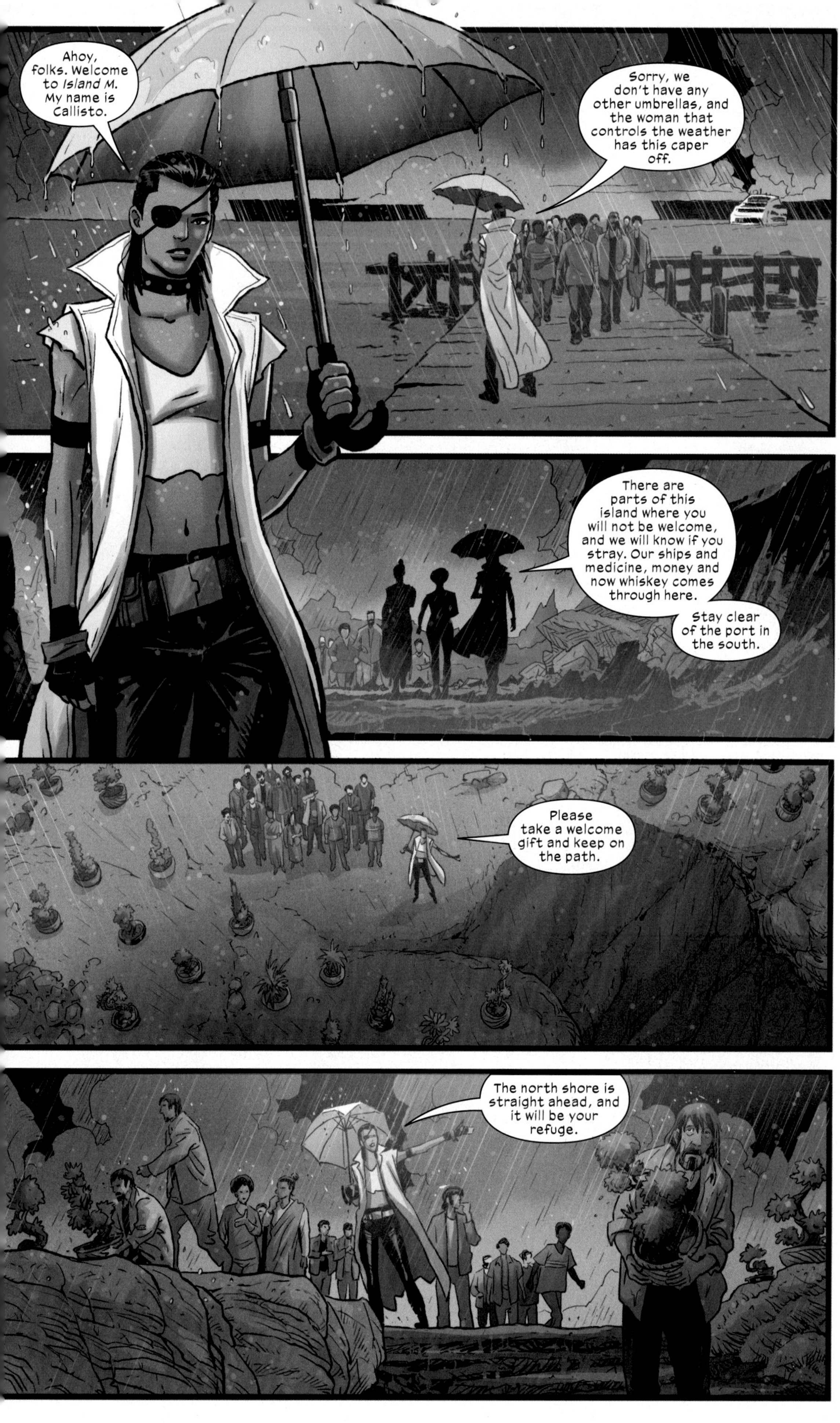
Ahoy, folks. Welcome to *Island M*. My name is Callisto.
Sorry, we don't have any other umbrellas, and the woman that controls the weather has this caper off.
There are parts of this island where you will not be welcome, and we will know if you stray. Our ships and medicine, money and now whiskey comes through here.
Stay clear of the port in the south.
Please take a welcome gift and keep on the path.
The north shore is straight ahead, and it will be your refuge.

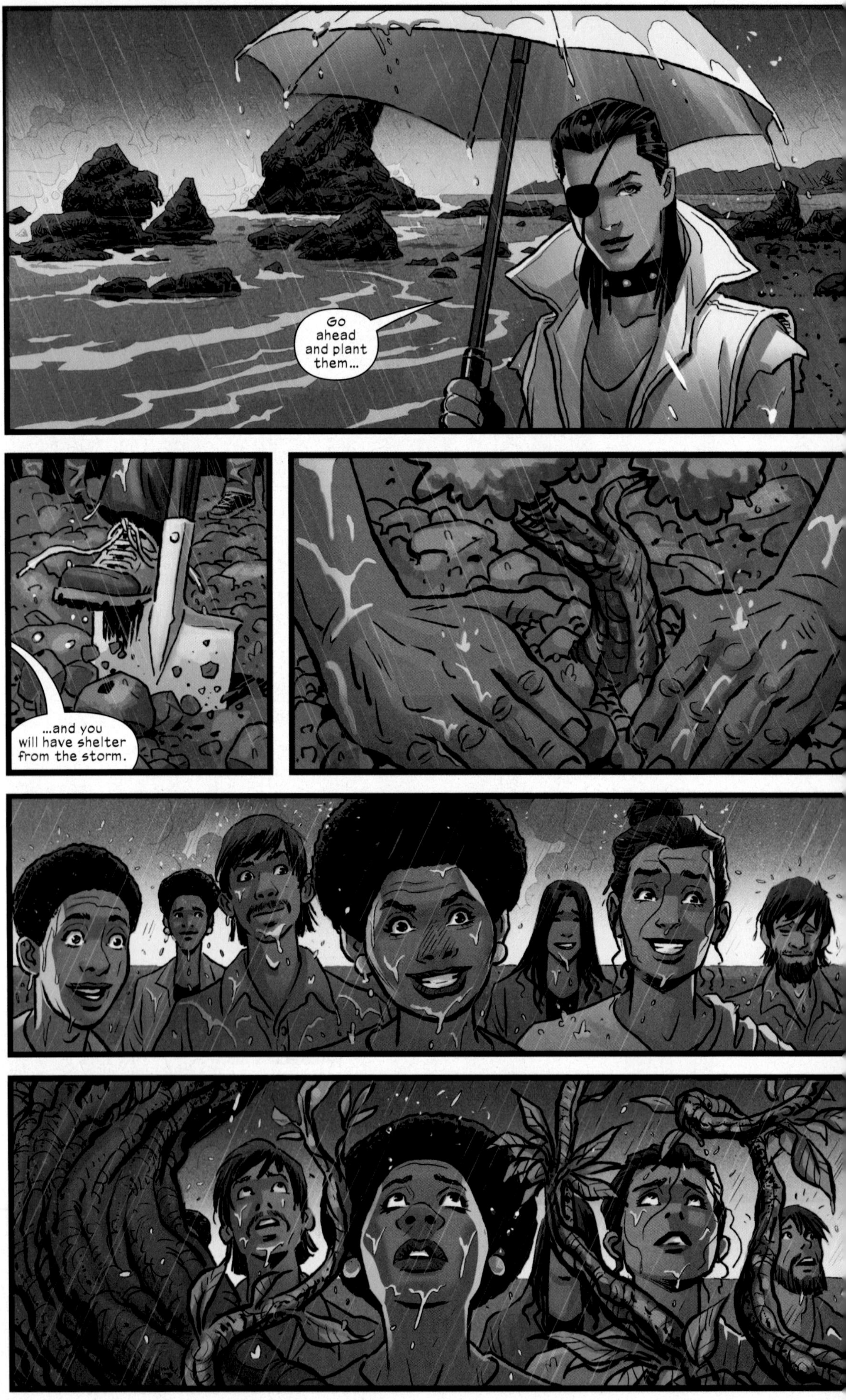
Go ahead and plant them...
...and you will have shelter from the storm.

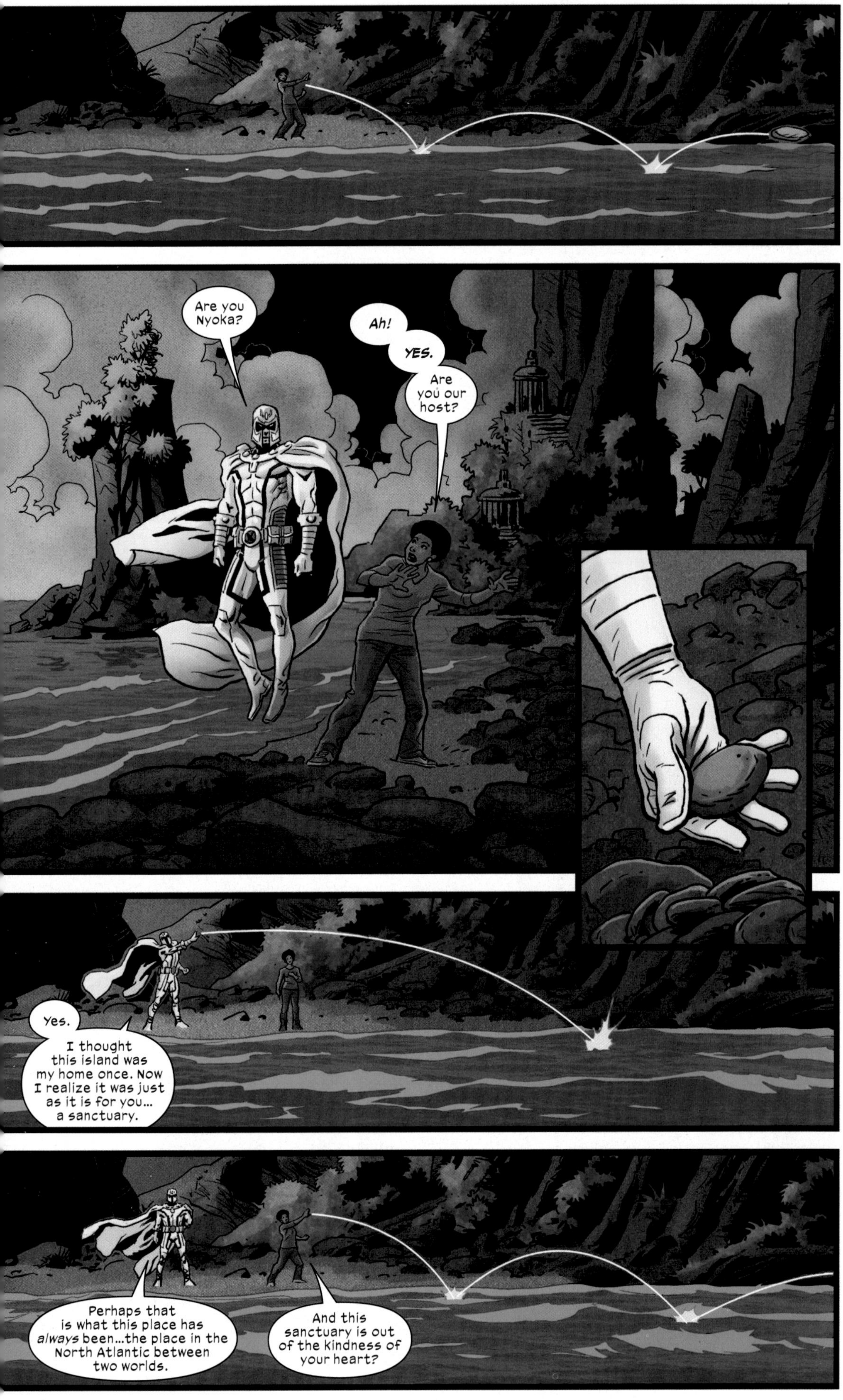
Are you Nyoka?
Ah!
YES.
Are you our host?
Yes.
I thought this island was my home once. Now I realize it was just as it is for you... a sanctuary.
Perhaps that is what this place has *always* been...the place in the North Atlantic between two worlds.
And this sanctuary is out of the kindness of your heart?

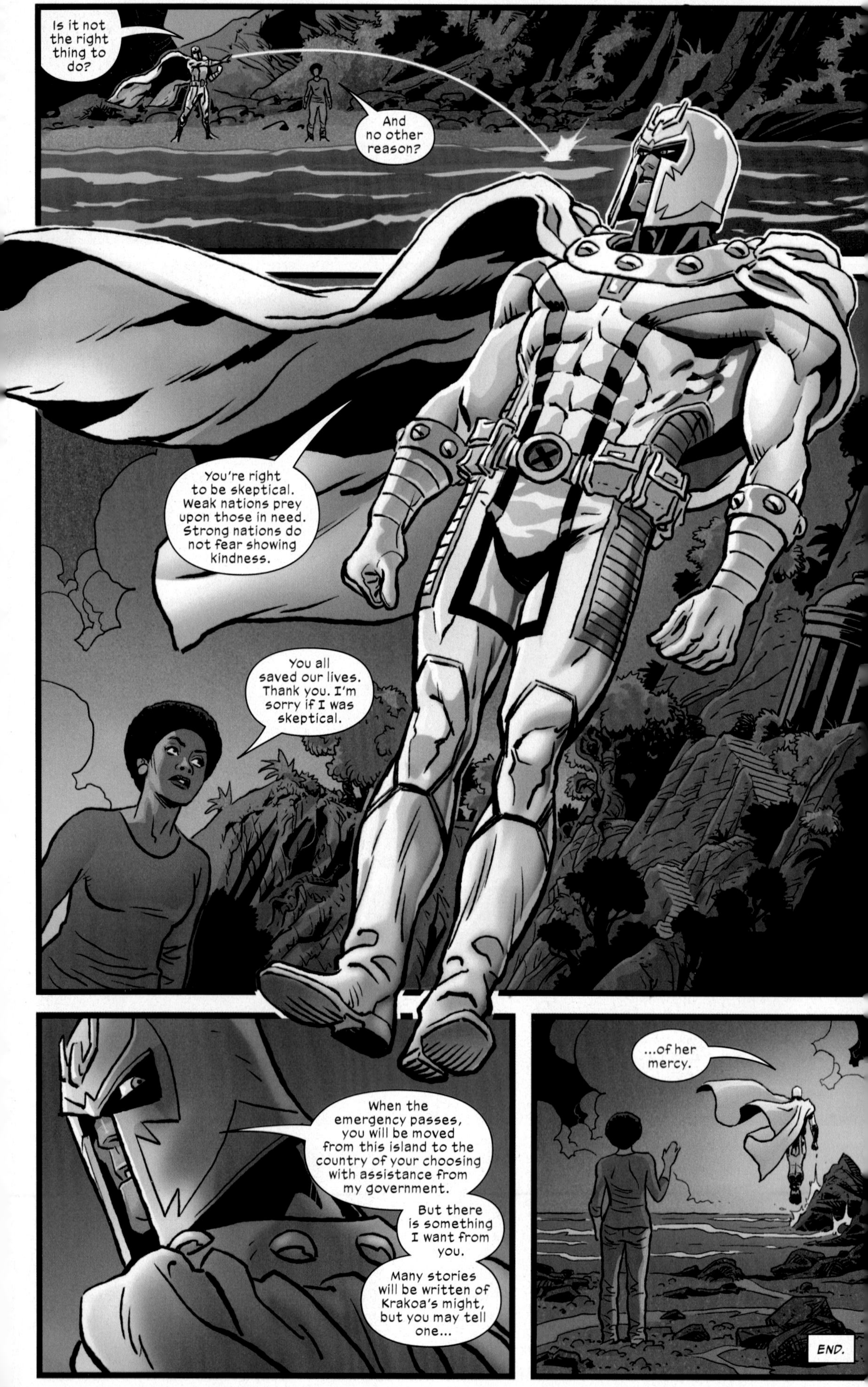
Is it not the right thing to do?
And no other reason?
You're right to be skeptical. Weak nations prey upon those in need. Strong nations do not fear showing kindness.
You all saved our lives. Thank you. I'm sorry if I was skeptical.
When the emergency passes, you will be moved from this island to the country of your choosing with assistance from my government.
But there is something I want from you.
Many stories will be written of Krakoa's might, but you may tell one...
...of her mercy.
END.

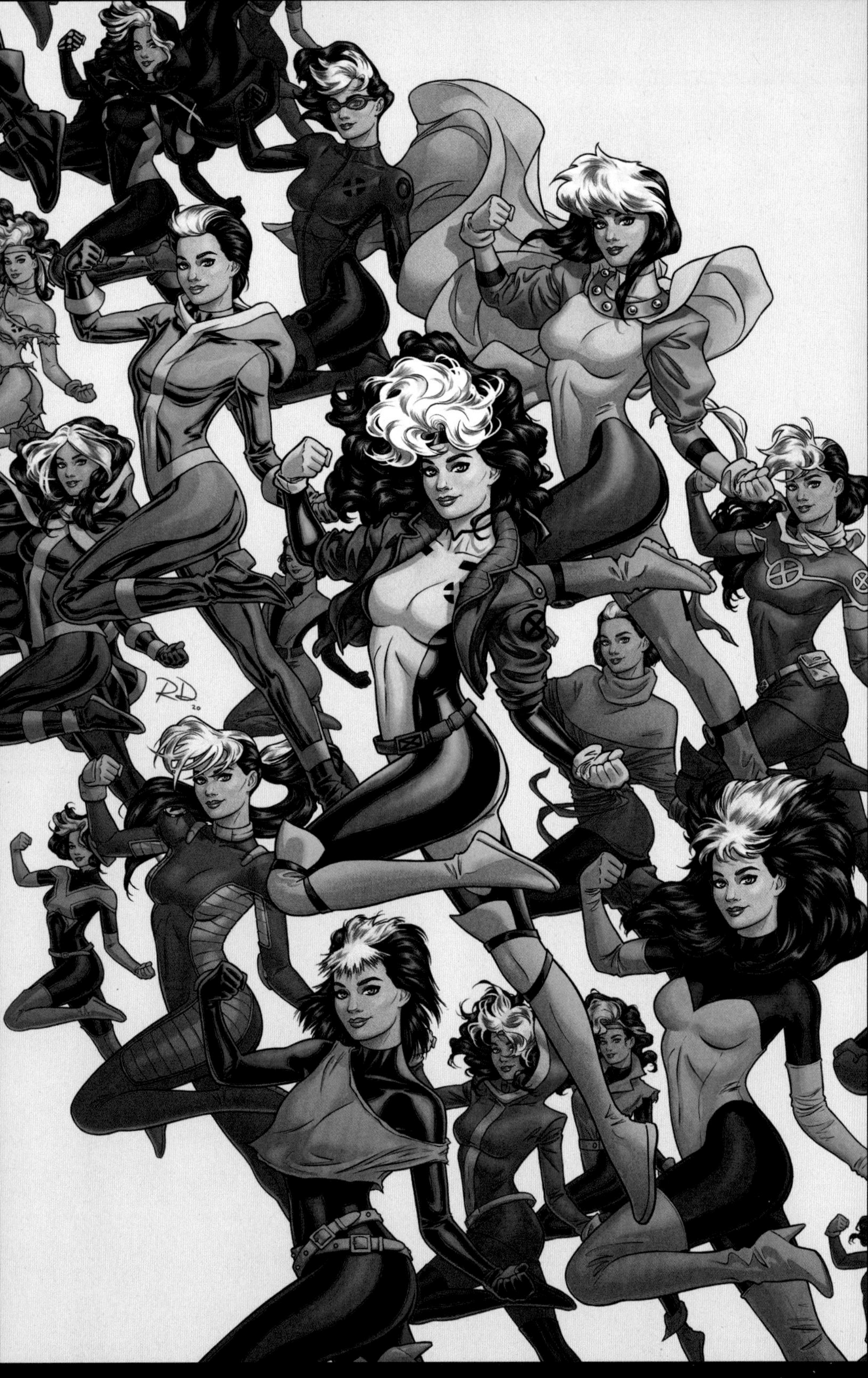

Excalibur #18 Variant by Russell Dauterman

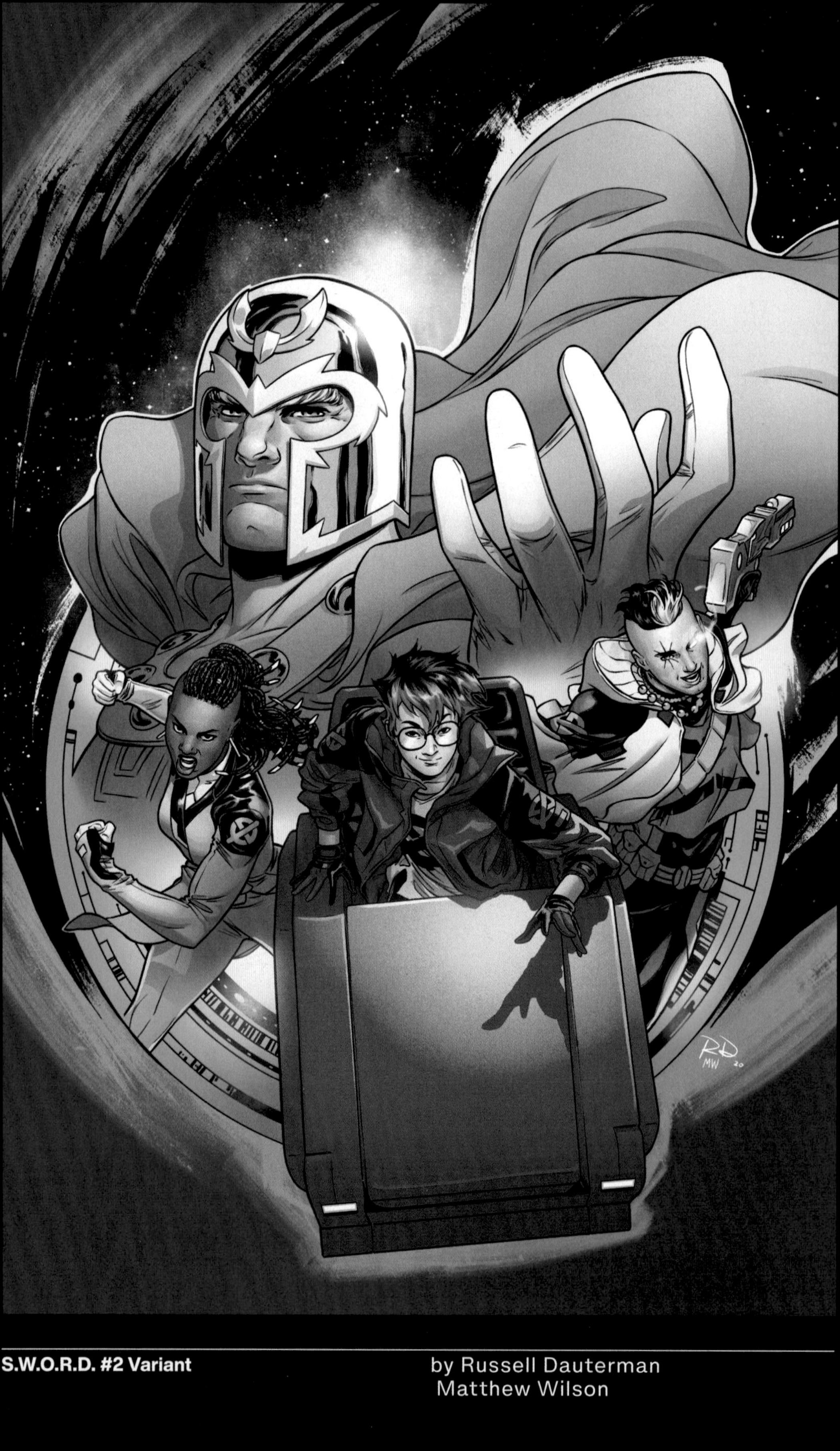

S.W.O.R.D. #2 Variant

by Russell Dauterman
Matthew Wilson

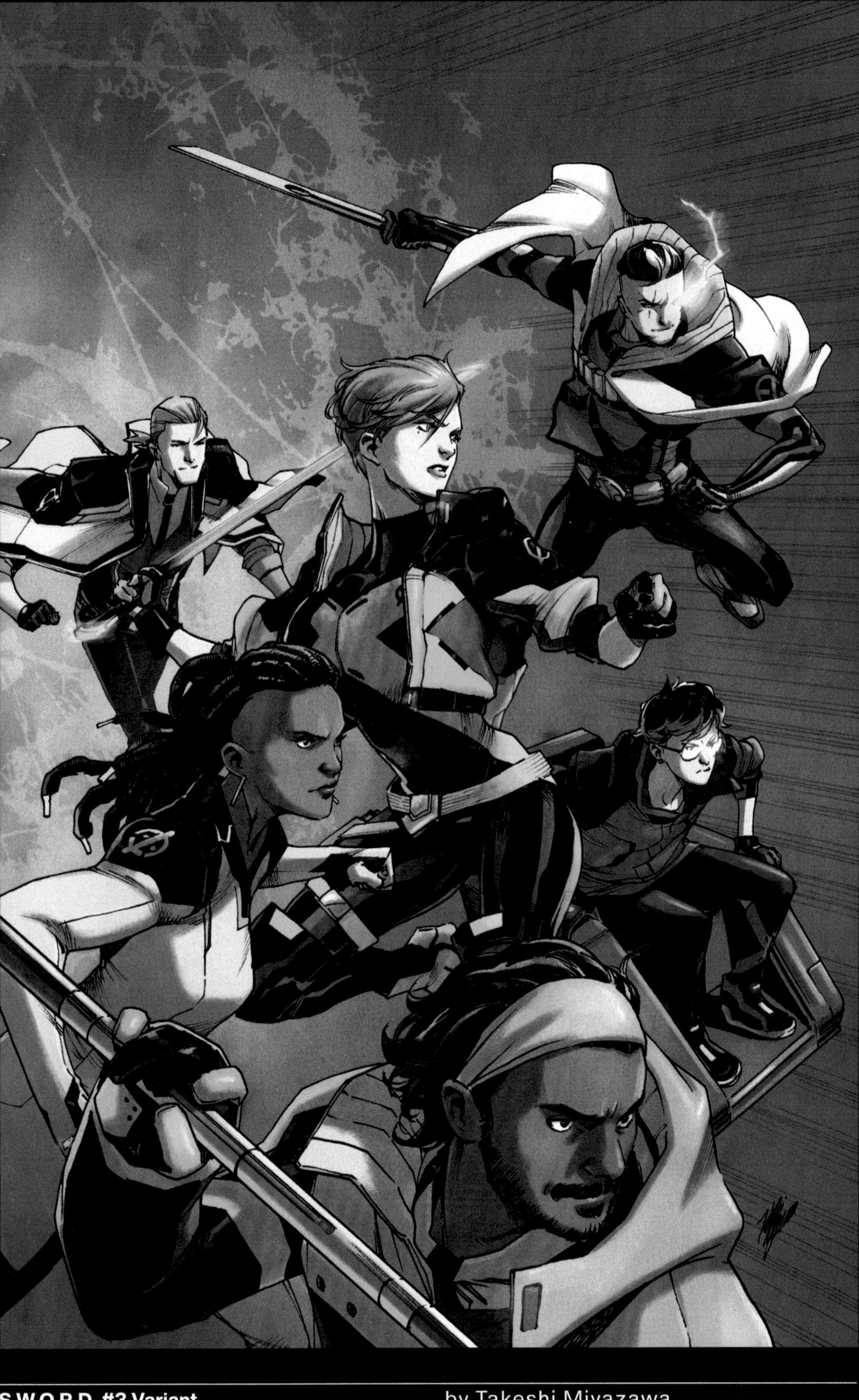

S.W.O.R.D. #3 Variant

by Takeshi Miyazawa
& Ian Herring

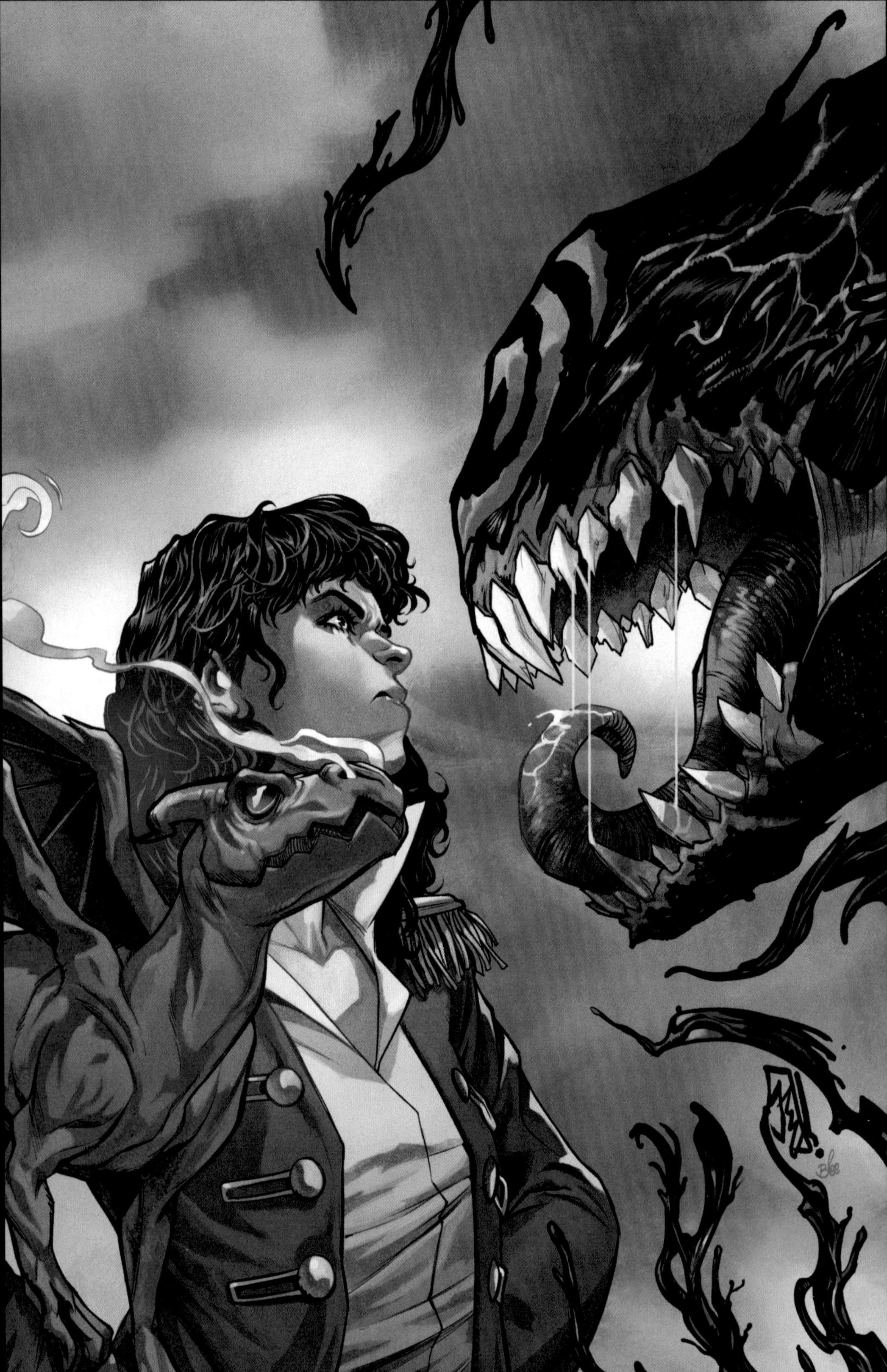
Blee

King in Black: Marauders #1

by Stefano Caselli
& Federico Blee

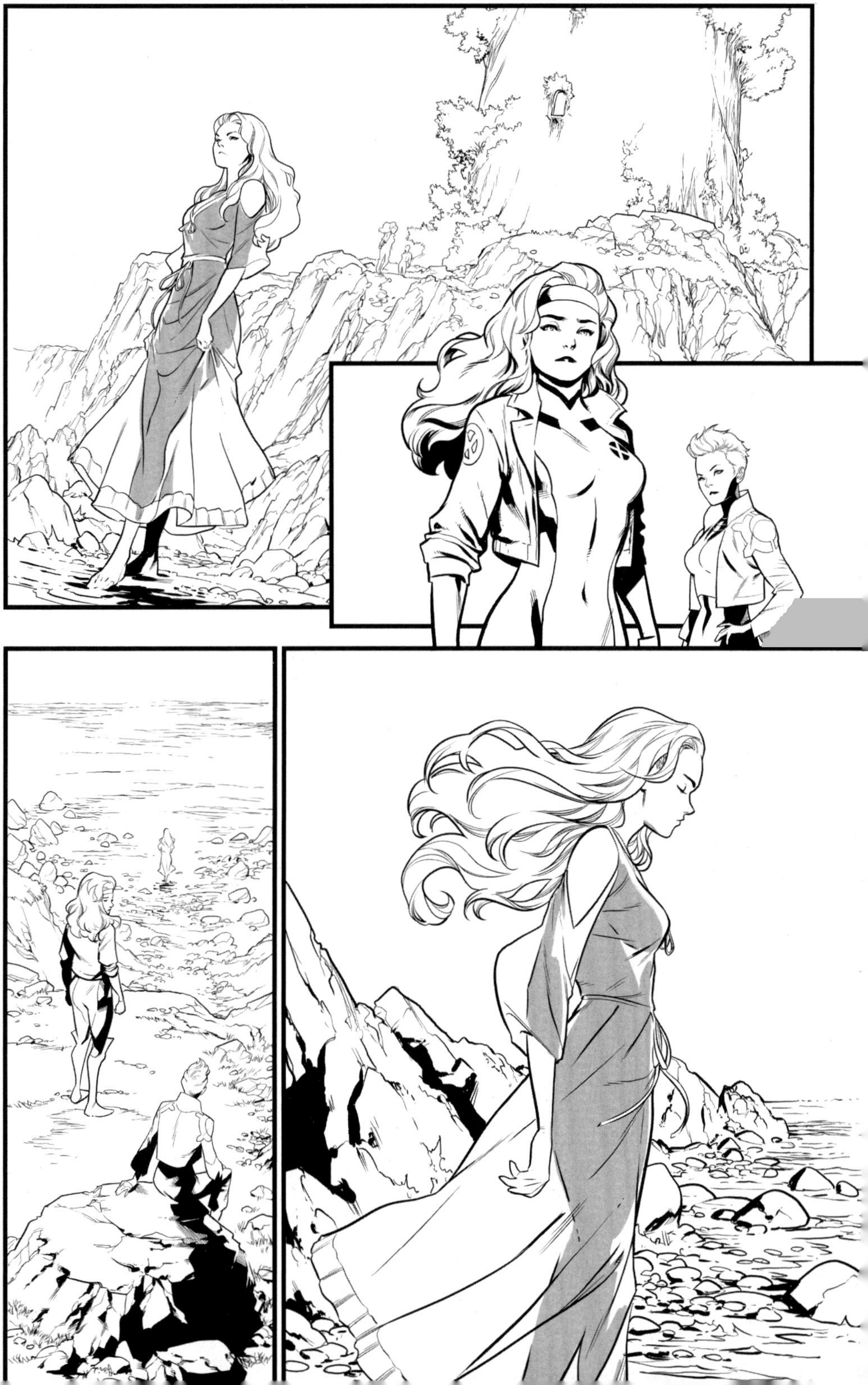

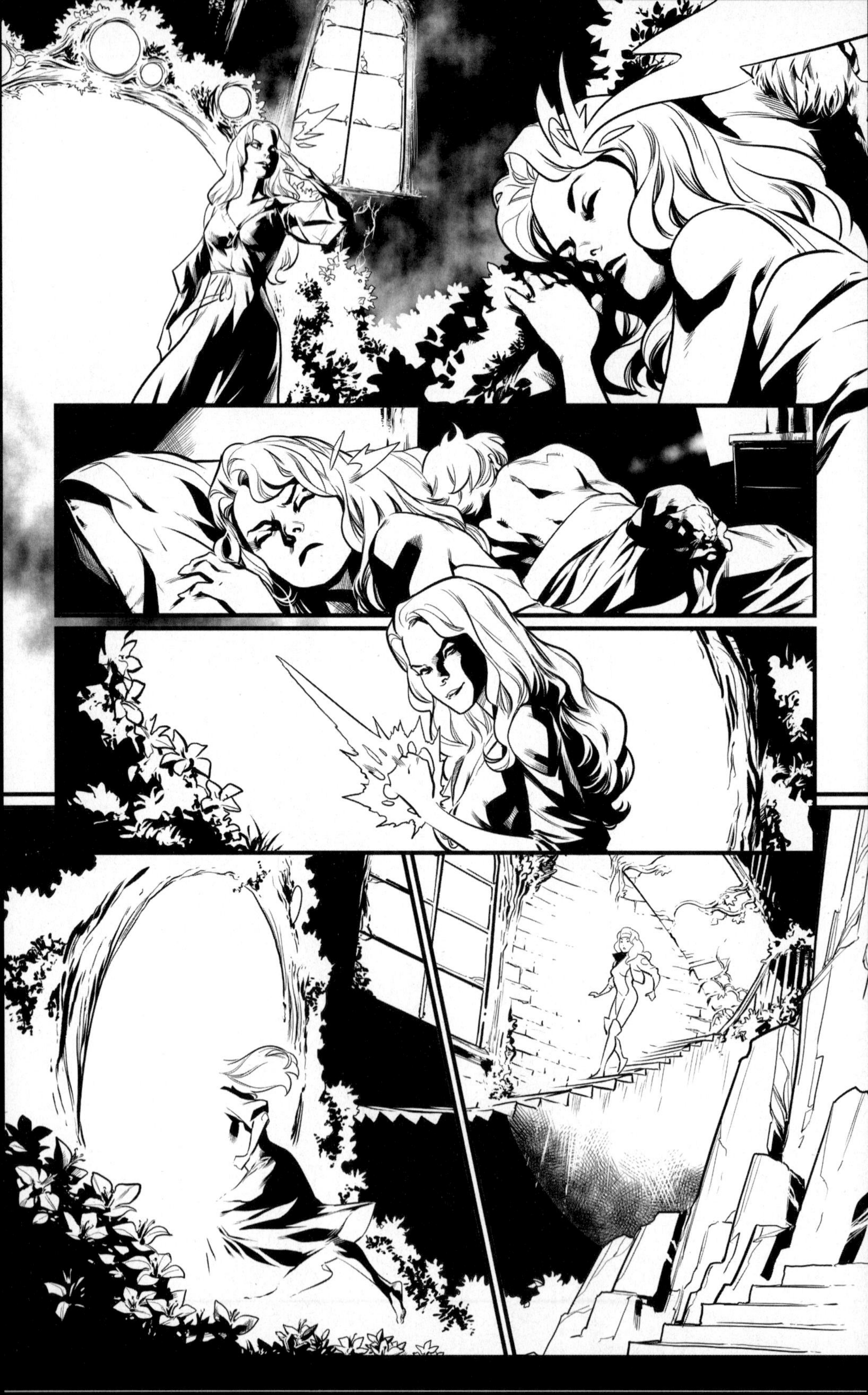

Excalibur #18, Page 10 Art by Marcus To

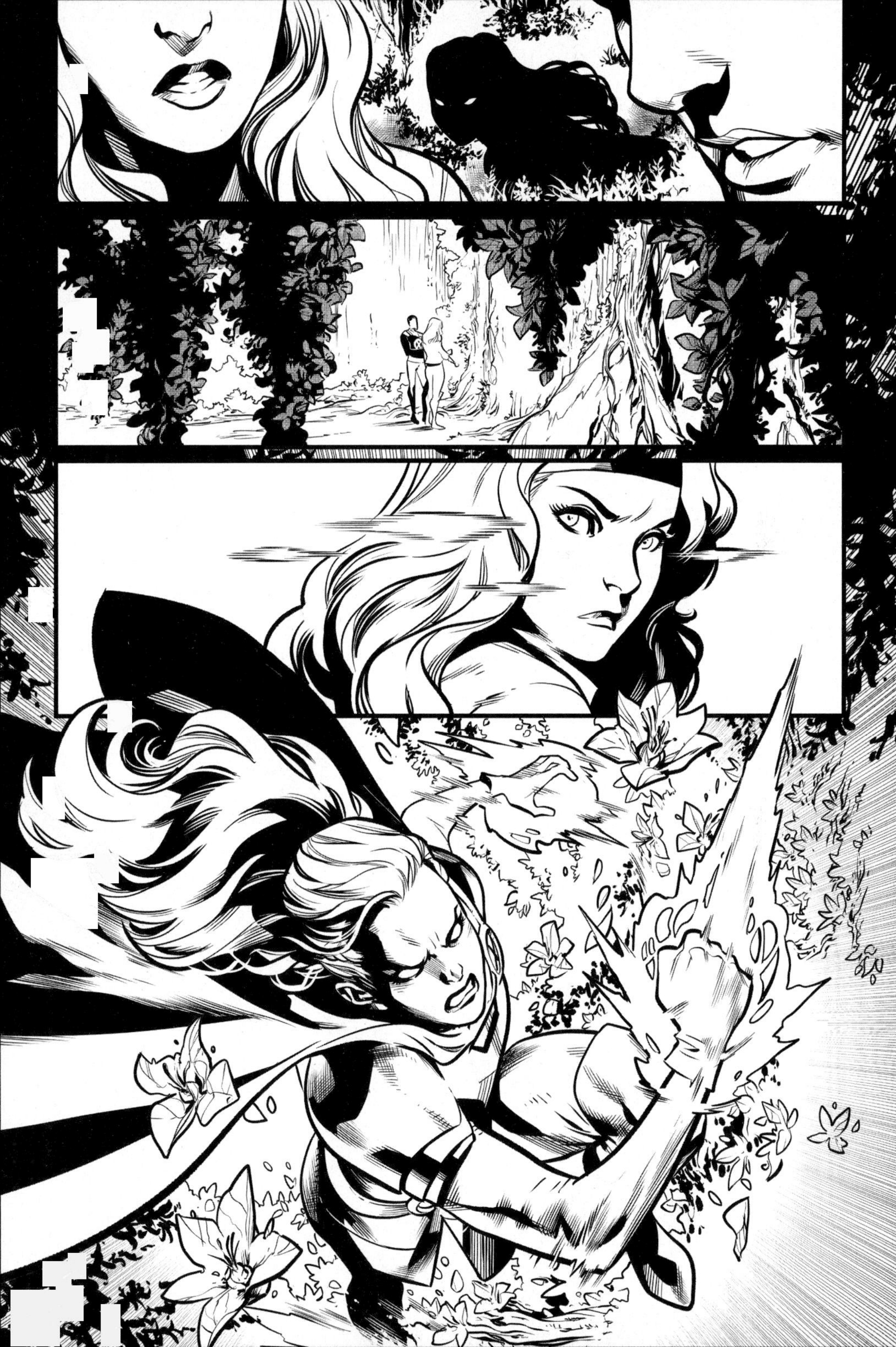

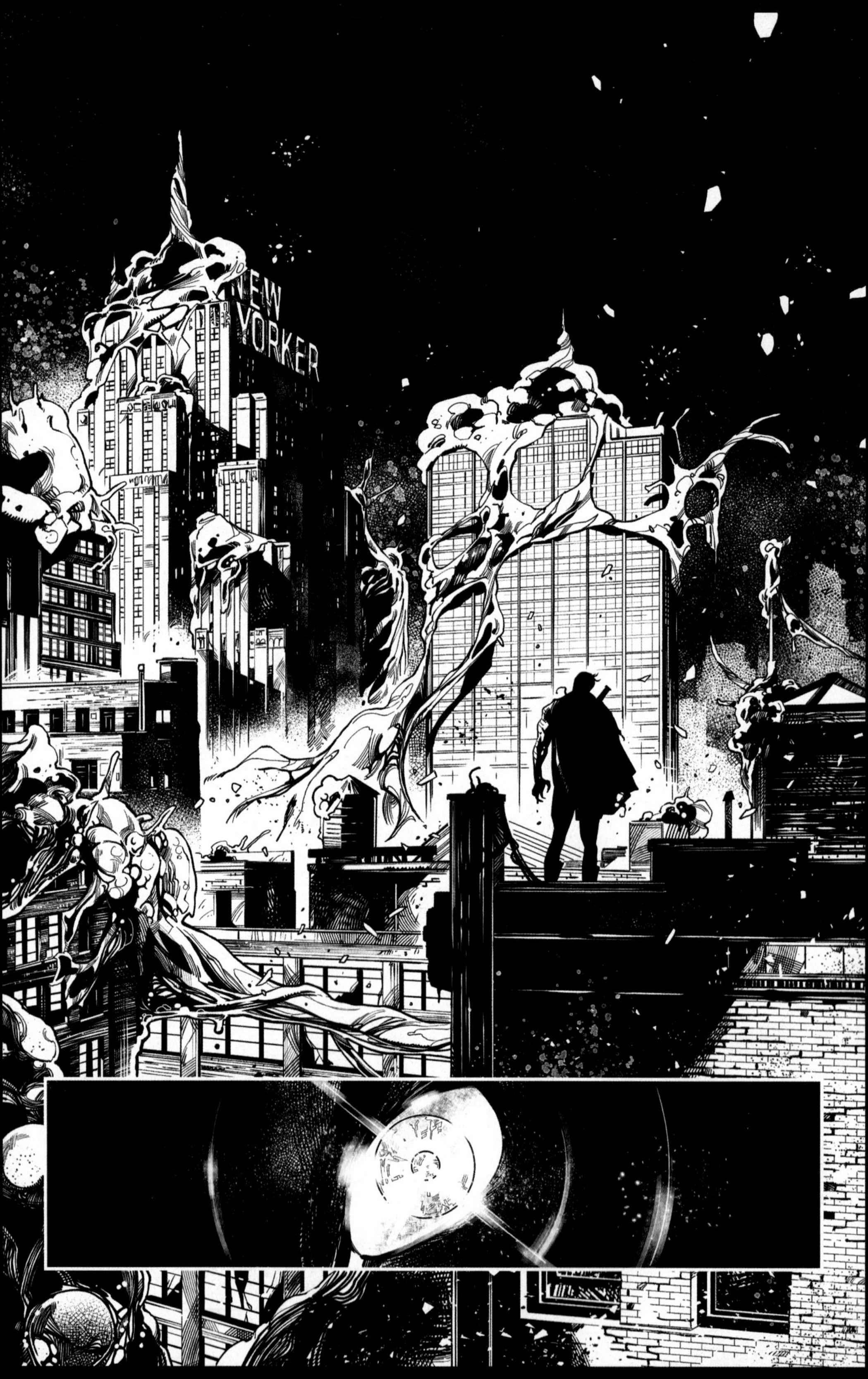
NEW YORKER

S.W.O.R.D. #2, Page 1 Art by Valerio Schiti

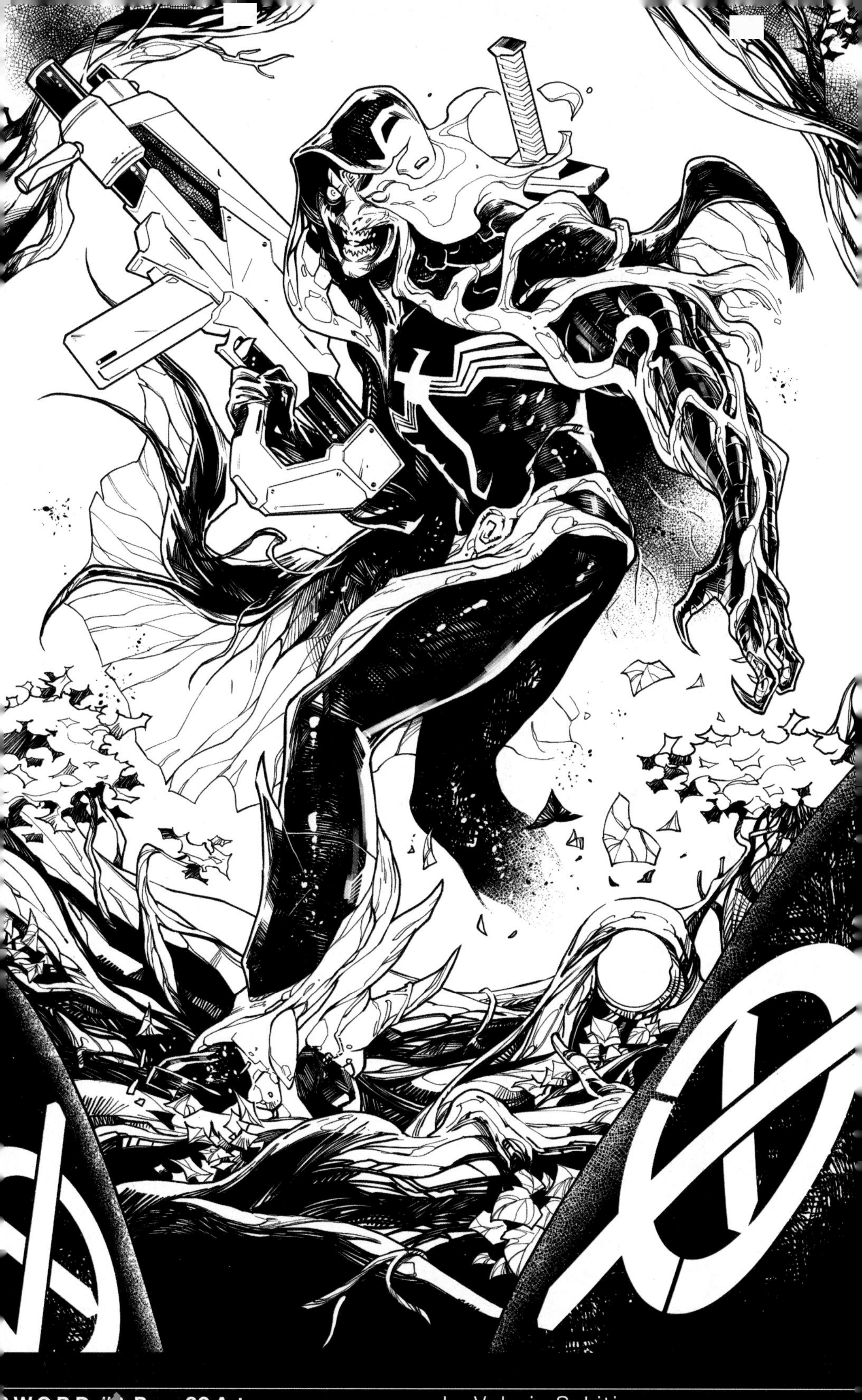

S.W.O.R.D. Page 20 Art by Valerio Schiti

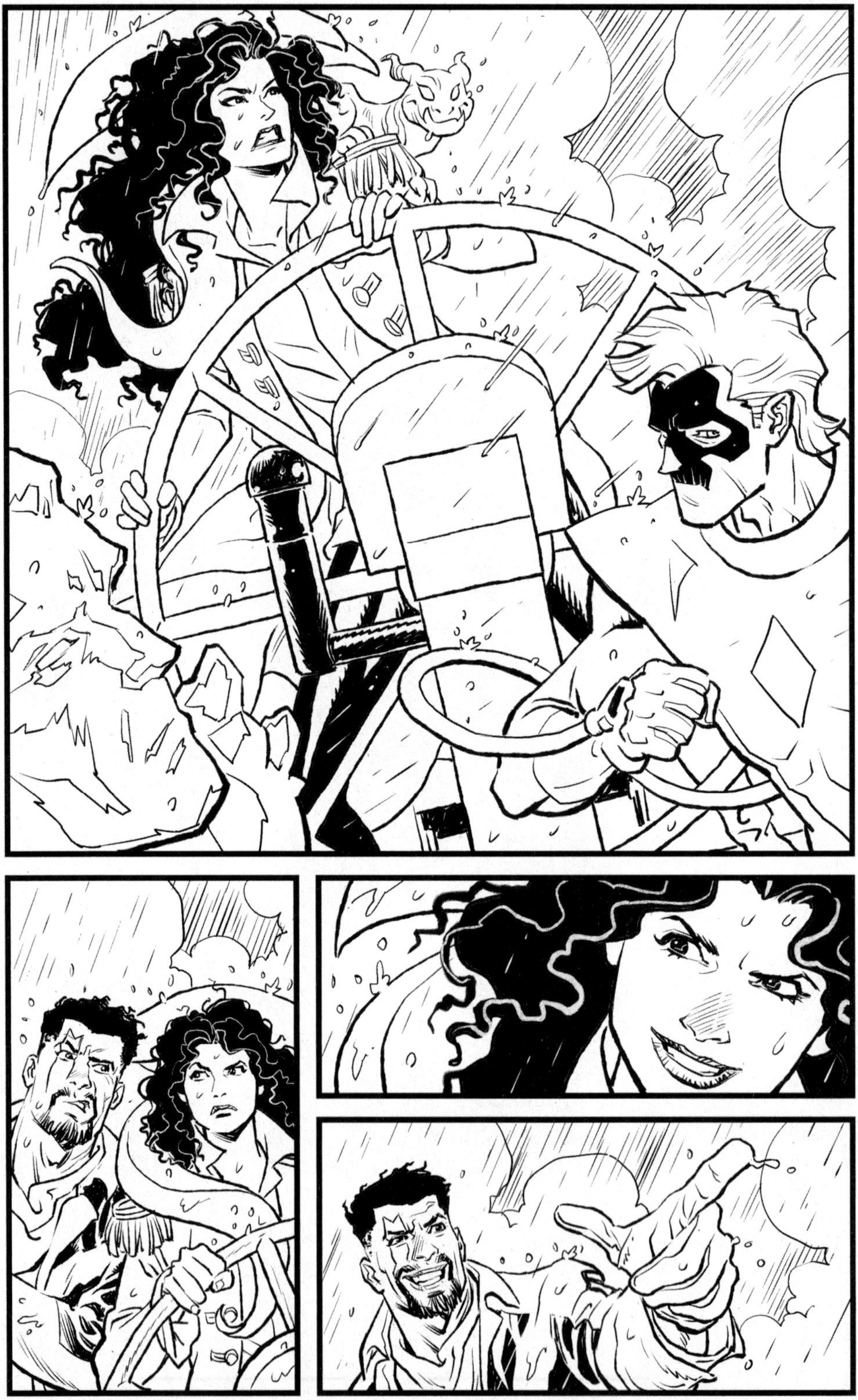

King in Black: Marauders #1, Page 5 Art by Luke Ross

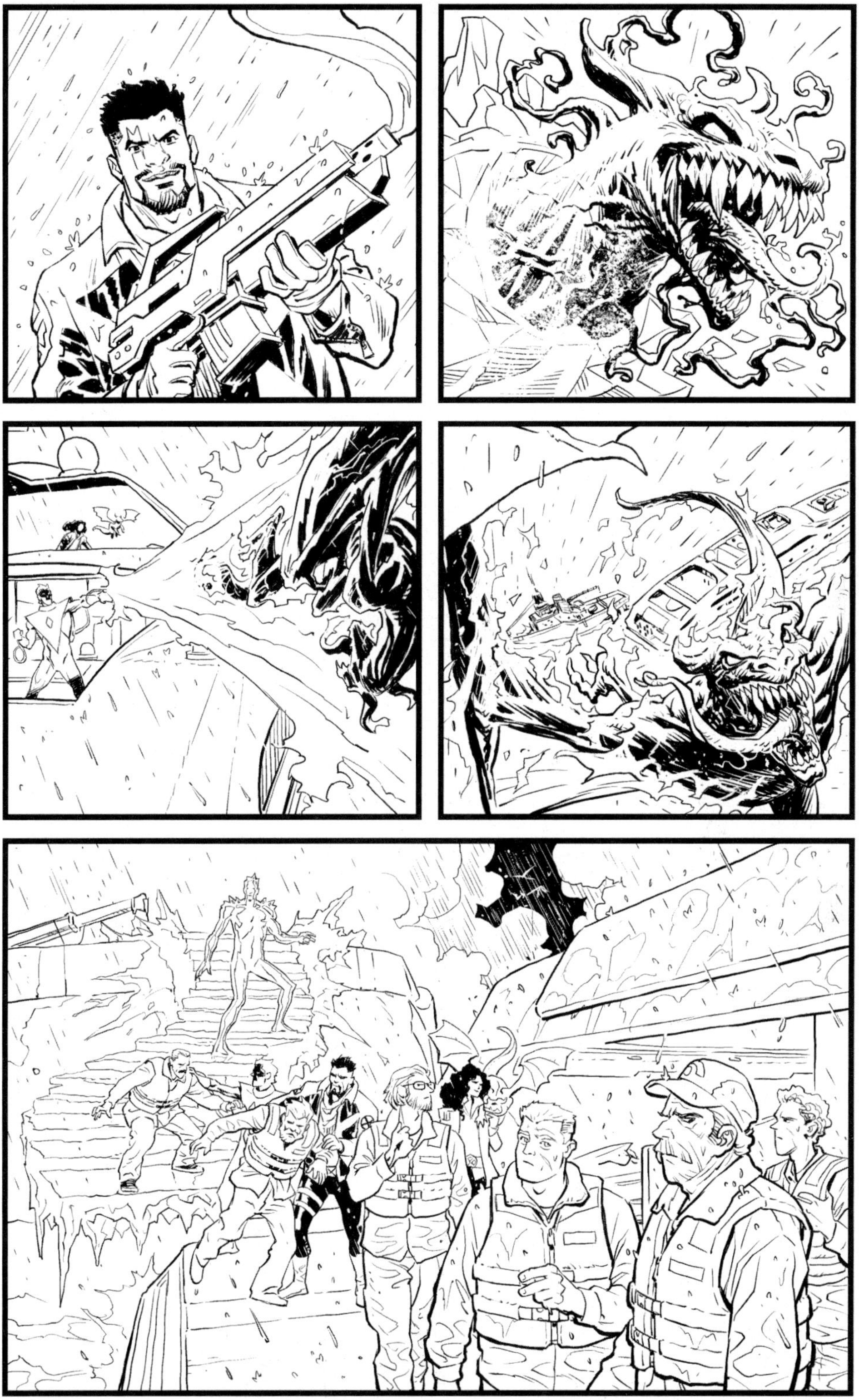

King in Black: Marauders #1, Page 8 Art by Luke Ross